QUEENS

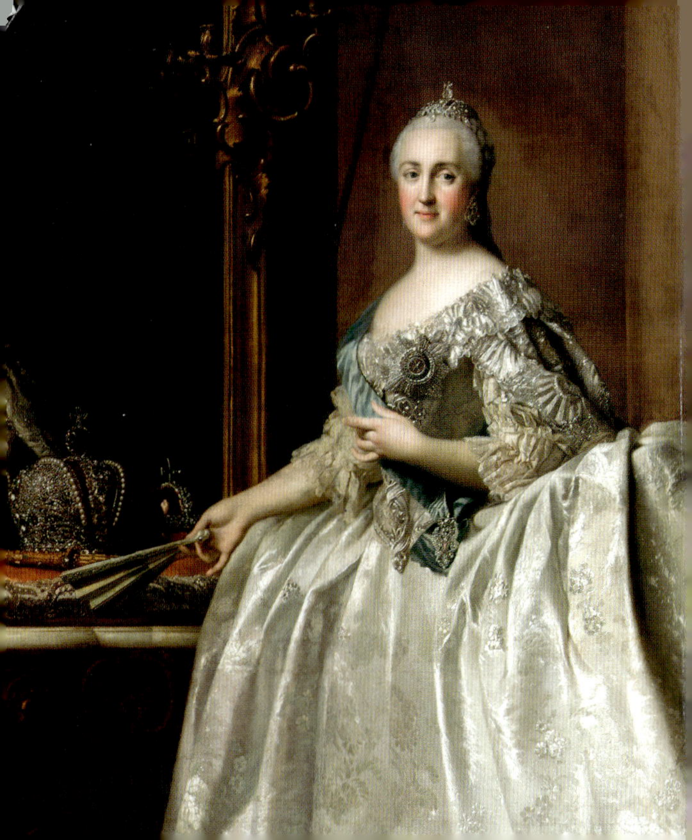

QUEENS
WOMEN WHO RULED

FROM ANCIENT EGYPT TO BUCKINGHAM PALACE

By Lauren Bucca

A Tiny Folio™
Abbeville Press Publishers
New York London

Many thanks to the team at Abbeville Press, and editor Amy K. Hughes, for bringing this book together. I am also grateful to Paul Bucca, Stacy Bucca, Jonathan Bucca, and Allison O'Flinn, for their unfailing support, and to Perry Orthey, for always encouraging me.

—Lauren Bucca

Front cover and p. 114 (detail): *Queen Elizabeth I*, c. 1600–1610. See p. 171.
Back cover: Bust of Nefertiti, 1352–32 BCE. See p. 23.
Front endpapers: Mortuary Temple of Hatshepsut. Photo by Ijanderson977.
Back endpapers: Principal facade of Buckingham Palace. Photo by Diego Delso.
p. 2: Vigilius Eriksen (1722–1782). *Portrait of Catherine II of Russia in Front of a Mirror* (detail), 1762–64. See p. 242.
p. 6: *Seated Portrait of Ningzong's Empress* (detail), c. 1202–33. See p. 103.
p. 14: Seated Statue of Hatshepsut (detail), c. 1479–58 BCE. See p. 19.
p. 54: Mosaic of Theodora, Basilica of San Vitale, Ravenna, Italy (detail), c. 547. See p. 61.
p. 182: Mahadev Visvanath Dhurandhar (1867–1944). *Tarabai—Founder of the Kolhapur Confederacy* (detail), 1927. See p. 219.
p. 246: Hubert Vos (1855–1935). *H. I. M., the Empress Dowager of China, Cixi (1835–1908)* (detail), 1905–6. See p. 264.

Copy Editor: Amy K. Hughes
Design: Misha Beletsky
Production Manager: Louise Kurtz

First edition
10 9 8 7 6 5 4 3 2 1

ISBN 978-0-7892-1401-0

Library of Congress Cataloging-in-Publication Data
Names: Bucca, Lauren, 1991– author.
Title: Queens : women who ruled, from ancient Egypt to Buckingham Palace / by Lauren Bucca.
Other titles: Women who ruled, from ancient Egypt to Buckingham Palace
Description: First edition. | New York : Abbeville Press Publishers, [2021] | Series: Tiny folio | Includes bibliographical references and index. | Summary: "An illustrated book of queens from around the world throughout time"—Provided by publisher.
Identifiers: LCCN 2020051873 | ISBN 9780789214010 (hardback)
Subjects: LCSH: Queens—History. | Queens—History—Pictorial works. | Queens in art—Pictorial works.
Classification: LCC D107.3 .B83 2021 | DDC 920.72—dc23
LC record available at https://lccn.loc.gov/2020051873

For bulk and premium sales and for text adoption procedures, write to Customer Service Manager, Abbeville Press, 655 Third Avenue, New York, NY 10017, or call 1-800-ARTBOOK.

Visit Abbeville Press online at www.abbeville.com.

CONTENTS

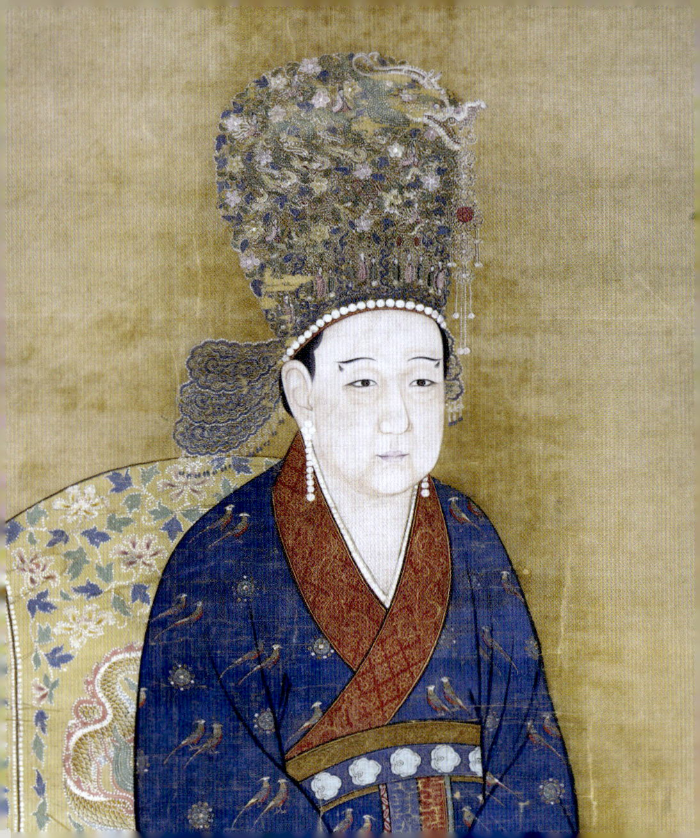

INTRODUCTION

Queens have immensely impacted the world. However, when considering rulers of the past, we do not often conjure to mind influential women like Kubaba of Sumer or Suhita of the Majapahit Empire. Their stories, and those of many others, have been excluded or marginalized in historical records. This book tells the story of sung, and unsung, queens from around the world and throughout time.

The title "queen" has several meanings. It refers to a consort, someone married to a king, like Tiye of Egypt; a regent, one who governs on behalf of a ruler too young or unable to reign, such as Cao of Song China; or a regnant, a queen who rules in her own right, like Liliuokalani of the Hawaiian Islands. This book includes regents and queens consort, but it focuses on the regnant queen, showcasing women who have wielded power, against all odds, in a world dominated by men. The titles "queen" and "empress" are used primarily throughout this book, though it should be noted that these titles may differ in the language of the queen depicted.

Most queens have been consorts, and their role has varied across cultures and eras. They were involved in business and political transactions between kingdoms, but their primary purpose was to produce a male heir. While men experienced danger and death on the battlefield, women underwent these things at home—childbirth was perilous, and many queens died young due to delivery complications. A woman's ability, or inability, to have children was perceived as a reflection of her character, and barrenness was grounds for divorce.

Though a queen consort had some power, her security was determined by her husband. Kings could be fickle, finding trivial reasons to divorce their wives, sometimes accusing them of offenses like adultery or witchcraft as justification for separation, so that they could remarry (a habit of Henry VIII). However, queens had their own affairs and even betrayed their husbands by leading political or military opposition against them, like Cleopatra VII (queen of the Ptolemaic Kingdom of Egypt), who enlisted Julius Caesar's army to help defeat her brother-husband, Ptolemy XIII. For hundreds of years, queens found solace by retiring to—or founding—monasteries or convents. Though we often consider monasteries as places inhabited solely by men, historically they could be occupied by men and women (though segregated by sex). These could be uniquely women's spaces, where queens pursued spiritual and intellectual activity, sheltered from death, plots at court, and the pressure to bear children. That many queens retired to monasteries or settled near temples, as did Shin Sawbu of Myanmar, is unsurprising, considering how dangerous their world could be.

Though a queen's role was primarily to bear children, she had other responsibilities. Queens-to-be often brought land as part of their dowry, which functioned as a peace transaction between the queen's old and new homes, and sometimes they wielded considerable influence over these lands. They performed a business role by managing the affairs of the household or the court, from its appearance to the oversight of income and goods. Queens would act as advisers to their husbands, influence political decisions that would ensure the success of their line, and preside over matters when their husband was away, from smoothing over tense diplomatic situations to enacting educational or religious initiatives.

As regents, queens had the power of kings, including the authority to make decisions affecting politics and society. Regents did all the same work as queens consort, but they often maximized the opportunity to govern. Many regents, even those who ruled for just a few months, made monumental decisions, from forging peace treaties to sending armies to war. Regent queens were legitimized by ruling on behalf of a male king or prince. This allowed women to greatly influence their kingdoms in ways that would have been unavailable, or disdained, if they were ruling in their own name. In some cases, especially for regencies representing infants and children, queens would govern for years or even more than a decade. Some regents wouldn't relinquish the throne to the heir when he came of age, while others deposed their own children. Regents would often try to take power and become the sole ruler, and some succeeded, like Irene of Athens, regent and empress of the Byzantine Empire.

Queens with sole power performed all the duties of consorts and regents, and more. Countless queens were acknowledged and respected as rulers in their own right, and in many cases their supporters worked to keep them on the throne despite opposition from male contenders. In the Americas, many women chiefs were respected as leaders with absolute authority. In Spain, there was a long tradition of women ruling, or co-ruling, with their spouses.

Throughout most of history, monarchs established their power through might. Most queens were banned from battle, and when the opportunity came for a woman to claim her throne, even having an army did not always guarantee success against her opponent—as Matilda, empress consort of the Holy Roman Empire until her husband's death, found when she tried to lay claim to the throne of England, which was hers by birth. Though queens were warriors at times, leading armies and coups, the societal bias that saw women as weaker than men often kept queens—and even well-positioned regents—from power.

There is no single way to categorize rulership throughout the world, especially with scant records in some places, but while many queens were respected, female rule was overwhelmingly met with resistance. Most kingdoms throughout history were patriarchal, and women were meant to conform to their society's definition of traditional feminine traits. The perception of female rule was often negative, and writers grasped for ways to interpret a woman in power. Since antiquity, women have been described as either angels or devils. In medieval Europe, Isabella of France (queen of England) was called a "She-Wolf," and the moniker stuck for queens after her; the name "Dame Hersent," a wily wolf in a story, was bestowed on Blanche of Castile (queen of France); and "Jezebel," the biblical temptress, on Urraca of Spain. Female rulers were also compared to other biblical women, such as Judith or the Virgin Mary, and sometimes both extremes—sinful and saintly—were applied to the same queen. This dichotomy of understanding women has been rampant in the English-speaking world and, indeed, everywhere.

Double standards for the sexes have existed throughout the world, particularly regarding sexual politics. Duong Van Nga of Vietnam was censured by a late medieval chronicler for her seemingly immoral relationship with the general and future emperor Le Dai Hanh, later her second husband, while an eighteenth-century dynastic historian took offense to her receiving a title parallel to that of her husband, "Bright Empress of Great Victory." (The emperor, evidently, was not to blame for the immorality of their relationship.) Such double standards persist in written records: kings were allowed to have mistresses, while queens were denounced for taking lovers. The husband of Isabeau of Bavaria (queen of France) approvingly took a mistress (creepily called "Little Isabeau"), while she was lambasted for an alleged affair with a duke that remains unsubstantiated to this day.

With these prevailing patriarchal biases against women, ruling queens had to find creative ways to adapt and establish their hold on their throne. They accomplished this by embracing and subverting the notions defining women at the time. They adopted their country as if they were its mother, made political allies, and aligned themselves with positive perceptions of women leaders from the past, whether it was Elizabeth I adopting the identity of the biblical prophet Judith, or later queens taking on the mantle of Elizabeth I. When possible, they used art to show the world how they wanted to be understood, commissioning portraits of themselves, their families, and scenes from their lives. Many queens accessorized their portraits with scepters, orbs, and crowns, or presented themselves as goddesses. Throughout much of history, however, queens lacked a choice in how they were characterized; in particular, many queens from African and Oceanian countries were depicted by Europeans or Americans with their own biases.

There are many queens we don't see in this book, but they are nevertheless important. Some cultures, such as ancient Egypt and England, loved to portray their queens, leaving us an abundance of images. Many parts of the world have oral rather than written traditions, including numerous African, Central and South American, and Oceanian countries, while some societies have chosen to highlight kings rather than queens in their records. For these reasons, many remarkable women have been lost to recorded history. History documented by text and image was most prominent in Europe and parts of Asia, and therefore we witness a great number of queens from these areas. The predominance of queens from particular parts of the world is an indicator of source availability, rather than their importance relative to other queens.

The women here are all exceptional and diverse in the ways they ruled and in how they were portrayed. The portraits in this book offer a glimpse of queens throughout history, revealing how they wanted to be viewed and how the world saw them—whether carved in stone, inked in a manuscript, or painted in a portrait the size of a wall. No matter how they were represented, their legacy lives on, in the women ruling today and the incredible rulers to come.

Note: In the following pages, the years of the queens' reigns are marked by a lowercase *r*.

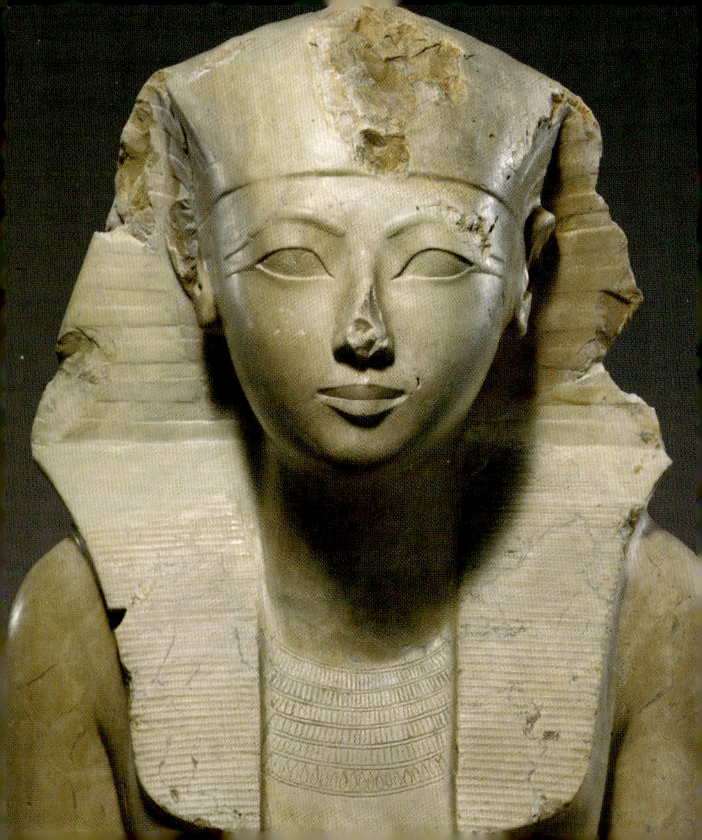

1. ANTIQUITY
2500 BCE–499 CE

The ancient world was anything but peaceful, and if you were royal, it was likely that you wouldn't have a long life. Family members were quick to turn on one another, and fratricide was commonplace, as was matricide: more than one queen was poisoned by her own son. This period was characterized by the growth of complex civilizations and the development of writing in various parts of the world, including China, India, the Fertile Crescent, Greece, Rome, and Mesoamerica. With powerful goddesses to serve as models, women ruled to a degree that wouldn't be seen again for centuries, as later societies influenced by written religions relegated women to the private sphere. Women often took charge to avoid a power vacuum in a place where a foreign entity threatened to take the throne, something that happened less often in later eras, when kingdoms were more consolidated.

Not every culture has a written history, as many relied on oral traditions; countless ancient records no longer exist. Some societies didn't write their histories until relatively late, such as Japan, whose earliest recorded history is from the seventh century CE. Other cultures, such as those of the ancient Greeks and Romans, absolutely loved to write. Early religions, among them Buddhism, Judaism, and Christianity, were used to unite lands and legitimize conquest, but they also served as conduits for recording history—though mentions of women were often tangential. Religious and classical writers, in particular, greatly shaped the perceptions of women that prevailed from ancient times to today—the biblical Eve showed women as morally weak, while the Virgin Mary transformed women into saintly mothers. Greek writers, including Aristotle, championed the idea that women were intellectually, ethically, and physically less proficient than men. In Roman law, women were regarded not as legal entities but completely under the control and protection of male power.

The role and perception of women varied across cultures, but it wasn't rare to see women ruling in ancient times. In Egypt, including the Ptolemaic Kingdom, brothers and sisters often married one another and ruled as equals. In the Roman Empire, empresses governed with their husbands or sons. Julia Agrippina of Rome co-ruled with her son, Nero, for many years, though she was really the one making the decisions, presiding at senate meetings from behind a curtain. Queens were powerful political movers, ordering the assassinations of their enemies, expanding trade routes, and fighting valiantly for their children to inherit the throne. They were warriors as well, leading troops into battle and commanding their own ships.

For many cultures, we have written accounts but few visual records. We know, for example, of the Trung sisters of first-century CE Vietnam, Trung Trac and Trung Nhi. The former was Vietnam's first woman monarch, and together the sisters led a revolt against Chinese occupation. Pharandzem, a fourth-century CE queen consort and regent of Armenia, was known for defending her fortress against Persian invasion. There are many others whose portraits we do not see, but who were still instrumental in shaping the world. Most extant ancient visual records are from societies that carved their histories in stone; many representations of queens in other mediums have been lost to time.

The most visually recorded queens during this time were Egyptian and Roman. The outstanding preservation of Egyptian art, with images of queens often coupled with written descriptions, provides an incredible opportunity to learn about women leaders. Egypt's goddesses served as a template for powerful women, and queens often took on the personas of deities, like Isis or Hathor, as a way to assert their authority. Yet, even in Egypt, where women had more power than in many other places, queens were still understood in terms of male leadership. The great Hatshepsut is adorned in masculine imagery in a fifteenth-century BCE statue (p. 19), wearing the *nemes*-headcloth and the *shendyt*-kilt (not pictured) typical of an Egyptian pharaoh. Because Egypt was a male-dominated society, after some of the most singular female rulers ended their reigns, their names were scratched from the official lists of kings. Later, Roman empresses likewise appeared in stone, often with their spouse or son. Their lifelike portrayals on coins would inspire a practice taken up by Renaissance artists and common to this day.

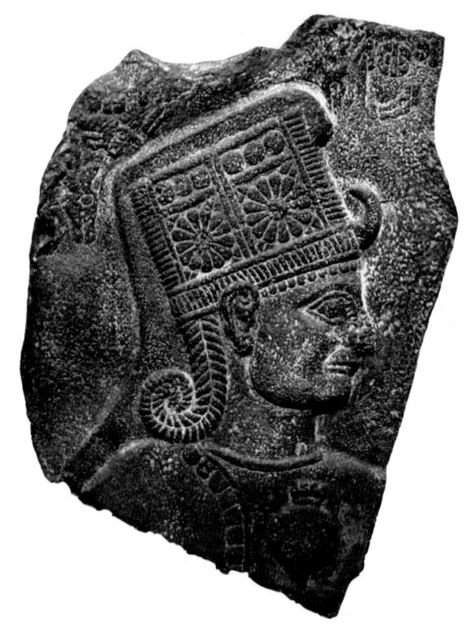

Kubaba, queen of Sumer (southern Iraq) (*r.* c. 2500–2330 BCE). The only queen listed in the record of Sumerian rulers, and one of the few women sovereigns in Mesopotamian history. (Plaster relief, c. twentieth century BCE.)

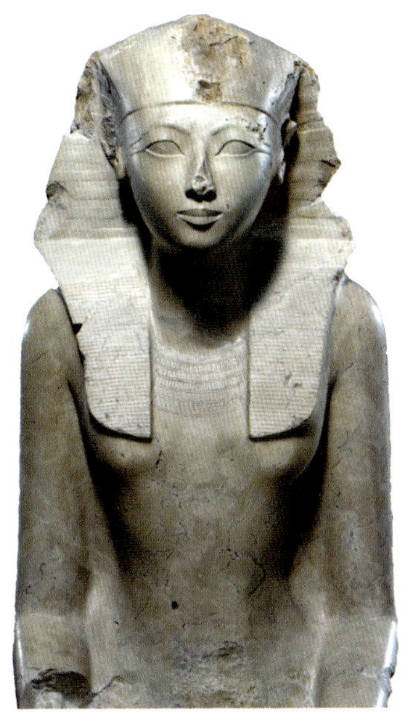

Hatshepsut, queen consort (*r.* 1493–1479 bce), regent (*r.* 1481–1472 bce), and pharaoh of Egypt (*r.* 1473–1458 bce). Hatshepsut's clever scheming transformed her from regent to pharaoh, bringing unprecedented female leadership to Egypt. (Sculpture, c. 1479–58 bce.)

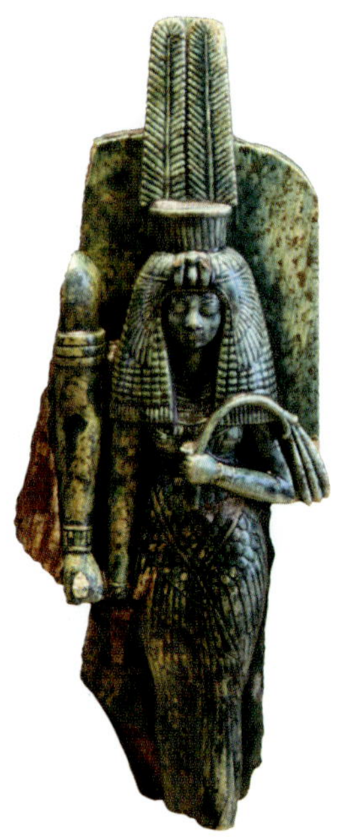

TIYE, QUEEN CONSORT OF EGYPT (*r.* 1390–1353 BCE). Entrusted with foreign affairs, she is the first queen in Egyptian history to have her name appear on legal documents. (Sculpture, 1391–53 BCE.)

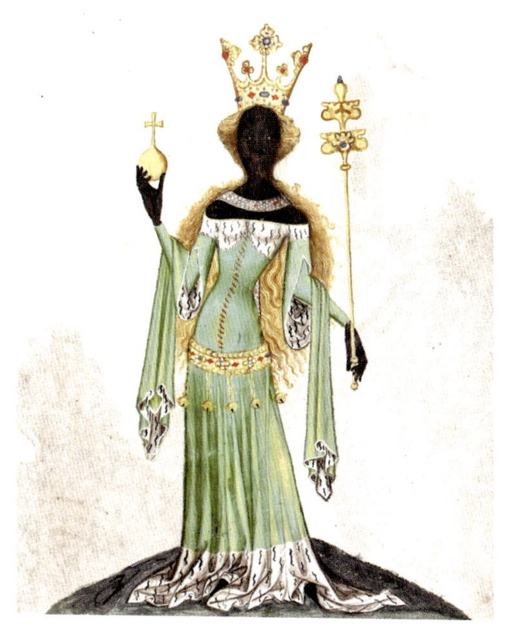

QUEEN OF SHEBA (ARABIA) (*r.* c. tenth century BCE).
The Queen of Sheba and King Solomon are traditionally credited with founding a dynasty that lasted a thousand years. (Manuscript illustration, c. 1405.)

More Than Appearances

In this sculpture, Nefertiti is distinguished by her elegant, enigmatic features and her idiosyncratic blue crown. Revered throughout history as a beauty, Nefertiti offered much more. In a unique move, Pharaoh Akhenaten elevated her to coruler, and she brought levelheadedness to a reign marked by her husband's religious extremism and self-aggrandizement. Akhenaten had completely disrupted the order of Egyptian worship and society, which Nefertiti is now credited with helping restore.

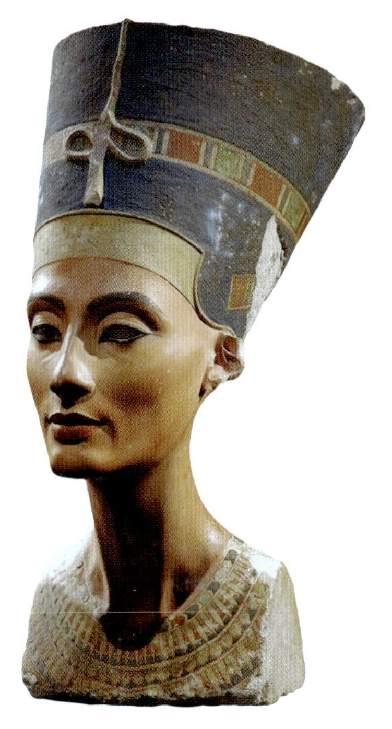

Nefertiti, queen consort of Egypt (*r.* 1353–1336 BCE).
(Sculpture, 1352–32 BCE.)

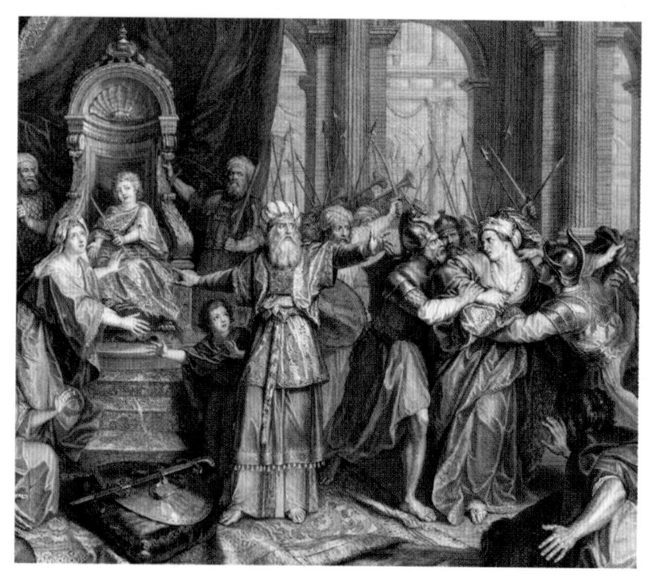

Athaliah, consort (*r.* c. 849–842 BCE) and queen of Judah (Middle East) (*r.* 841–835 BCE).
Seized the throne and sentenced all other possible claimants to death.
(Right; print, detail, by Jean Audran after Antoine Coypel, c. 1677–1756.)

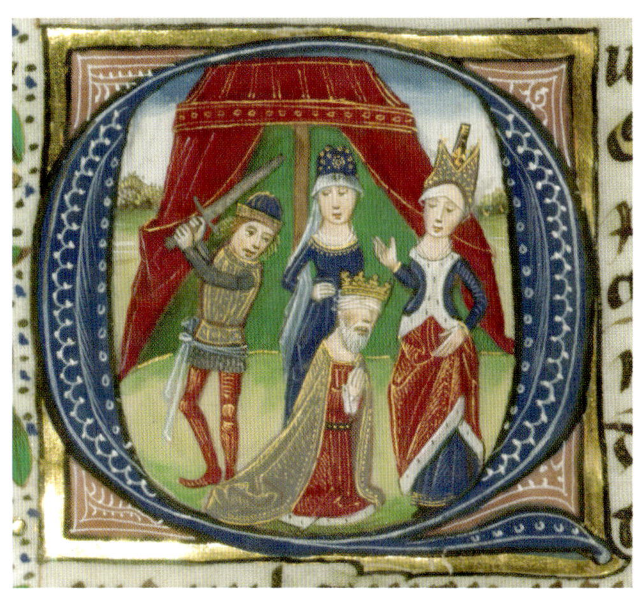

Tomyris, queen of the Massagetai (central Asia) (*r.* c. 530 bce). Led her troops into battle against Cyrus II, the Great, of Persia, whom she had beheaded. (Right; manuscript, detail, c. 1470–80.)

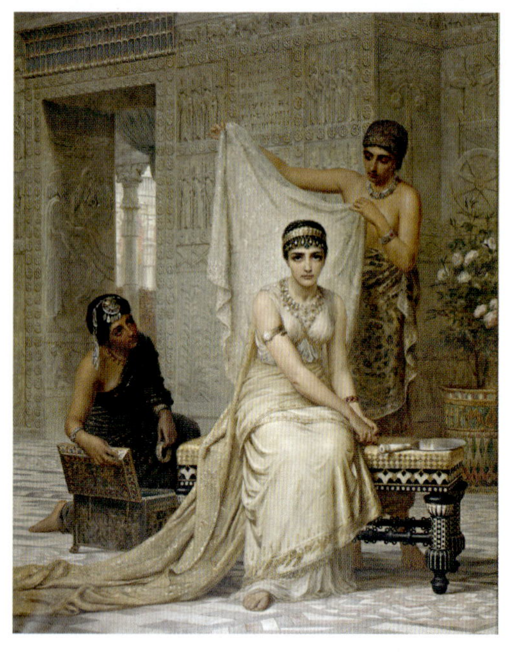

Esther, queen consort of Persia (Iran) (*r.* c. fifth century BCE). Famed in biblical tradition for supplicating the king to spare the Jewish people from death. (Painting by Edwin Long, 1878.)

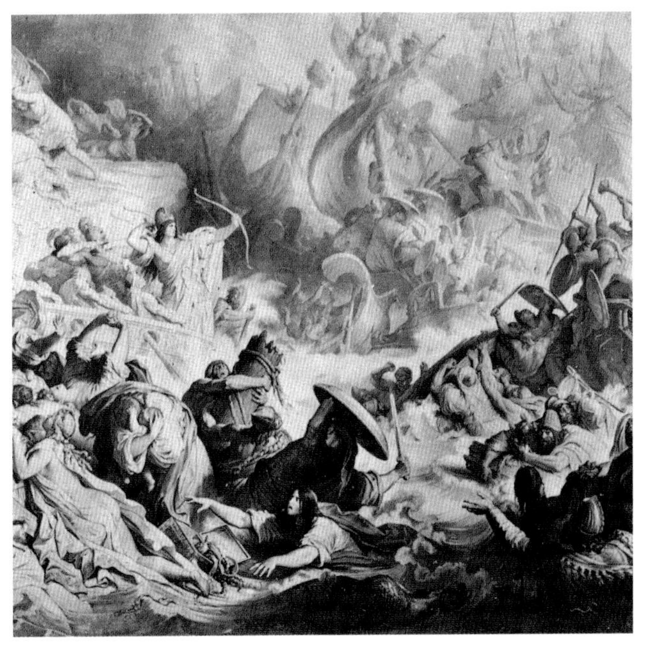

Artemisia I, queen of Halicarnassus, Cos, Nisyrus, and Calymnos, Caria (Greece and Turkey) (*r.* 484–460 BCE). Commanded her own ships at the Battle of Salamis. (Left, shooting an arrow; print, detail, after Wilhelm von Kaulbach, c. 1875–80.)

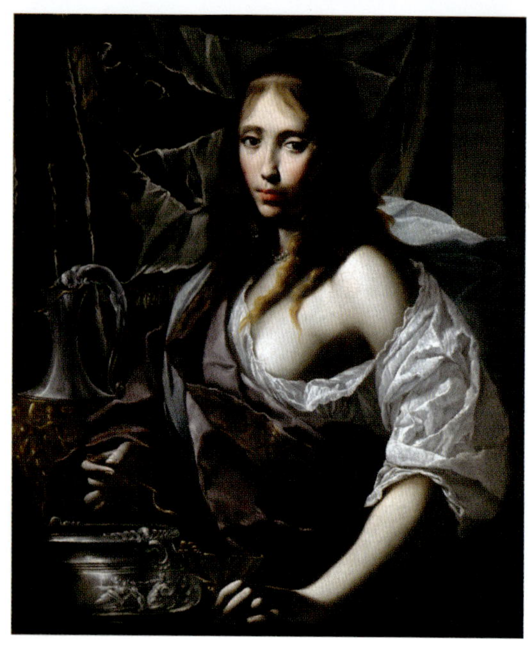

Artemisia II, queen of Caria (Turkey) (*r.* 353–351 bce). Though she was a naval strategist and commander, she is famous for (reputedly) drinking her husband's ashes. (Painting attributed to Francesco Furini, c. 1630.)

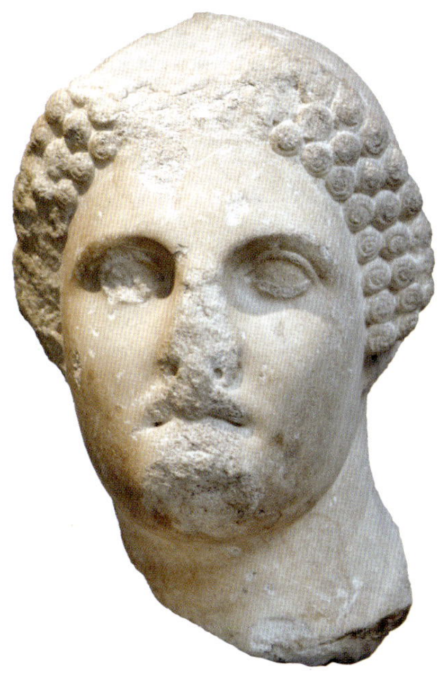

Ada, queen of Caria (Turkey) (*r.* 344–340; 334–326 BCE). Became Alexander the Great's adoptive mother and granted him the inheritance of Caria in exchange for his help regaining her throne. (Sculpture, c. 350 CE.)

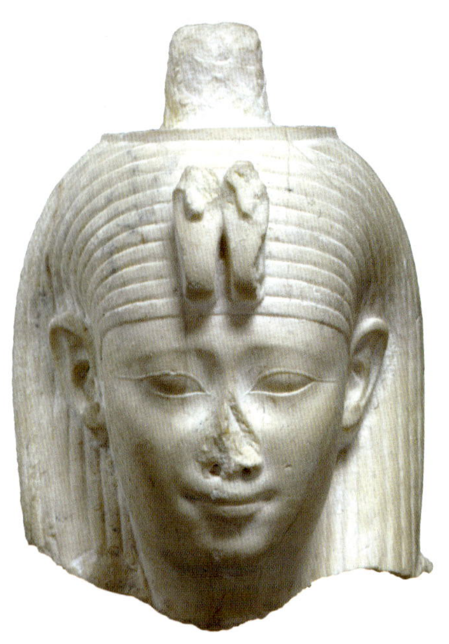

Arsinoe II, queen consort (coruler) of Thrace, Anatolia, and Macedonia (*r.* c. 300–281 BCE), and pharaoh (coruler) of the Ptolemaic Kingdom (Egypt) (*r.* 281–c. 270 BCE). She was deified after her death, and her cult flourished throughout the Ptolemaic period. (Sculpture, 278–70 BCE.)

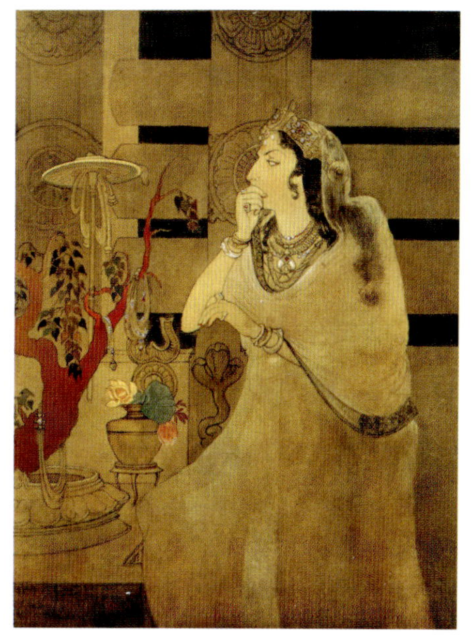

TISHYARAKSHA, QUEEN CONSORT OF MAURYAN INDIA (*r.* c. 260–235 BCE).
Poisoned a sacred Buddhist tree because she was jealous of her husband's attentions to it. (It grew back.) (Chromoxylograph, 1911.)

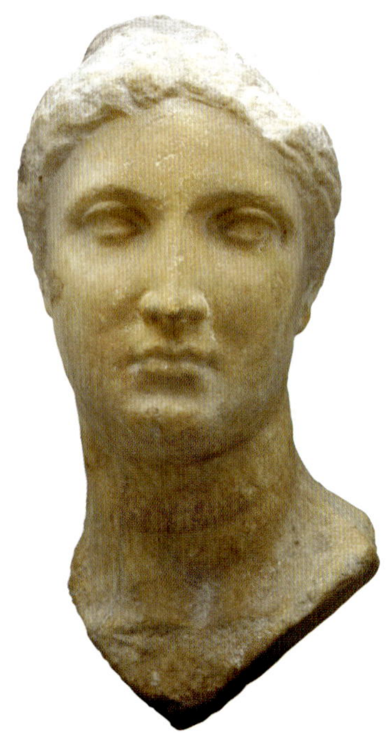

Arsinoe III, pharaoh (coruler) of Egypt (*r.* 220–204 BCE). Successfully led 55,000 troops against Antiochus the Great with her brother-husband. (Sculpture, late third–second century BCE.)

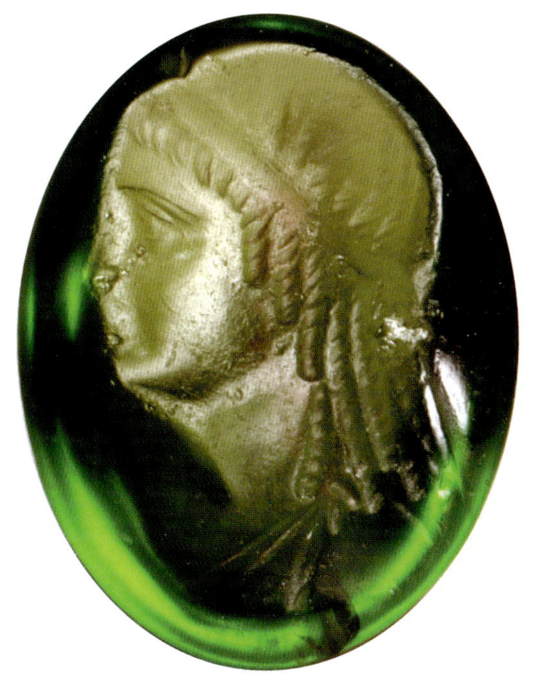

CLEOPATRA II, PHARAOH (CORULER) OF EGYPT (*r.* 175–116 BCE). Deposed briefly by her brother, she got revenge by driving him out of Egypt. (Peridot engraving, c. 175–15 BCE.)

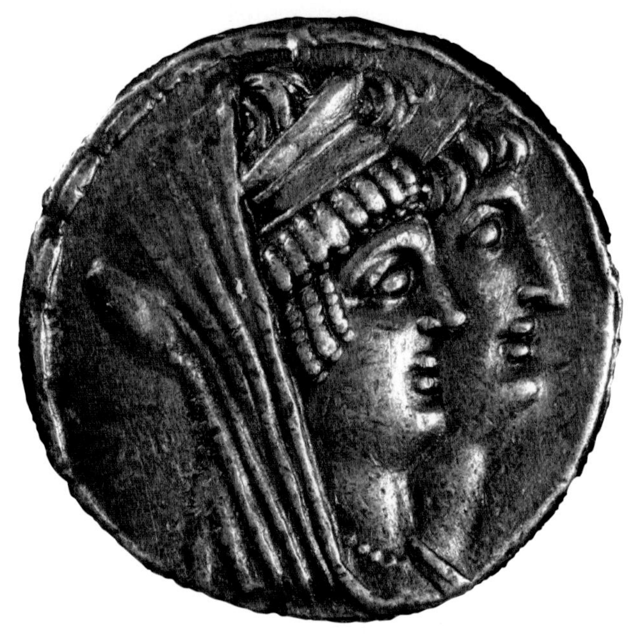

Cleopatra Thea, consort (*r.* 150–126 BCE) and queen of the Seleucid Empire (Syria) (*r.* 125–121 BCE). The first Hellenistic female ruler to issue coins in only her name. (Left, with her son, Antiochus VIII; coin, 123–20 BCE.)

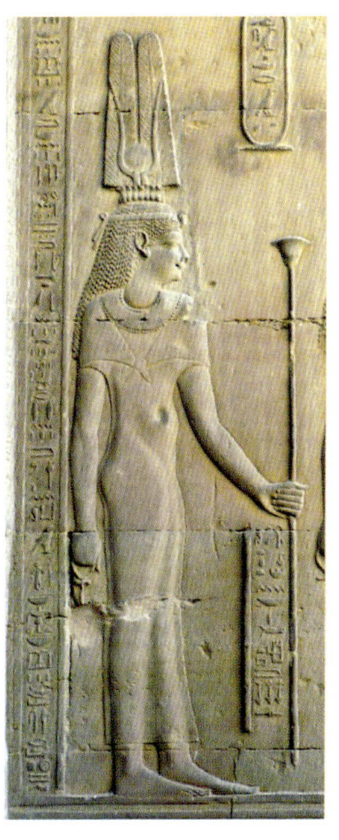

Cleopatra III, pharaoh (coruler) of Egypt (*r.* 130–101 BCE). Governed with her son and was later murdered, likely at his command. (Relief, detail, c. 175–47 BCE.)

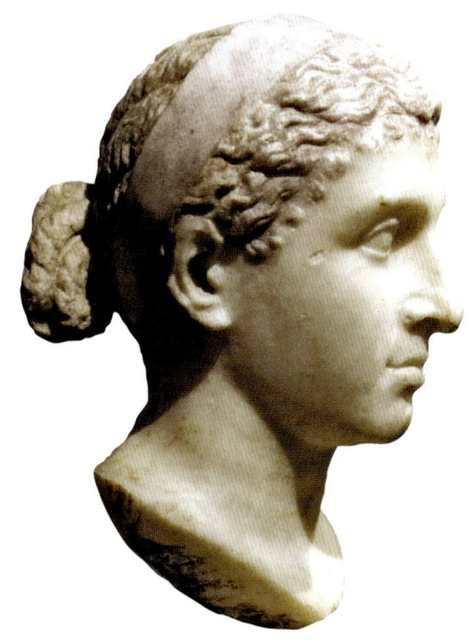

Cleopatra VII Thea Philopator, queen (coruler) of the Ptolemaic Kingdom (Egypt) (*r.* 51–30 BCE). This ambitious queen's alliances with Julius Caesar and Marc Antony, and her tragic suicide, have made her an enduring subject in art and literature. (Sculpture, 50–38 BCE.)

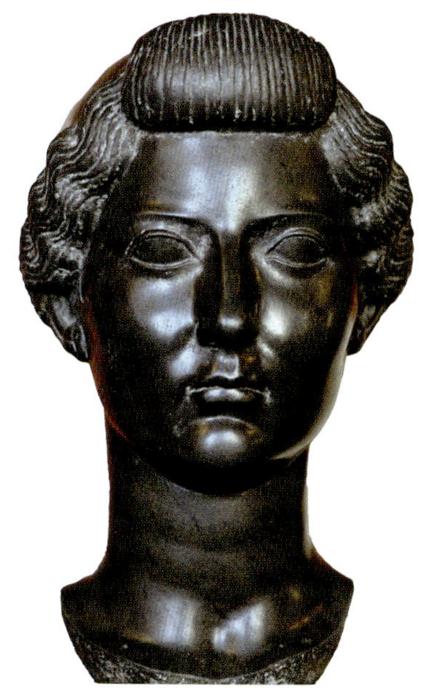

Livia Drusilla, empress consort of the Roman Empire (*r.* 38 BCE–14 CE).
Honored as "Mother of Her Country" upon her death but later vilified by historians for her use of authority. (Sculpture, 31 BCE.)

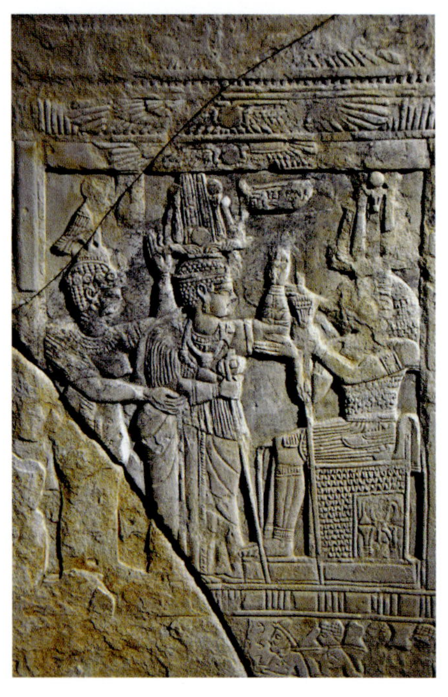

Amanishakheto of Meroë, Queen of Kush (Sudan) (*r.* 10 BCE–1 CE). Led the Nubians in a successful attack against the invading Romans. (Center; sculpture, first century CE.)

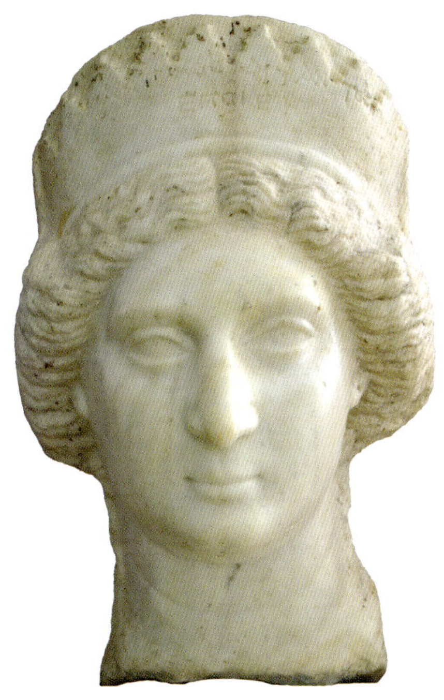

MUSA, QUEEN OF THE PARTHIAN EMPIRE (IRAN) (*r.* 2 BCE–4 CE).
Arranged her husband's poisoning so she could
co-rule with her son. (Sculpture.)

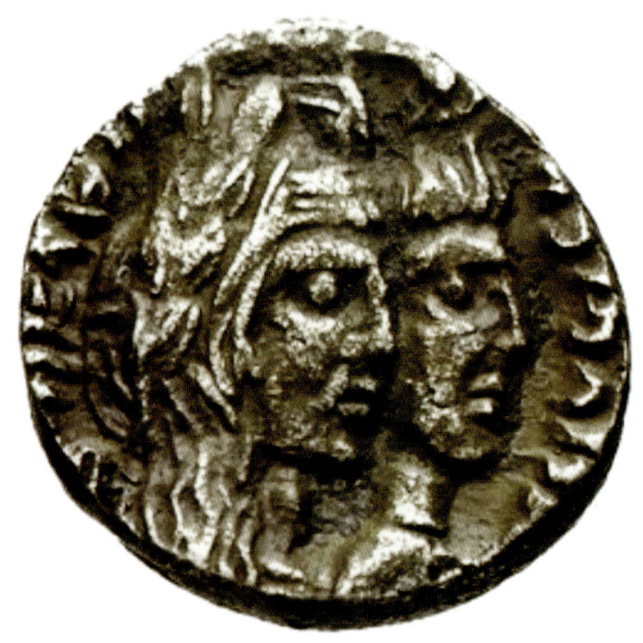

Shaqilath, queen (coruler) of the Nabataeans (Arabia) (*r.* c. early first century ce).
Significantly expanded international trade during her reign.
(Right, with her husband, Aretas IV; coin, 21–22 ce.)

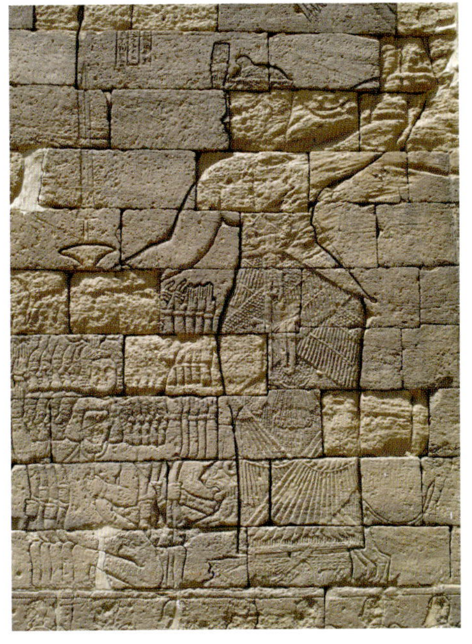

Amanitore, queen of Meroë (Sudan) (*r.* 1–20 CE). Building projects flourished during her reign, including the restoration of the Temple of Amun. (Relief, first century CE.)

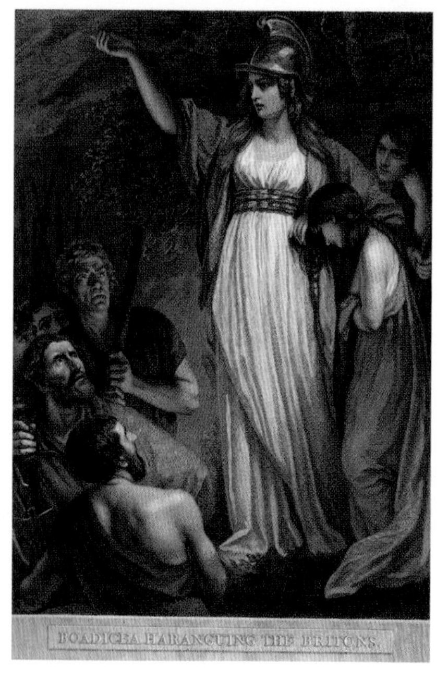

Boudicca, queen (coruler) of the Iceni (England) (*r.* mid-first century ce). Commanded her tribe in an uprising against the invading Roman Empire. (Engraving by William Sharp after John Opie, 1793.)

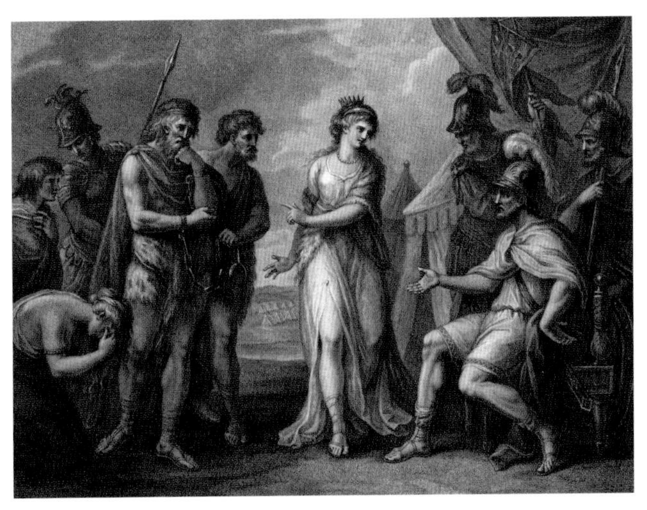

CARTIMANDUA, QUEEN (CORULER) OF THE BRIGANTES (ENGLAND) (*r.* mid-first century CE).
Twice avoided, with Rome's help, being overthrown by her husband. (Center; print by Francesco Bartolozzi, 1788.)

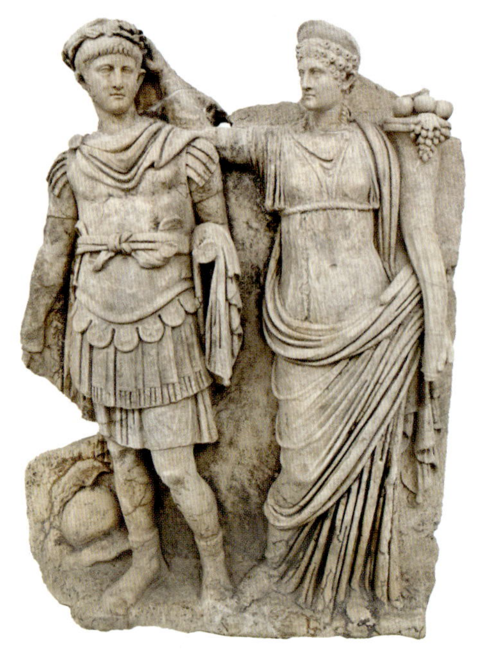

Julia Agrippina, or Agrippina the Younger, consort (*r.* 49–54 CE) and empress (coruler) of the Roman Empire (*r.* 54–57 CE). Her son, Nero, had her assassinated because she was too powerful. (Right, with Nero; sculpture, 54–68 CE.)

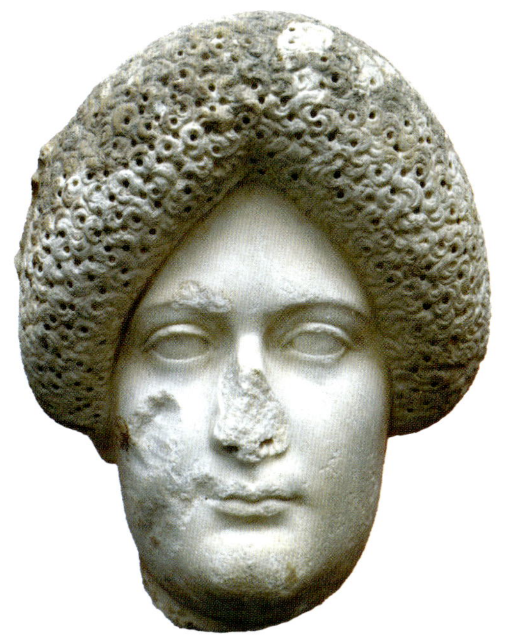

Domitia Longina, empress consort of the Roman Empire (*r.* 81–96 CE).
There is fierce disagreement: she either co-conspired in the murder of her husband, Domitian, or was loyal to her dying day. (Sculpture, c. 110 CE.)

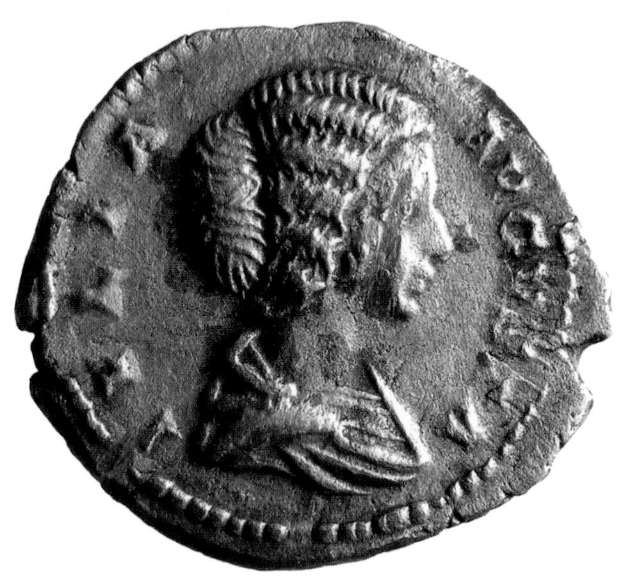

Julia Domna, empress consort (*r.* 193–211 CE) and de facto regent of the Roman Empire (*r.* 211–217 CE). Friend of the philosopher Philostratus, whom she commissioned to write the *Life of Apollonius of Tyana*. (Coin, 193–222 CE.)

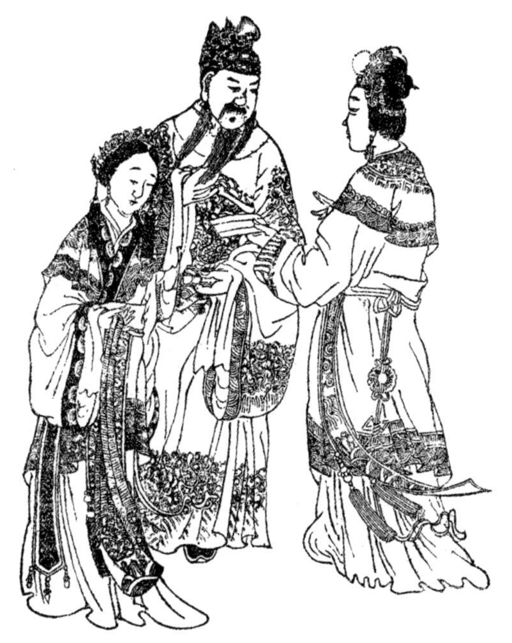

Fu Shou, empress consort of Eastern Han China (*r.* 195–214 CE). Bravely, but unsuccessfully, conspired to remove a court usurper, Cao Cao. (Right, with Consort Dong and Emperor Xian; illustration, 1928.)

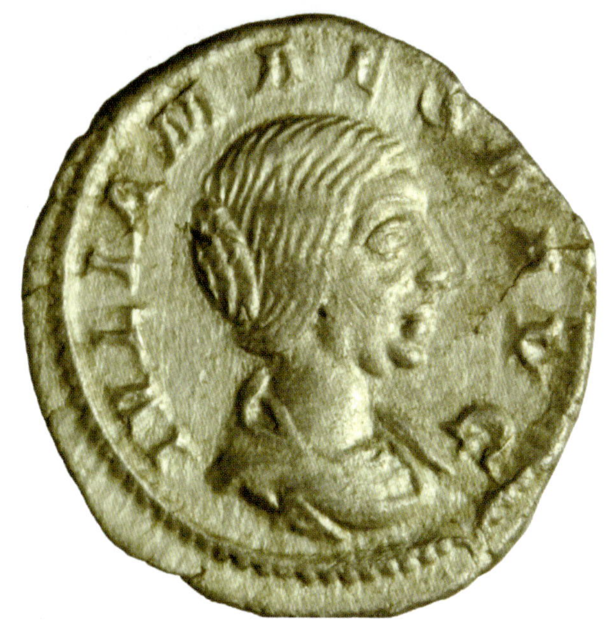

Julia Maesa, de facto regent (*augusta*) of the Roman Empire (*r.* 222–224/27 CE). Her savvy scheming restored the Severan dynasty to the throne. (Coin, c. 222 CE.)

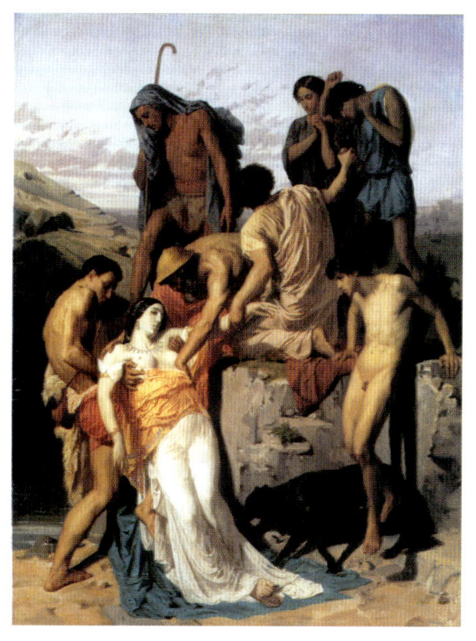

ZENOBIA, CONSORT (*r.* 260–267 BCE), REGENT (*r.* 267–272 BCE), AND EMPRESS OF PALMYRA (SYRIA) (*r.* 272 BCE).
A conqueror of Egypt and Asia Minor, she fought to establish independence from Rome, until her armies lost to Emperor Aurelian. (Painting by William-Adolphe Bouguereau, 1850.)

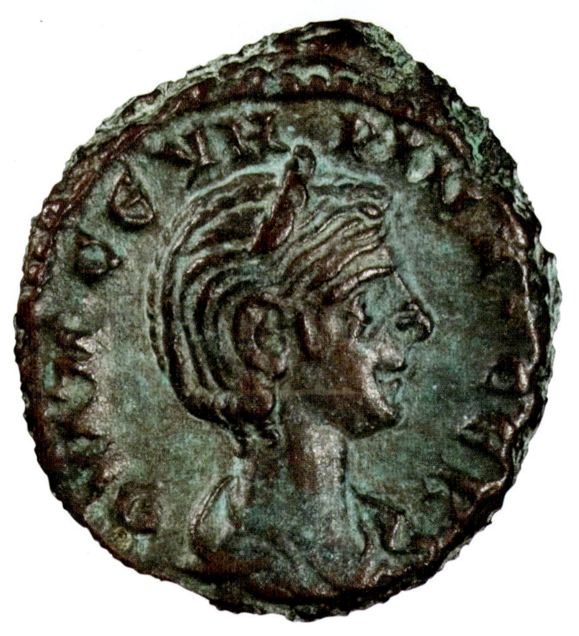

Ulpia Severina, empress (*r.* 270–275 ce) and regent of the Roman Empire (*r.* 275 ce).
She may have been the only woman to rule the Roman Empire in her own right. (Coin, c. 274–75 ce.)

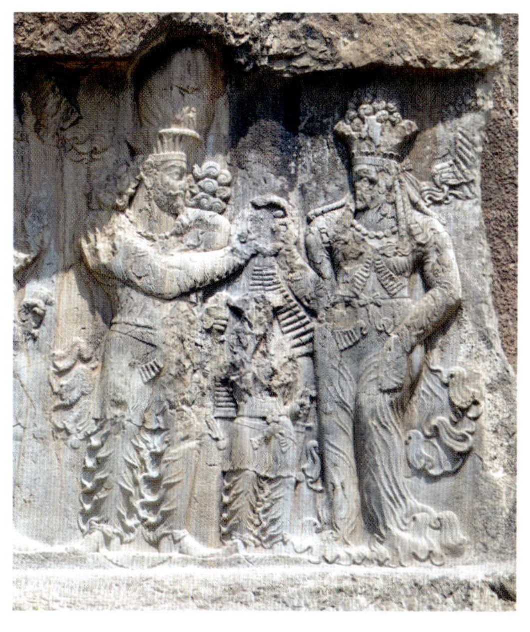

Shapurdukhtak, queen consort of the Sasanian Empire (Iran) (*r.* 293–302 CE).
In the pictured relief, the queen is believed to be the figure handing her husband, Narseh, the ring of kingship.
(Right; relief, detail, 293–303 CE.)

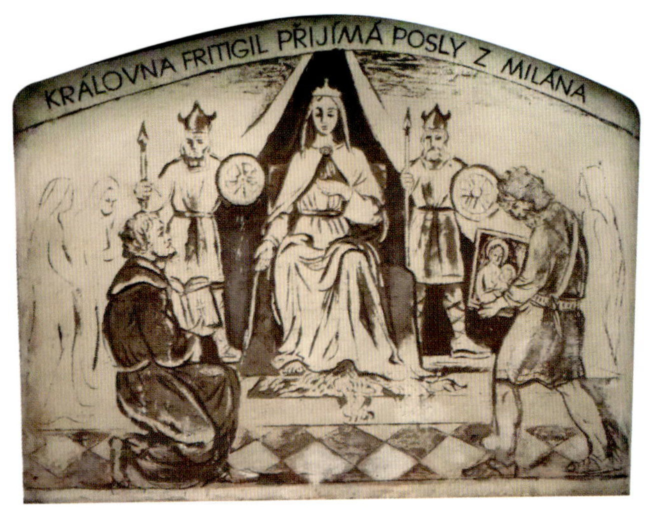

Fritigil, queen of the Marcomanni
(Germanic peoples, eastern Europe) (*r.* c. 350 CE).
Traveled to Milan to meet her correspondent and religious adviser
Bishop Ambrose, but he died before she arrived. (Mural, detail.)

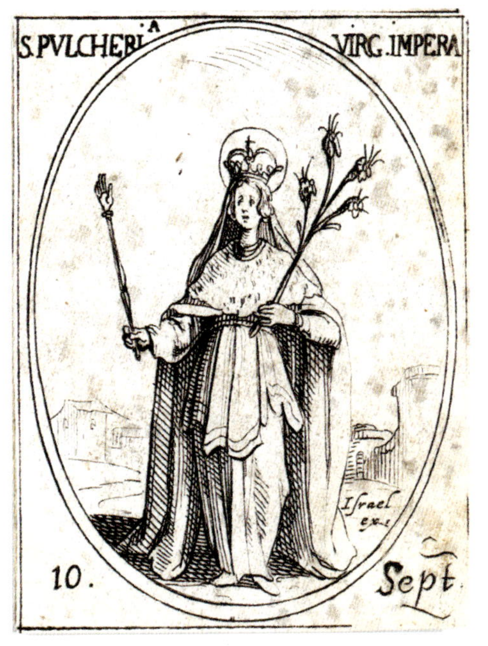

Saint Pulcheria, regent (*r.* 414–416 CE) and empress (coruler) of the Roman Empire (*r.* 450–453 CE). A key player in religious councils and prolific builder in Constantinople. (Print, detail, by Jacques Callot, 1636.)

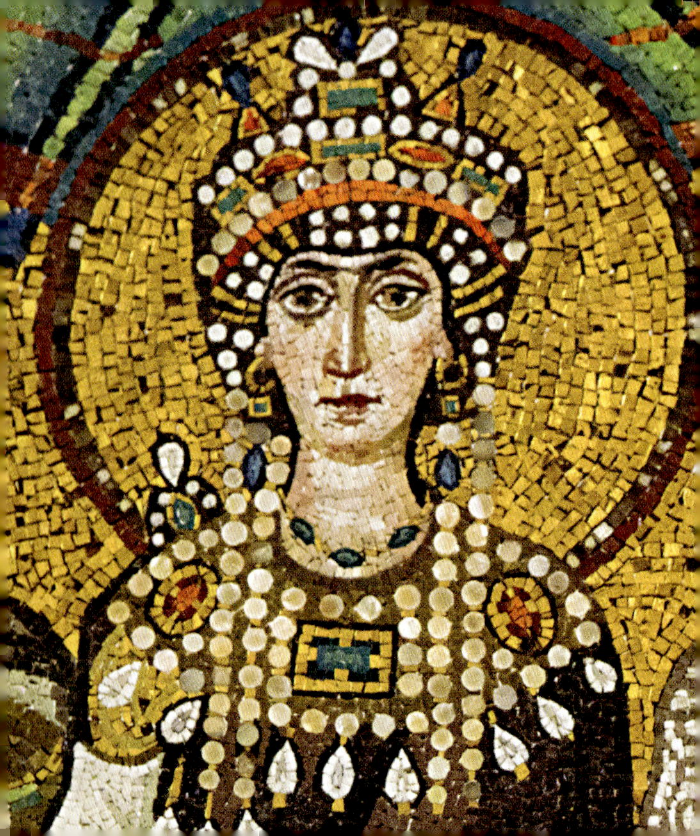

2. MIDDLE AGES

500–1299

Italian humanists, enamored with antiquity, created the term "Middle Ages" to describe the period between the fall of Rome and the Renaissance. The Middle Ages were a culturally rich time, despite what the humanists believed, encompassing creative activity such as the flourishing known as the Islamic Golden Age. Though the term is European, the Middle Ages' chronological breadth is useful for describing a nearly global trend of artistic production shifting from stone to manuscript illumination and painting. In this period, the world was poised to exalt women as mothers, child bearers, and advisers for kings, rather than as rulers in their own right. It was remarkably uncommon for a woman to claim absolute power. Patriarchal views of women persisted in many cultures and were buoyed by interpretations of religious texts that positioned women as inferior to men.

As in ancient times, the right to reign was often secured by violence, either assassination or war. Women were not typically permitted to be warriors, and it was fighters who seized land and throne. However, this didn't mean that women were content to stand on the sidelines. Gemmei became the fifth of eight empresses to rule on their own in Japanese history, and named her daughter, Gensho, as heir. Gensho's ascent is the only example of a daughter inheriting the throne from her mother in the history of Japan. Both empresses made considerable political and cultural contributions in their time.

In Europe, cultural stereotypes of women seeped into matters of the law. Codified in the early sixth century by the Frankish king Clovis, Salic law explicitly excluded women from inheriting property, fiefs, and most significantly, the throne. This would influence European law for centuries to come. The advent of Islam in seventh-century Arabia also prohibited the role of women in authority, and interpretations of scriptures were used to subjugate women. At the beginning of the eleventh century, Neo-Confucianism in China imposed a social hierarchy where men ruled over women, which by extension restricted women from obtaining the throne.

Women who tried to exercise their own authority met considerable opposition. A woman aspiring to power was perceived as an adulteress or a witch—the personification of a woman deviating from socially held ideas of femininity. Kings, for the most part, concurred with this mental framework, and many were quick to accuse their wives of these transgressions in order to justify divorce. Queens, on the other hand, mostly obtained divorces by claiming consanguinity—that the married couple was too closely related for the union to be lawful. This was a notably ironic claim, considering the relational closeness of marriages at the time.

Though beset with limitations and challenges, medieval royal women were shrewd politicians. Many advised on diplomatic matters, using the perception and stereotype of their sex as sensitive intercessors to influence the king to make political gains by showing mercy to his enemies. These women sent armies to battle, fought in wars (more often than you might think), and ordered the assassinations of their enemies. Queens often outlived their husbands, usually due to the militaristic nature of life, and would act as an adviser for their reigning son, skillfully ensuring the success of their line. Queens were also concerned with matters outside of war and politics. They managed their households, founded universities and libraries, supported scriptoria, and commissioned illuminated manuscripts.

Hostile and demeaning perceptions of women abounded during the Middle Ages, but despite this, the period became an exceptional time for female regents. In many cultures, regency was perceived as a God-given right. By governing on behalf of a male royal, a female regent was seen as unthreatening and traditionally feminine enough to satisfy the prejudices of society. Eleanor of Aquitaine, queen of France (as consort to Louis VII) and England (as consort to Henry II), presided over her namesake region and inheritance, and issued numerous charters in her own name. She acted as regent for her son Richard the Lionheart while he was on a crusade. As regent, she protected England from the machinations of her son's enemies, who wanted to conquer the king's lands while he was away. She secured Richard's ransom when he was captured while returning to England, and traveled in person to escort him back home. As Eleanor demonstrated, regents could nearly grasp full rulership, though there were often stipulations, put in place because of their sex. In many parts of the world, such as medieval China, it was common for female regents to attend councils behind screens.

Representations of queens—indeed, of nearly everyone—during this period are generic, usually in the form of donor portraits or inside historiated initials in illuminated manuscripts. In these artworks, rulers are commonly cast as a type, with the colors of their clothes and metaphorical objects showing them as virtuous or honorable; sometimes queens are represented as goddesses or saints—and quite few, in fact, would even be granted sainthood. The Middle Ages captured the imagination of artists for centuries afterward, particularly in the nineteenth century, with romanticized renderings of queens. The representations of queens in this chapter, however, are dominated by European art, due to the output of royal imagery of that period; other notable queens ruled during this time who have not been captured in this way.

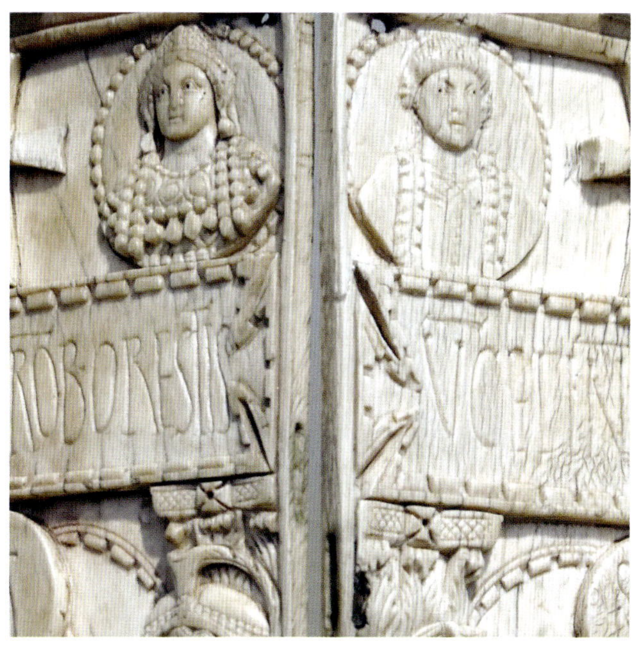

AMALASUNTHA, REGENT (*r.* 526–534) AND QUEEN OF THE OSTROGOTHS (BALKANS) (*r.* 534–535).
Spurned by Ostrogoth nobility for being an intellectual and patron of the arts. (Left, with her son, Athalaric; relief, detail, 530.)

Actress to Empress

Theodora had been an actress as a means to survive, but she gave up the profession after converting to Christianity. When she met Justinian, the future Byzantine emperor, he was immediately enamored of her. The law forbade marriage to actresses because they were seen as prostitutes; Justinian had the law changed so he could marry Theodora. She ruled closely with her husband, intermittently performed as regent for short periods, governed her own court, and played a vital role in religious affairs.

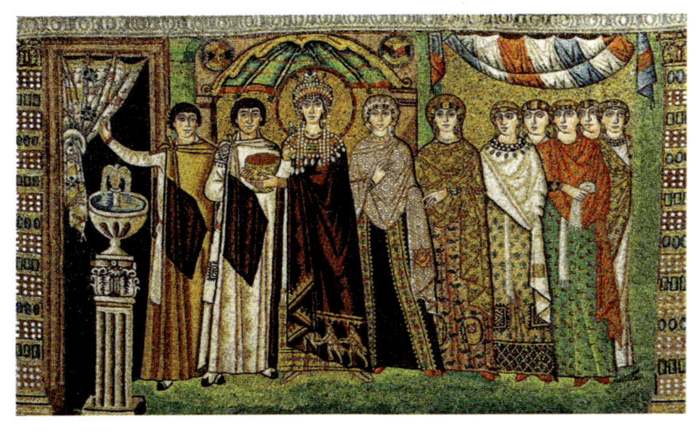

Saint Theodora, empress consort of the Byzantine Empire (*r.* 527–548). (Center, with halo; mosaic, c. 547.)

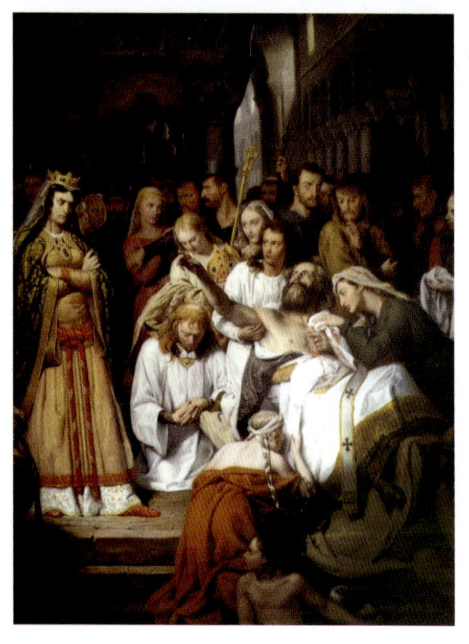

Fredegund, queen consort (*r.* c. 568–584) and regent of the Franks (Germany) (*r.* 584–597).
She was responsible for her brother-in-law Sigebert I's death, and supposedly had Bishop Praetextatus stabbed during Easter Mass. (Far left; painting by François-Édouard Cibo, 1832.)

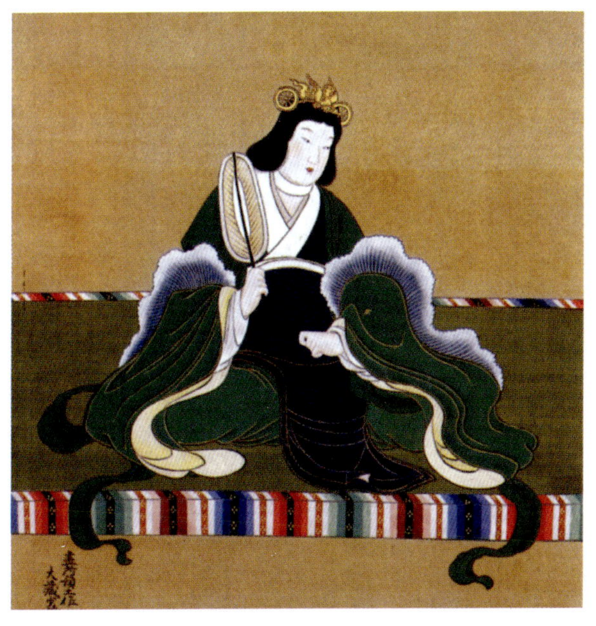

Suiko, consort (*r.* 576–585) and empress of Japan (*r.* 592–628). She was the first reigning empress of Japan in recorded history. (Painting by Tosa Mitsuyoshi, 1726.)

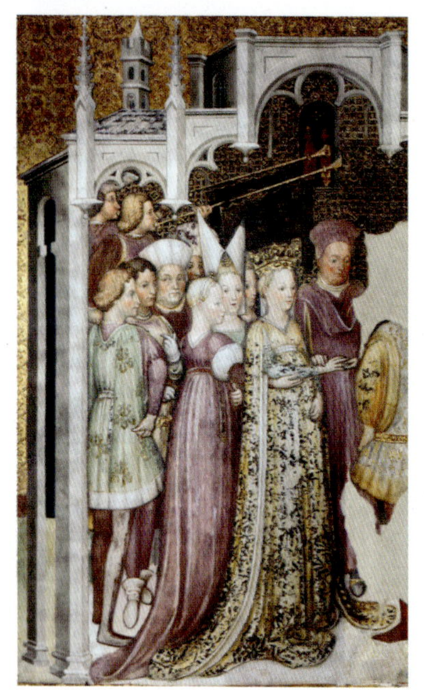

THEODELINDA, QUEEN CONSORT (*r.* 588–616) AND CO-REGENT OF LOMBARDY (ITALY) (*r.* 616–626). Positioned Nicene Christianity to dominate over its rival sect, Arianism. (Right, in flowered gown; fresco, 1444.)

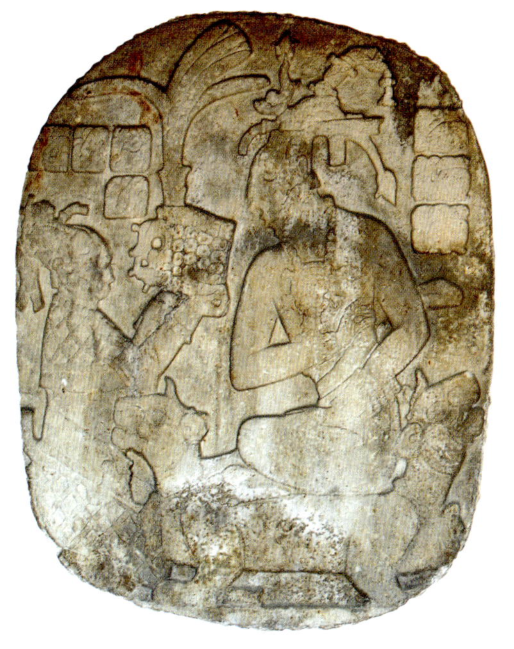

Lady Sak K'uk, or Muwaan Mat, queen (or regent)
of Palenque (Mexico) (*r.* 612–615).
Passed the crown to her son, K'inich Janaab' Pakal, as seen here, which broke with patrilineal tradition. (Left, with her son; relief, c. 612–900.)

Trailblazing Empress

When Wu Zetian's husband, Emperor Gaozong, died, his throne was bequeathed to their third son. Wu Zetian exiled this son and placed her youngest son on the throne, so that she could push him aside and reign as de facto ruler. Her followers begged her to become the sole empress, and even her son asked to resign his role. In 690, she became "Emperor, Son of Heaven," the title remaining masculine because there was no alternative, or precedent, for a female ruler. This sculpture of the goddess Vairocana is probably modeled on Wu Zetian.

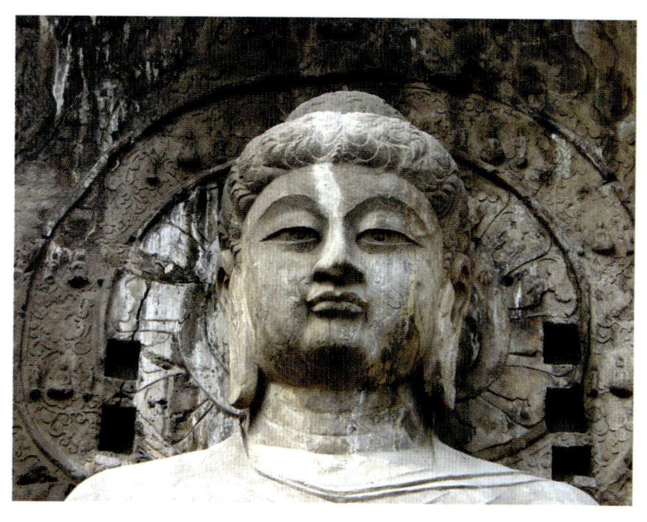

Wu Zetian, empress consort (*r.* 655–683) and dowager of Tang China (*r.* 683–690), and empress of Zhou China (*r.* 690–705). (Cave sculpture, 672–76.)

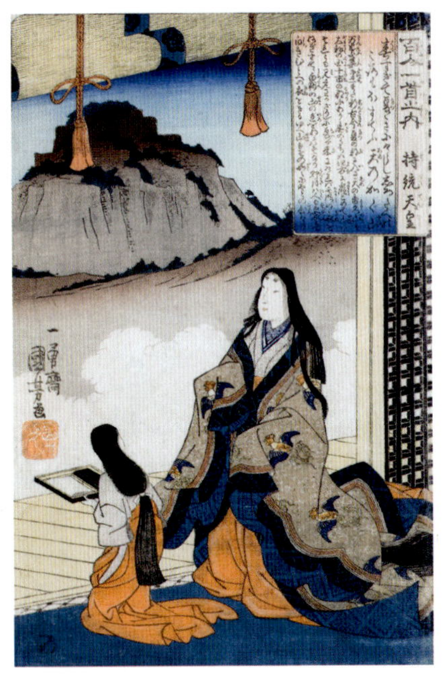

Jito, consort (*r.* 673–686), dowager (*r.* 686–690), and empress of Japan (*r.* 690–697).
She was granted authority over the government after the emperor's death. (Right; print, c. 1840.)

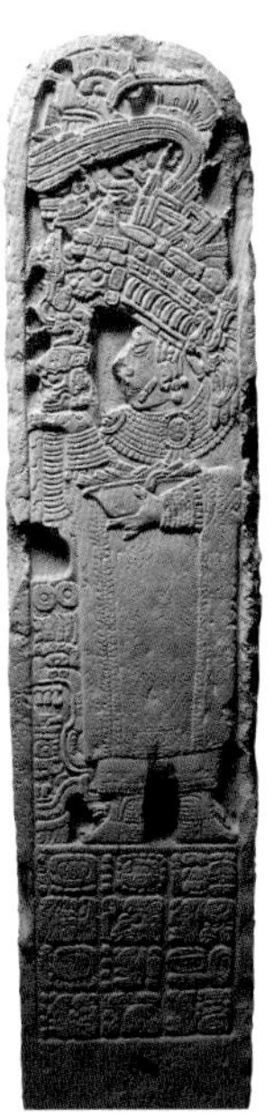

Lady Ik' Skull, or Lady Eveningstar, queen consort (or regent) of Yaxchilan (Mexico) (*r.* early to mid-eighth century). Lady Ik' Skull's son commissioned many stone carvings in her honor, as she was publicly ignored by the king. (Sculpture, c. eighth century.)

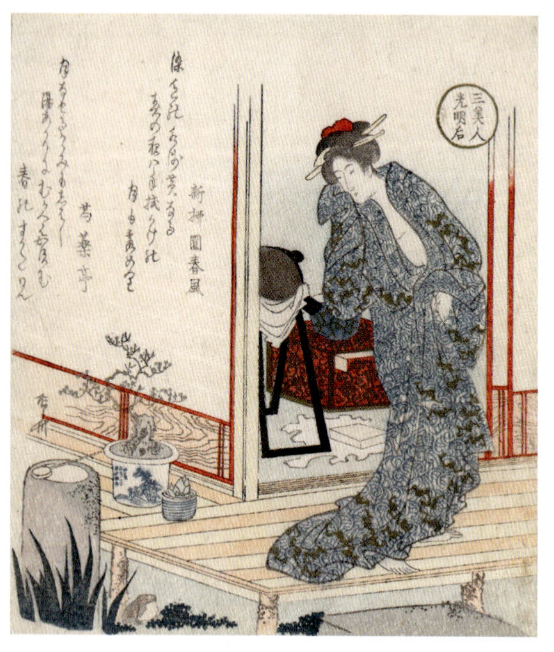

Komyo, empress consort of Japan (*r.* 730–749).
She and her husband became Buddhist priest and nun upon their retirement from royal life. (Print by Ryuryukyo Shinsai, c. 1820–25.)

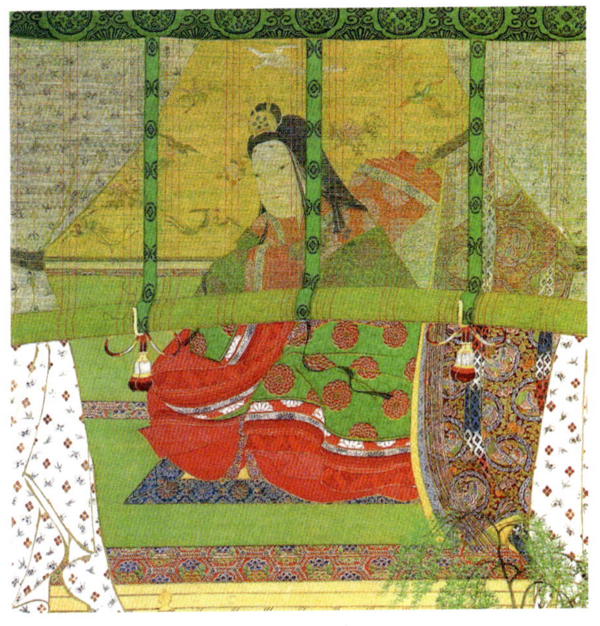

Koken, or Shotoku, empress of Japan (*r.* 749–758; 764–770). Koken granted the Buddhist monk Dokyo immense authority; this resulted in female succession being prohibited in Japan. (Painting, eighteenth century.)

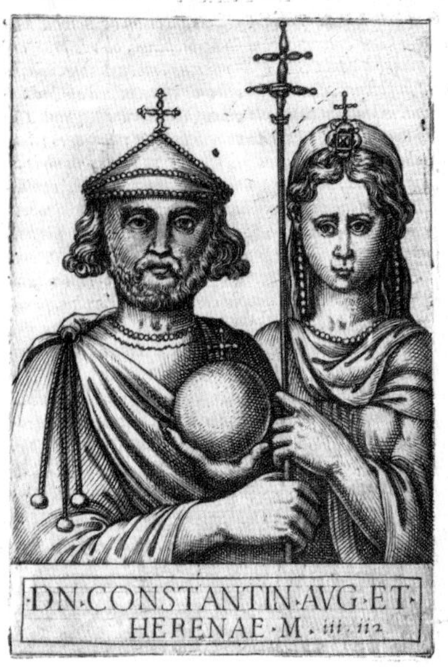

IRENE OF ATHENS, CONSORT (*r.* 775–780), REGENT (CORULER) (*r.* 780–790; 792–797), AND EMPRESS OF THE BYZANTINE EMPIRE (*r.* 797–802).
The first empress regnant of the Byzantine Empire; allegedly gouged out her son Constantine VI's eyes so she could take control. (Right, with her son; engraving, detail, by Giovanni Battista de' Cavalieri, 1583.)

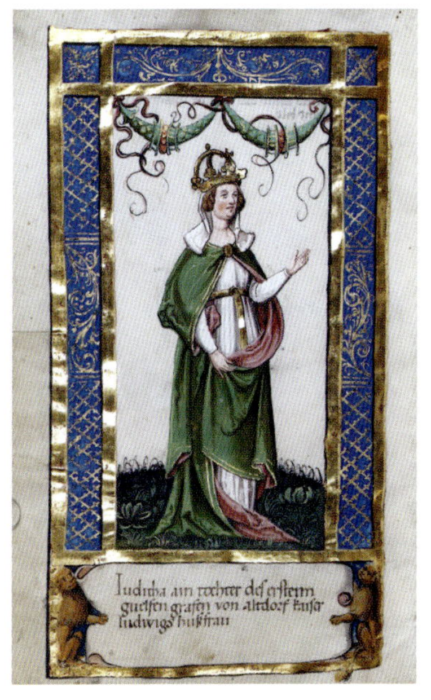

Judith of Bavaria, empress consort of the Holy Roman Empire and the Franks (Germany) (*r.* 819–840).
While her husband campaigned, she ran the court and strategized for her son to inherit the throne. (Manuscript miniature, c. 1510.)

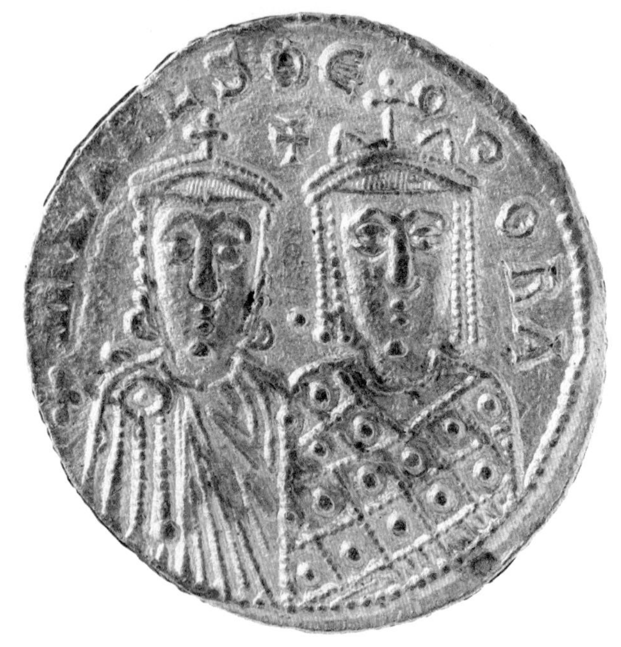

Saint Theodora, empress consort (*r.* 830–842) and regent of the Byzantine Empire (*r.* 842–855).
She reinstituted the veneration of icons.
(Right, with her son, Michael III; coin, c. 843–56.)

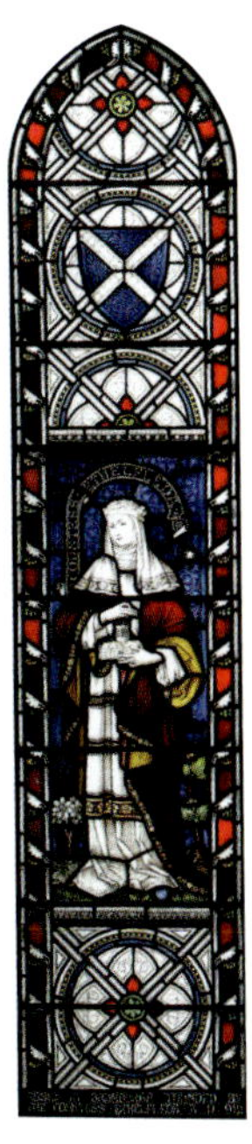

AETHELFLAED, CONSORT (*r.* c. 880–911) AND QUEEN OF MERCIA (ENGLAND) (*r.* 911–918).
Successfully strategized for her army to reclaim Viking-held territory. (Stained glass, c. 1862–64.)

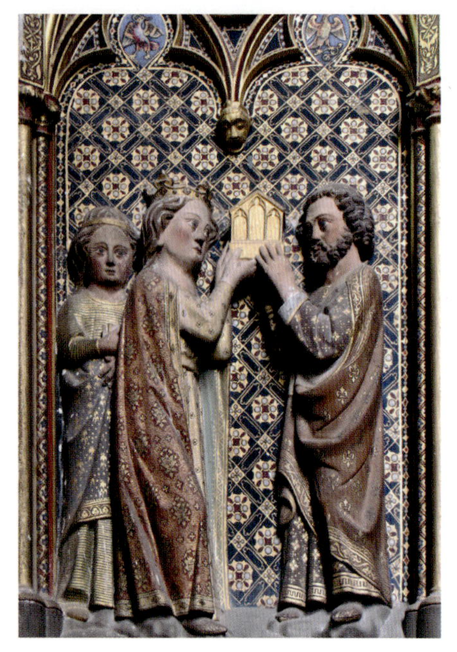

Saint Richardis, empress consort of the
Holy Roman Empire (*r.* 881–888).
She was the protégée of the mystic and writer Saint Hildegard
of Bingen. (Center; relief, eleventh century.)

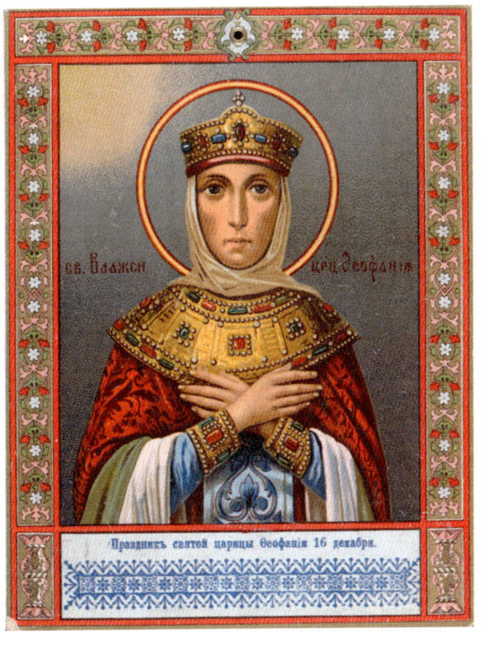

Saint Theophano Martinakia, empress consort of the Byzantine Empire (*r.* 886–893). Retired to a monastery after her husband started having an affair. (Print, detail, 1901.)

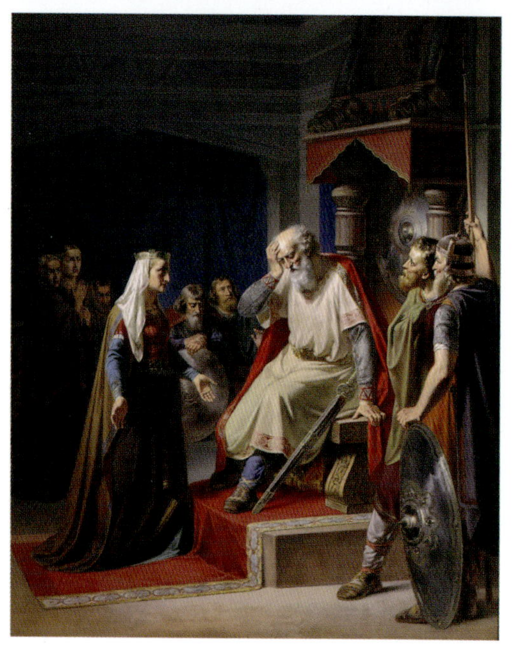

THYRA, QUEEN CONSORT OF DENMARK (*r.* c. 936–c. 958). Thyra's husband raised a memorial rune stone with an inscription describing her as the "Pride of Denmark." (Left; painting by August Carl Vilhelm Thomsen, c. 1860.)

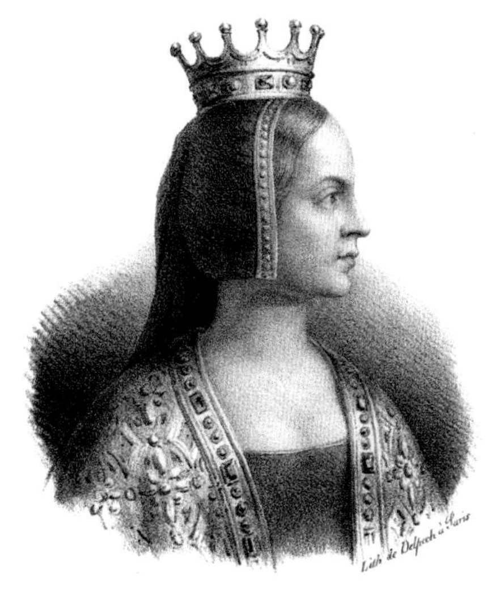

Gerberge,
Femme de Louis IV.

GERBERGA, QUEEN CONSORT (*r.* 939–954) AND REGENT OF FRANCE (*r.* 954–959). Used her army to maintain power and ensure that her son would inherit the throne. (Print, detail, 1818–42.)

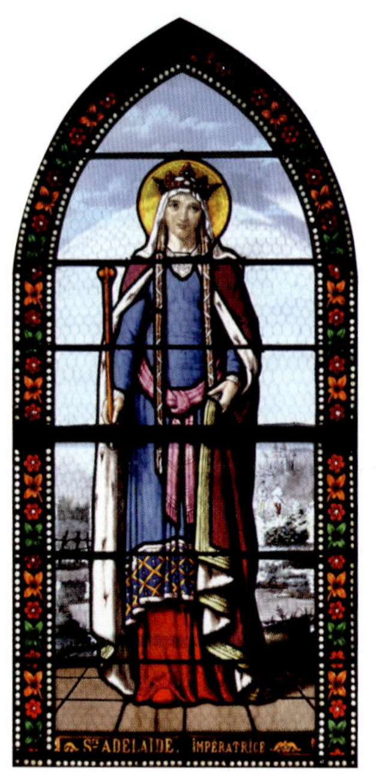

SAINT ADELAIDE OF LUXEMBOURG, EMPRESS CONSORT (*r.* 962–973) AND REGENT OF THE HOLY ROMAN EMPIRE (*r.* 991–995). The imprisoned Adelaide reputedly escaped her usurper through a tunnel under the castle walls. (Stained glass, c. 1890.)

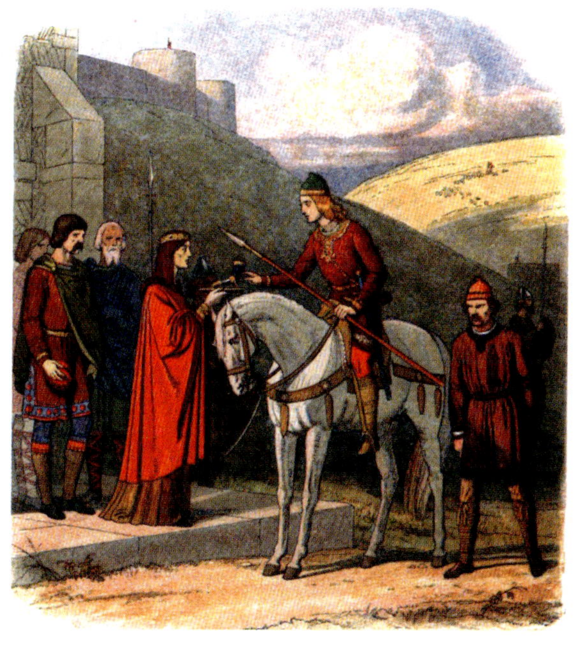

AELFTHRYTH, QUEEN CONSORT (*r.* 964/65–975) AND REGENT OF ENGLAND (*r.* 979–984).
Accused of arranging the murder of her stepson in order for her son to take the throne. (Left, in red cloak; illustration by Edmund Evans, 1864.)

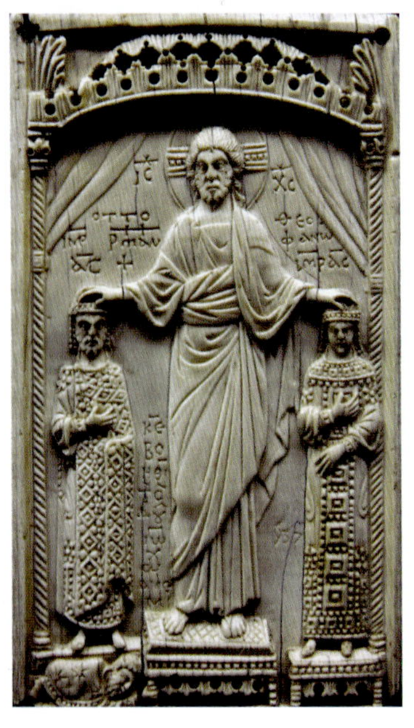

THEOPHANU, EMPRESS CONSORT (*r.* 973–983) AND REGENT OF THE HOLY ROMAN EMPIRE (*r.* 985–991). Referred to herself in official documents as *imperatrix*, empress, and sometimes even as *imperator*, emperor. (Right; carving, 982–83.)

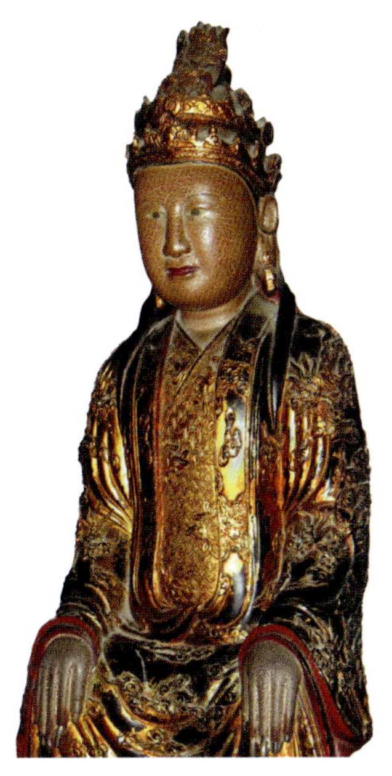

Duong Van Nga, regent (*r.* 979–980) and empress consort of Vietnam (*r.* 981–1000).
She elevated her second husband, General Le Hoan, to emperor in order to lead a defense against invaders. (Statue, c. tenth–eleventh century.)

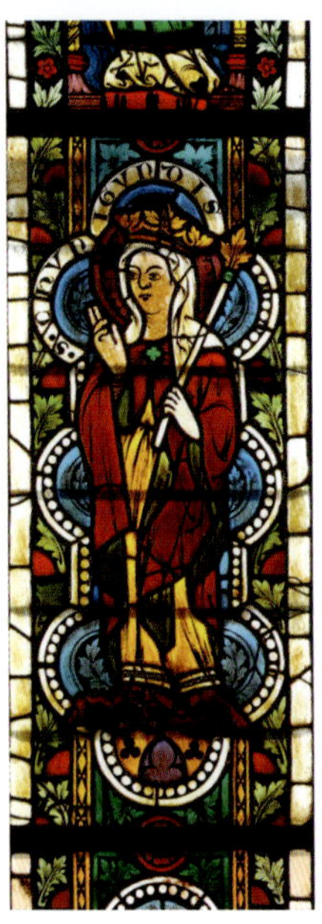

Saint Cunigunde, empress consort (*r.* 1002–1024) and regent of the Holy Roman Empire (*r.* 1024). She advised Henry II on all matters religious and secular, and her participation was recorded in one-third of her husband's surviving charters. (Stained glass, 1340–50.)

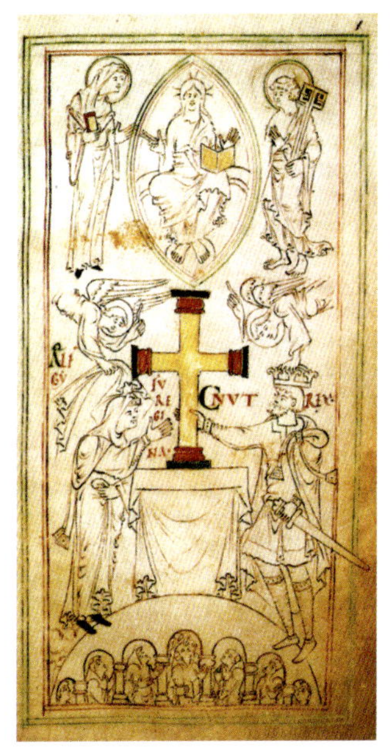

Emma of Normandy, queen consort of England (*r.* 1002–1035), Denmark (*r.* 1018–1035), and Norway (*r.* 1028–1035). Commissioned the richly illuminated manuscript *Encomium Emmae Reginae*, which served to unite her two sons. (Standing, lower left; manuscript illustration, c. 1031–71.)

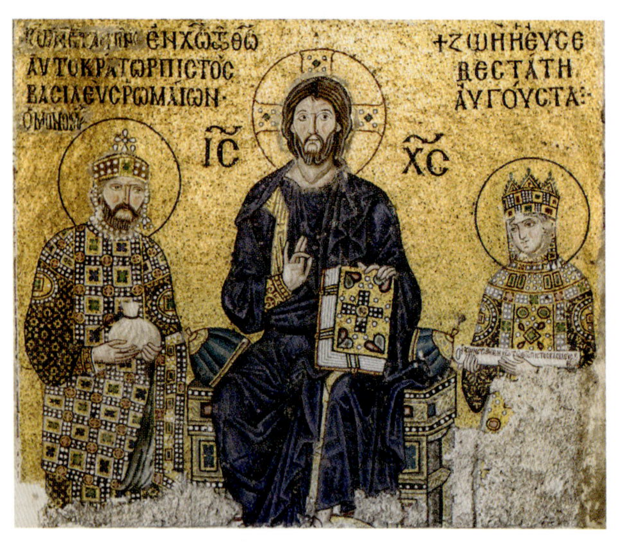

Zoë Porphyrogenita, empress (coruler) of the Byzantine Empire (*r.* 1028–1050).
Zoë's supporters ousted her husband and restored the exiled queen to the throne; she ruled as joint empress with her sister Theodora III. (Right, with Constantine IX Monomachos; mosaic, c. eleventh century.)

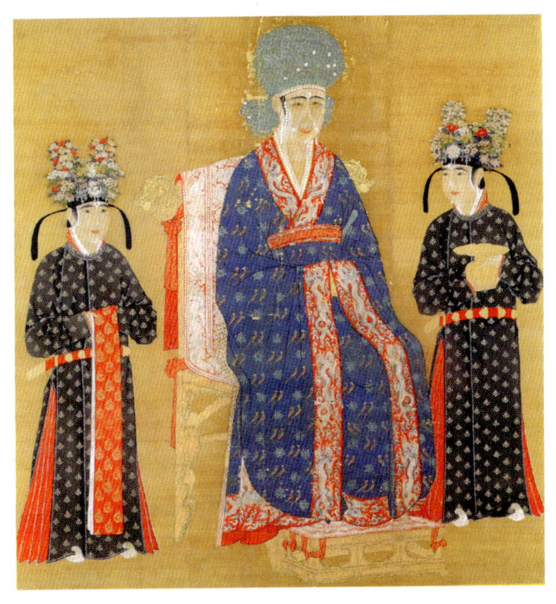

Cao, empress consort (*r.* 1034–1067), regent (*r.* 1063–1064), and dowager of Song China (*r.* 1063–1079). She refused, unsuccessfully, to step down as regent when her son recovered from an illness. (Center; painting, c. 1022–63.)

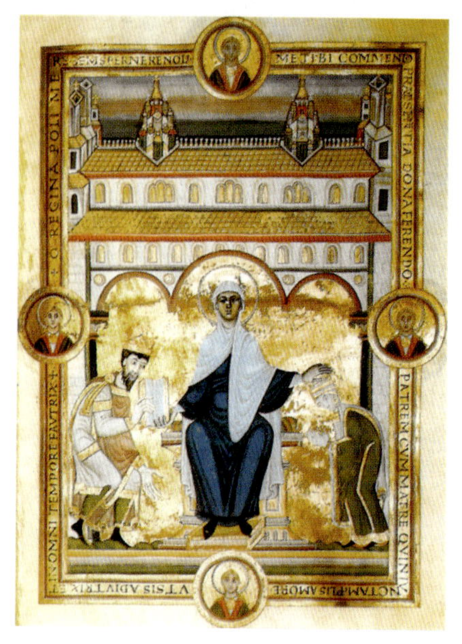

Agnes of Poitou, queen consort of Germany (*r.* 1043–1056), and empress (*r.* 1046–1056) and regent of the Holy Roman Empire (*r.* 1056–1062). Active in politics even after her retirement to a convent, when she mediated between her son and the pope. (Lower right; manuscript illustration, c. 1050.)

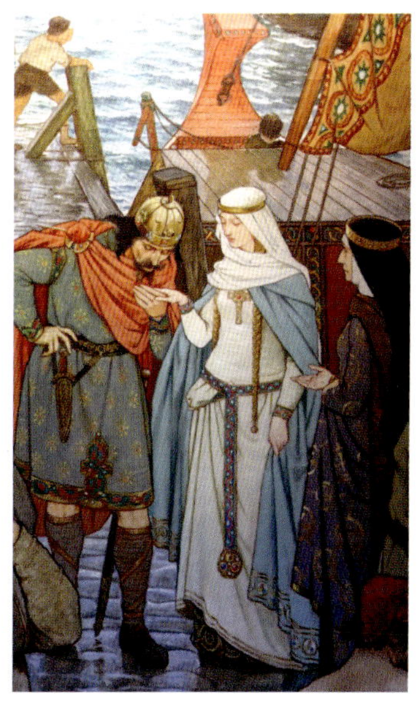

Saint Margaret, queen consort of Scotland (*r.* 1070–1093). Established a pilgrim's ferry to Saint Andrews, since named South Queensferry and North Queensferry. (Center; mural, detail, by William Hole, c. 1899.)

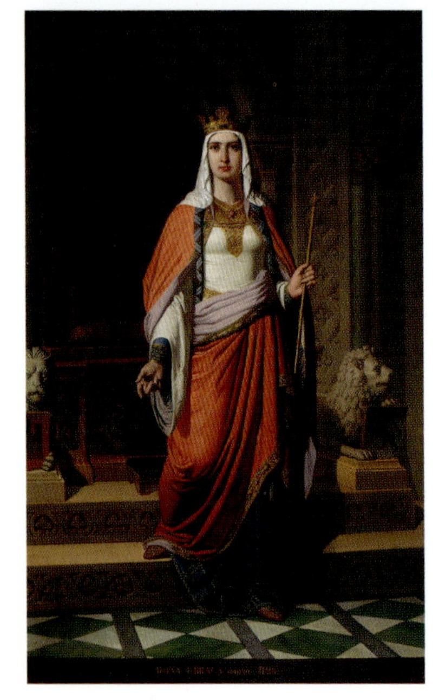

Urraca, queen of León, Castile, and (as coruler) Spain (*r.* 1109–1126).
Governed León and Castile independently after her marriage to Alfonso I of Aragon. (Painting by Carlos Múgica y Pérez, 1857.)

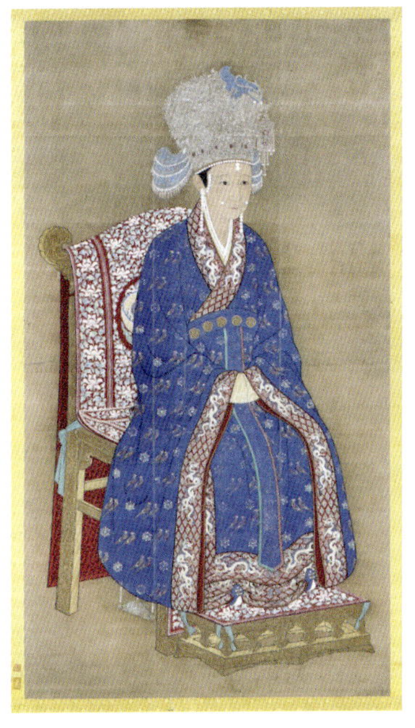

Zheng, empress consort of Northern Song China (*r.* 1110–1126).
Despite Zheng's lowly social status, she charmed the emperor into elevating her from concubine to empress. (Painting.)

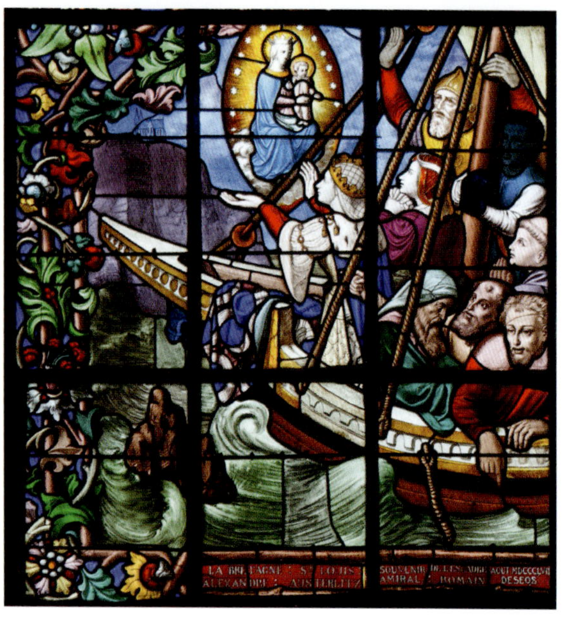

Matilda, empress consort of the Holy Roman Empire (*r.* 1114–1125), and (disputed) queen of England (*r.* 1141–1148). She was made "lady of the English" by her supporters and ruled part of England before Stephen took the throne. (Center, in crown; stained glass, detail, by Workshop of Adolphe Napoléon Didron, 1857.)

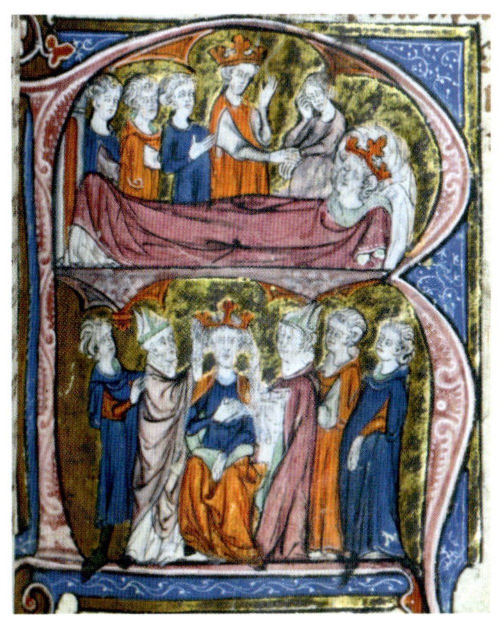

Melisende, queen (coruler) (*r.* 1131–1153) and regent of Jerusalem (*r.* 1153–1161).
Refused to abdicate the throne when her son came of age, dividing the kingdom with him instead. (Bottom, far right; manuscript, historiated initial, c. 1275–1325 CE.)

A Queen's Rebellion

Eleanor led a revolt against her second husband, King Henry II of England, with three of her sons. At the time, Henry was threatening the autonomy of her beloved Aquitaine, and her sons were upset to find their inheritance in jeopardy, as the king planned to give the princes' castles to their youngest brother. The uprising was unsuccessful. Her sons got a fresh start, but she was imprisoned for fifteen years, released only after her husband's death. She was a strong force during her son Richard I's rule, notably by freeing prisoners on the condition that they swear fealty to him, Richard the Lionheart.

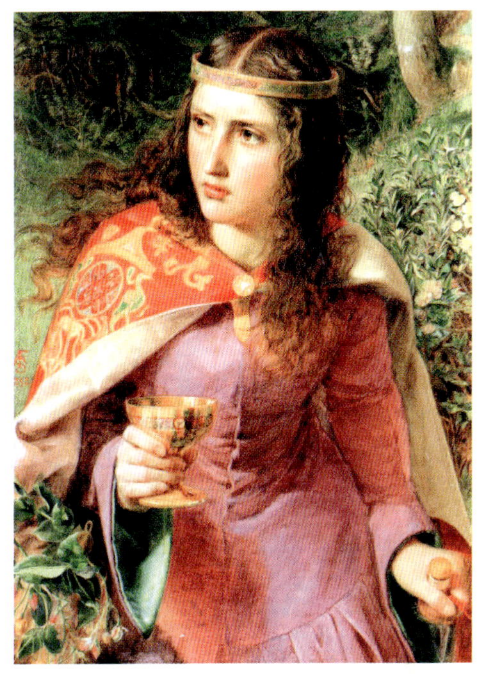

Eleanor of Aquitaine, queen consort of France (*r.* 1137–1152) and England (*r.* 1154–1189), and regent of England (*r.* 1191–1194). (Painting by Frederick Sandys, 1858.)

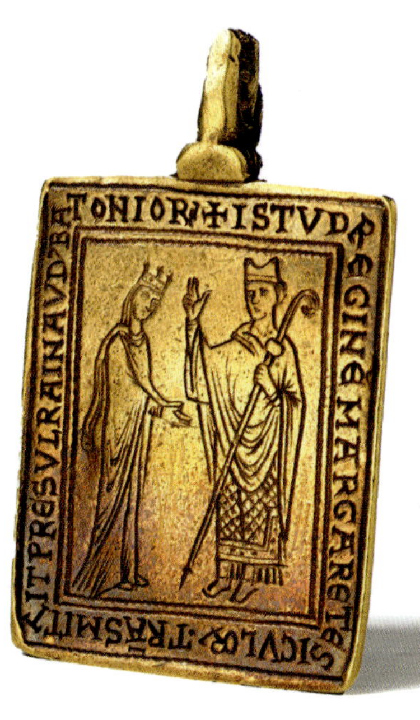

Margaret of Navarre, queen consort (*r.* 1154–1166) and regent of Sicily (*r.* 1166–1171).

Friend and longtime correspondent of Archbishop (and later saint) Thomas Becket of Canterbury. (Left; the queen's reliquary, 1174–77.)

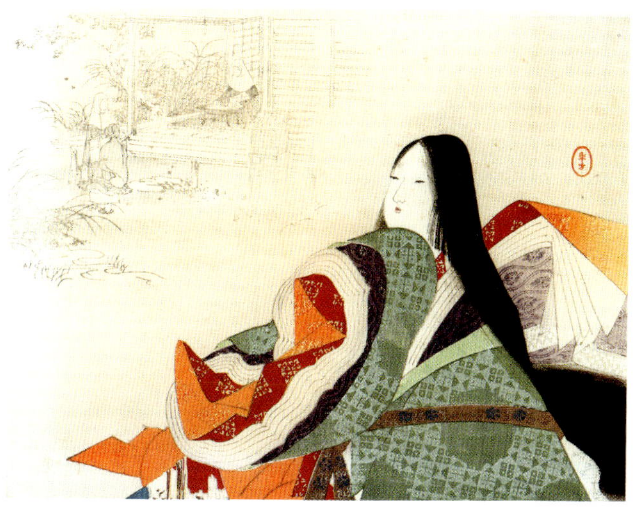

Taira no Tokuko, empress consort of Japan (*r.* 1172–1182). She jumped overboard during a sea battle—desiring to end her life rather than be captured by the enemy—but was rescued. (Print by Toshikata Mizuno, 1901.)

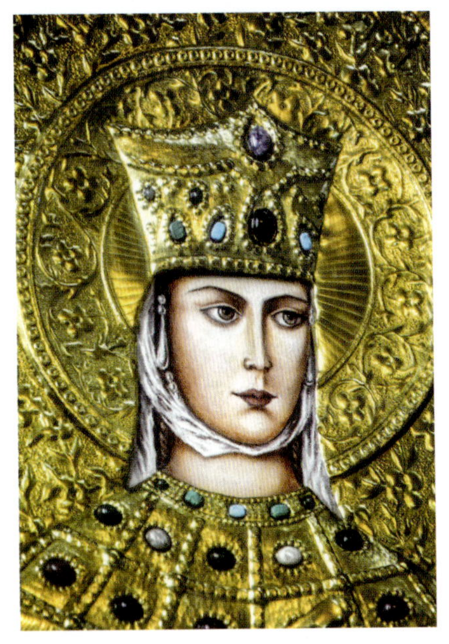

Saint Tamar the Great, co-regent (*r.* 1178–1184) and queen of Georgia (*r.* 1184–1213). The first woman in Georgia to rule on her own, she divorced her coup-attempting husband, remarried, and consolidated her empire. (Icon.)

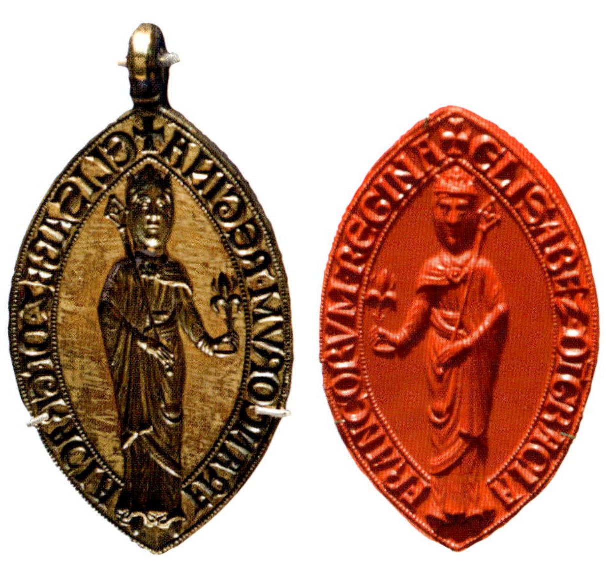

Isabella of Hainaut, queen consort of France (*r.* 1180–1190).
The king threatened to divorce her, so she traveled
as a barefoot penitent throughout the local churches
to gain the people's support. (Seal, c. 1180.)

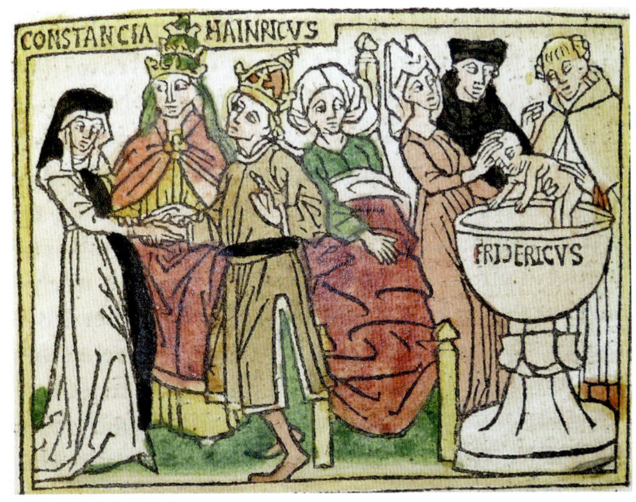

Constance, empress consort of the Holy Roman Empire (*r.* 1191–1197), and queen (coruler) of Sicily (*r.* 1194–1198). Dante's *Divine Comedy* places this clever queen in Paradise. (Far left; illustration, detail, c. 1474.)

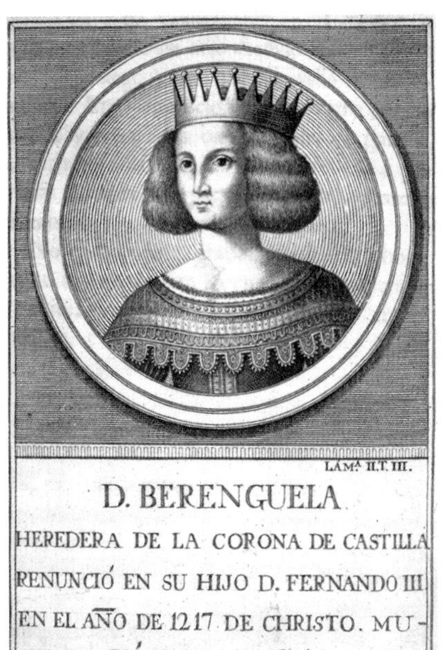

BERENGARIA OF NAVARRE, QUEEN CONSORT OF LEÓN (*r.* 1197–1217), AND QUEEN OF CASTILE AND TOLEDO (SPAIN) (*r.* 1217). She orchestrated the reunion of a divided León and Castile. (Illustration, detail, by Manuel Mariano Rodríguez, 1788.)

A Sneaky Dinner Date

In Song China, Yang and a rival, Cao, were both up for the position of empress, to be decided after Emperor Ningzong dined with them separately. To defeat her competitor for the role of empress, Yang pretended to defer to Cao, allowing her to have a banquet first. At Yang's dinner with the emperor, she convinced him—inebriated from his dinner with Cao—to sign an edict to make her empress. The signed edict was intercepted, but luckily she had another on hand, which the emperor readily inscribed during the evening when no interceptors were about.

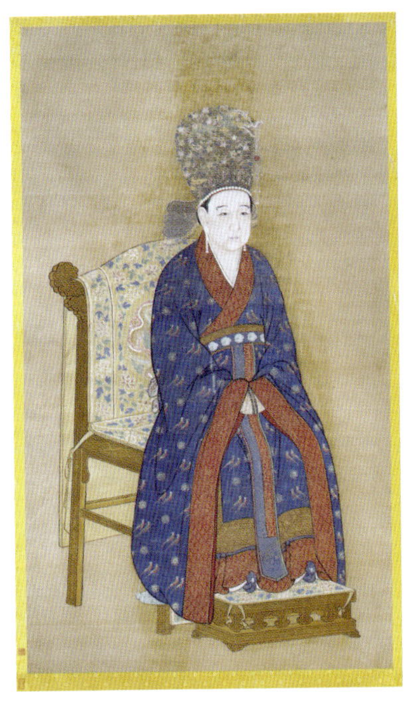

YANG, EMPRESS CONSORT (*r.* 1202–1217), CO-REGENT AND DOWAGER OF SONG CHINA (*r.* 1224–1233). (Painting, c. 1202–33.)

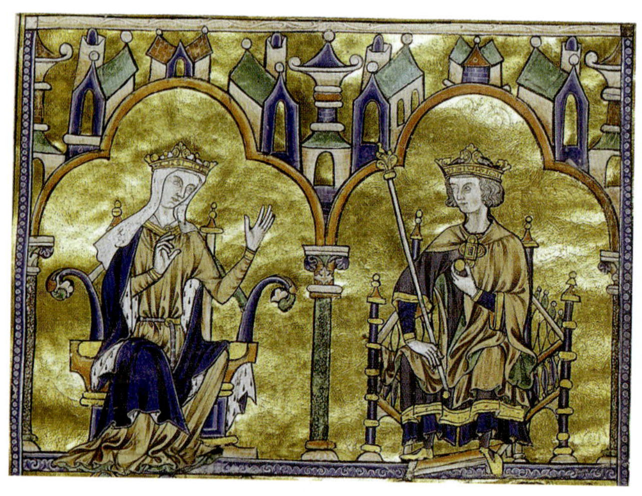

Blanche of Castile, queen consort (*r.* 1223–1226) and regent of France (*r.* 1226–1234; 1248–1252).
She summoned and traveled—but didn't fight—with an army to meet the forces that denounced her son's authority. (Left, with her son, Louis IX; manuscript illumination, detail, thirteenth century.)

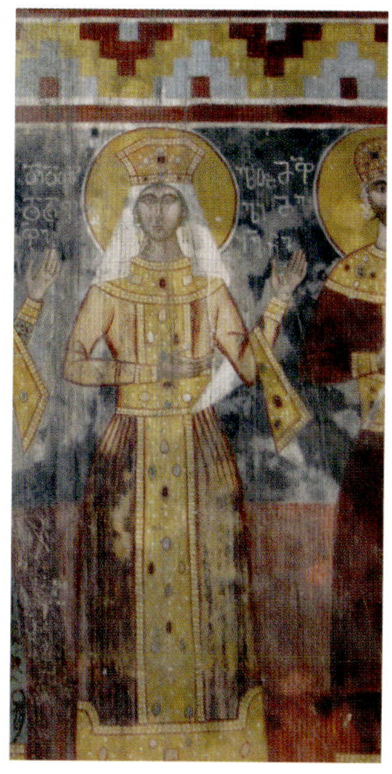

RUSUDAN, QUEEN OF GEORGIA (*r.* 1223–1245). Imprisoned her illegitimate nephew to ensure that her son would inherit the throne. (Fresco, detail, sixteenth century.)

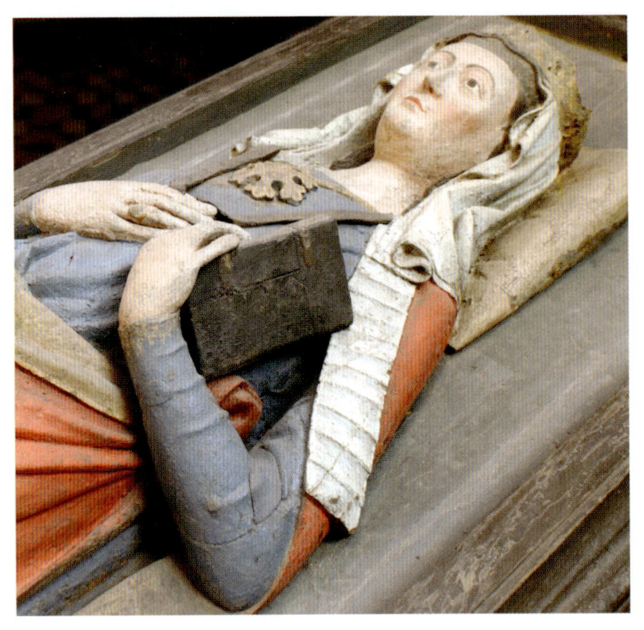

MARGARET SAMBIRIA, QUEEN CONSORT (*r.* 1252–1259) AND REGENT OF DENMARK (*r.* 1259–1264).
The first known regent in Denmark's history, she obtained Pope Urban IV's permission for women to inherit the Danish throne. (Relief, c. 1282.)

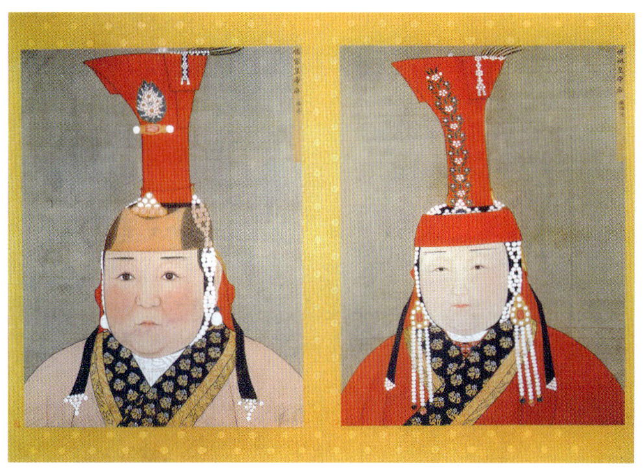

Chabi, empress consort of Yuan China (*r.* 1260–1281). She was a key political adviser to her husband, Kublai Khan (pictured, left); her red robes, a color used for elite women, symbolize Mongol power. (Painting, fourteenth century.)

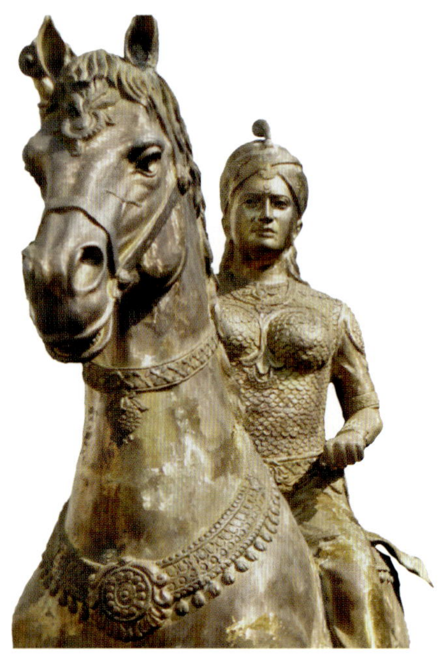

RUDRAMA DEVI, QUEEN OF ORUGALLU (INDIA) (*r.* 1262–1289). Rudrama, a victorious warrior, adopted a male persona to establish herself in a patrilineal society. (Statue, detail, 2015.)

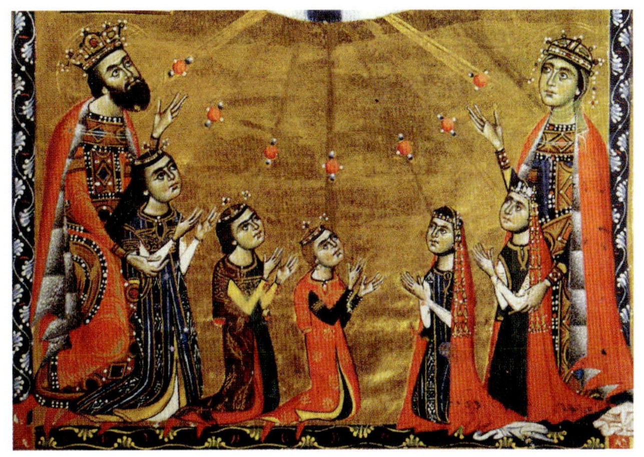

Keran of Lampron, queen consort of Armenia (*r.* 1270–1283/84). Became a nun after she had her last (and sixteenth) child; she commissioned the pictured manuscript by esteemed artist Toros Roslin. (Far right; manuscript illustration, 1272.)

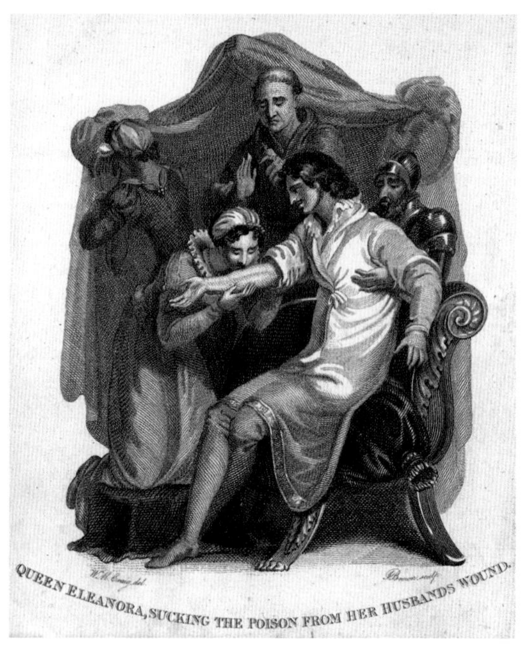

Eleanor of Castile, queen consort of England (*r.* 1272–1290). Oversaw the only scriptorium in northern Europe during her reign. (The pictured event is likely fictional.) (Left, with Edward I; print by Joseph Brown after W. M. Craig, 1820–56.)

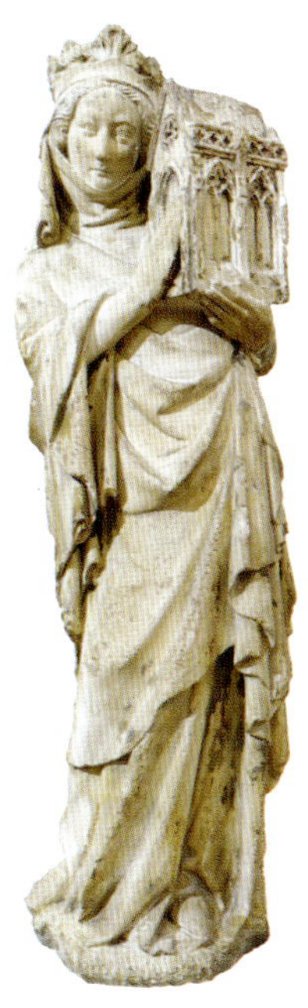

JOAN I, QUEEN OF NAVARRE (*r.* 1274–1305), AND QUEEN CONSORT OF FRANCE (*r.* 1285–1305). Founded the College of Navarre for students of modest means. (Statue, c. 1305.)

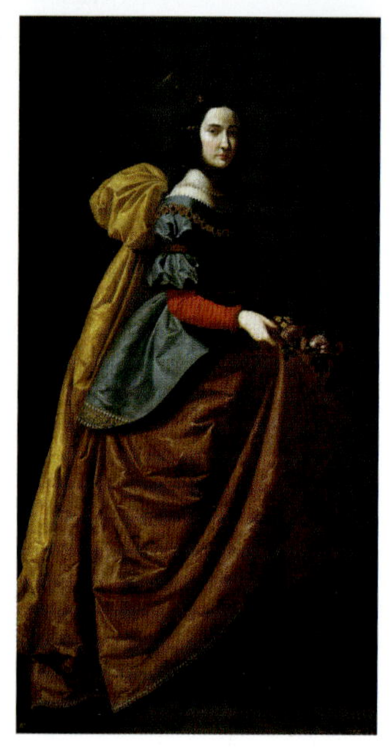

SAINT ELIZABETH OF ARAGON, QUEEN CONSORT OF PORTUGAL (*r.* 1282–1325). Known as "The Peacemaker," she rode out between her son's and husband's armies and made them reconcile. (Painting by Francisco de Zurbarán, c. 1635.)

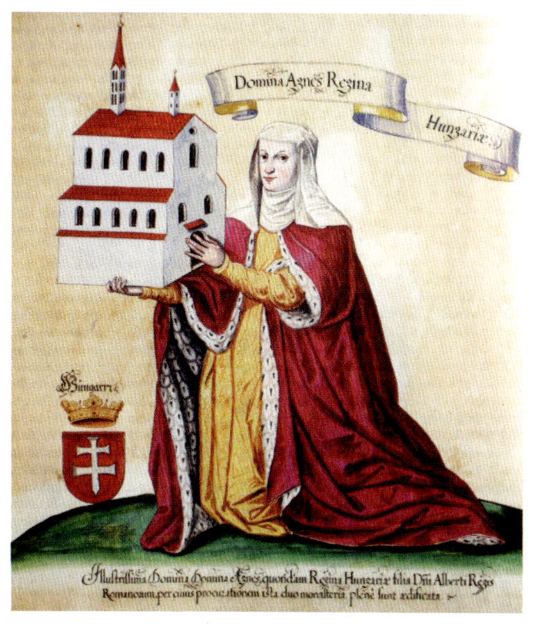

Agnes of Austria, queen consort of Hungary (*r.* 1296–1301). After she retired, Agnes still offered advice, even facilitating a treaty during the Gümmenen war. (Manuscript illustration, c. eighteenth century.)

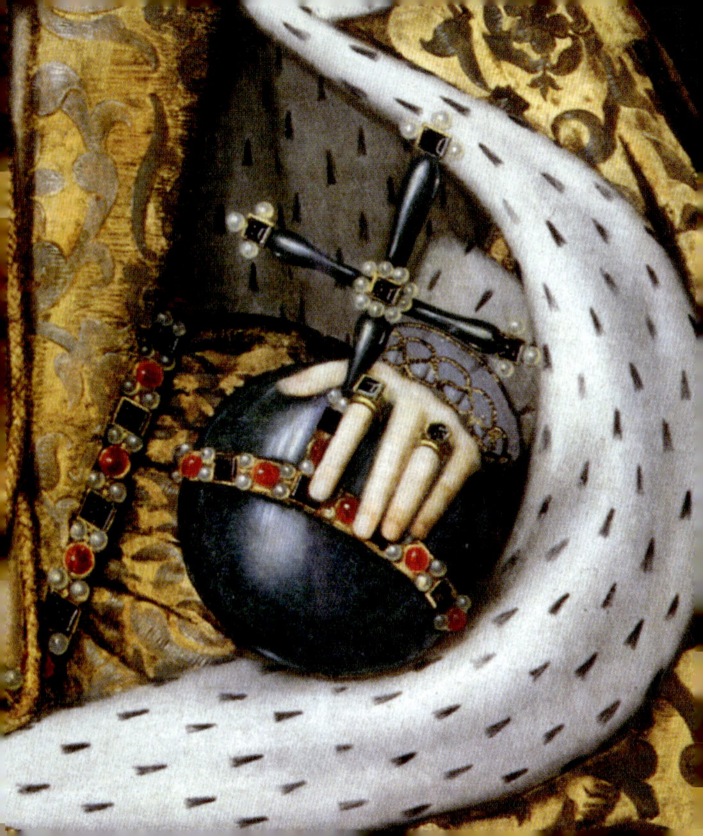

3. RENAISSANCE
1300–1599

Her left hand clutches an orb while her right holds a scepter. Sitting regally, with a king's crown upon her head, Elizabeth I (p. 171) represents a sovereign who has assumed the symbols of power, legitimizing her rule as a woman in a time when traditional views of femininity prevailed. Elizabeth harnessed symbols of authority and womanhood subversively and unashamedly, which marks her as one of the first European queens to portray herself exactly as she wanted to be seen. The Renaissance, a term for the robust cultural activity springing from Italy in the fourteenth century, spread throughout Europe up to the seventeenth century. Though the term describes a European phenomenon, the queens in this chapter are global, and its use serves to signal an important artistic trend during this time—portraits. The period's renewed interest in antiquity and humanism was manifested in realistic and individualized representations, departing from the generic portraits of ages before. We start to observe women with the trappings of wealth and power. Yet in other parts of the world, where meager or no visual images of queens exist, we must rely on written narratives to understand such queens as Seble Wongel of Ethiopia, an important actor during the Abyssinian-Adal War, and Suriyothai of Ayutthaya (Thailand), who is credited with giving her life to defend her husband.

A variety of factors contributed to Elizabeth becoming queen regnant—not least the succession act that, in 1553, named Henry VIII's daughters, first Mary ("Bloody Mary") and then Elizabeth, as heirs after their younger brother, Edward VI, died. It took a politically turbulent time, when the only eligible heirs were female, to bring these sisters to the throne. Elizabeth, as queen, laid a blueprint for women after her to follow, showing that a courageous and intelligent queen could rule without a husband and be respected in her own right. Elizabeth, and Mary before her, compensated for the degrading perception of women by adopting a male persona and embracing the role of wife and mother—but to the kingdom rather than a family. Elizabeth's portraits are full of symbols echoing these themes. Sometimes she is shown wearing an enameled pelican emblem, which exemplifies motherhood, or donning pearls to represent her virginity. In one painting she stands majestically on the globe.

A woman ruler, in any capacity, was more common during this period than the preceding one. In the Ottoman Empire, although royal women were barely visible in public and could not rule in the same way as men, they were still influential, and the period between 1533 and 1656 became known as the "Sultanate of Women." Queens in this era faced the difficult challenge of maintaining power and control while being considered inferior to men. When spoken of positively, they were compared favorably to men and said to have "masculine" characteristics. If viewed in a negative light, they were described as perversions of what society thought a woman should be—monstrous and promiscuous.

While navigating a world hostile to them, queens continued to manage the business affairs of their household, advise the king, secure their children's futures, and safeguard the land they inherited. Their most significant decisions affected the running of the kingdom, from signing armistices to introducing unified monetary systems and making laws. Queens took an active part in the cultural activity of the Renaissance by bringing artists and scholars to their courts and commissioning architectural and artistic projects. In Europe, with the beginning of the Protestant Reformation and Catholic Counter-Reformation, queens vitally influenced the religious practices of their countries. There were still warrior queens, like Durgavati of India, though they were less prevalent.

Elizabeth perhaps epitomized a queen striking the balance between society's perceptions of the feminine and the masculine, and the qualities from these categories that define a ruler. She represents many queens from throughout time who sought to define themselves within the confining structures and impossible standards of their world.

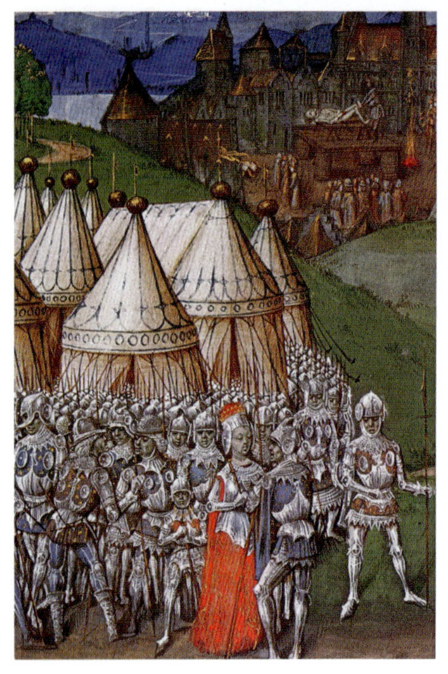

Isabella of France, queen consort (*r.* 1308–1327) and regent of England (*r.* 1327–1330). Nicknamed the "She-Wolf" by contemporary chroniclers. (Center, in red; manuscript illustration, detail, 1471–83.)

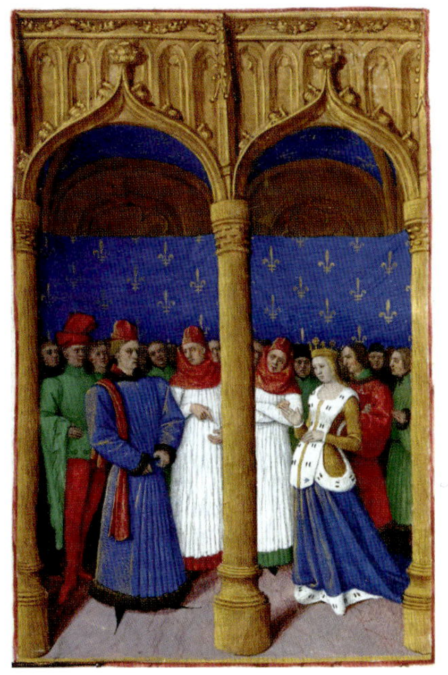

Jeanne of Évreux, queen consort of France (*r.* 1324–1328). The owner of Jean Pucelle's exceptional minuscule manuscript now known as the Hours of Jeanne d'Évreux. (Right foreground; manuscript miniature by Jean Fouquet, fifteenth century.)

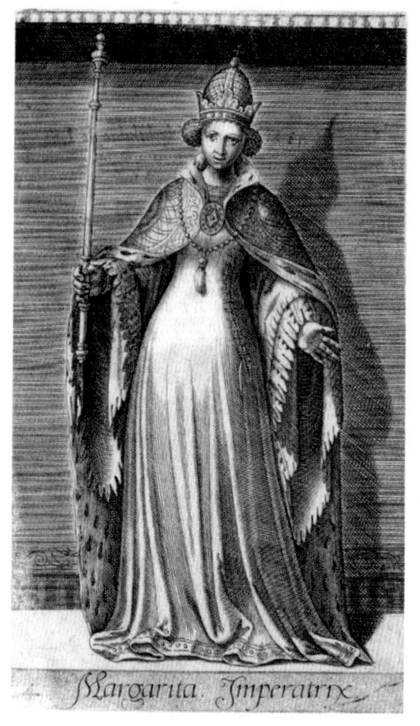

Margaret II of Avesnes, queen consort of Germany (*r.* 1324–1347) and the Holy Roman Empire (*r.* 1328–1347). Margaret's army was defeated by her son's in a battle for the rule of Holland. (Print after Willem Tybout, 1586.)

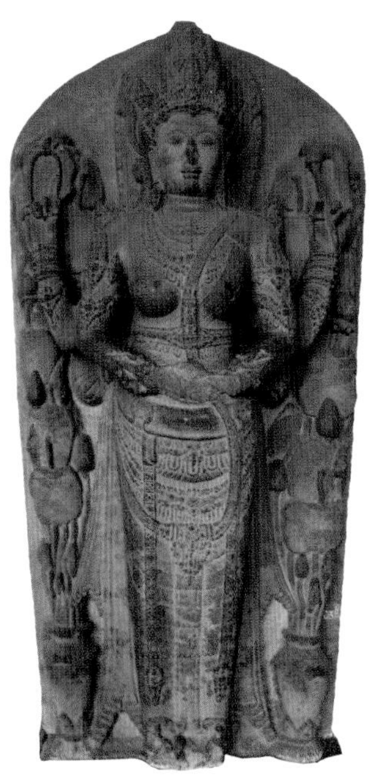

TRIBHUWANA WIJAYATUNGGADEWI, QUEEN OF THE MAJAPAHIT EMPIRE (JAVA, INDONESIA) (*r.* 1328–1350). The empire greatly expanded during her reign; she also led an army to quell a rebellion. (Statue, fourteenth century.)

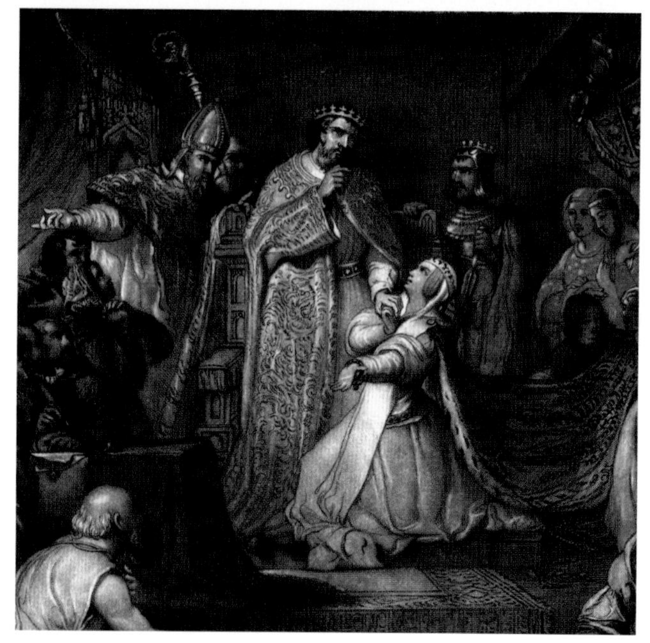

Philippa of Hainaut, queen consort (*r.* 1328–1369)
and regent of England (*r.* 1346).
Interceded for the lives of the burghers of Calais, France, held under siege by her husband. (Kneeling; engraving, detail, by John Sartain, 1847.)

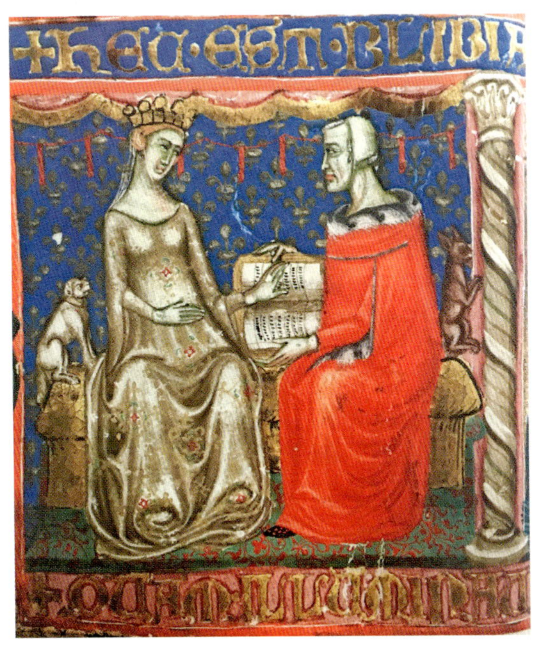

Joanna I, queen of Naples (*r.* 1343–1382).
Joanna, a patron of the arts and a skilled ruler, was tragically assassinated by her usurper. (Manuscript illustration by Cristoforo Orimina, fourteenth century.)

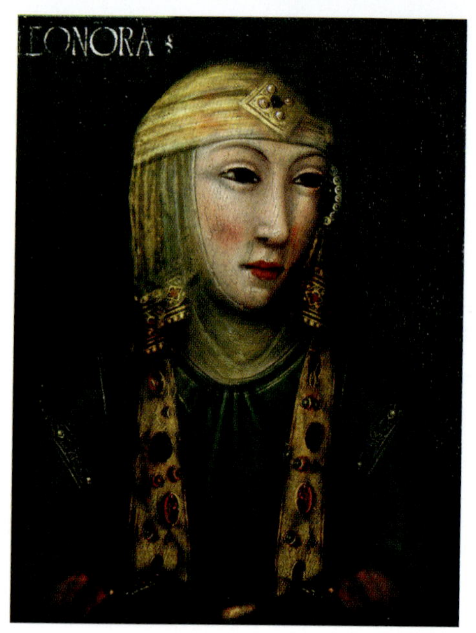

LEONOR TELES, QUEEN CONSORT (*r.* 1372–1383) AND REGENT OF PORTUGAL (*r.* 1383–1384). After her lover was murdered by her usurper, she fled Portugal, and later died while imprisoned in a convent. (Painting, c. fifteenth century.)

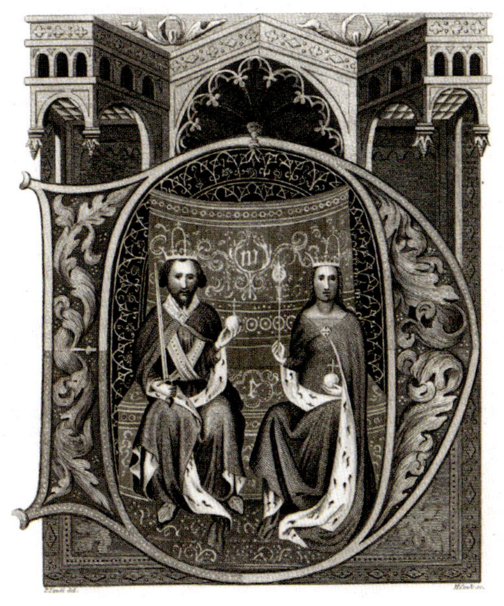

Joanna of Bavaria, queen consort of Germany and Bohemia (*r.* 1376–1386).
Her husband, Wenceslas IV (pictured, left), was a cruel king; one of his hunting dogs may have been responsible for Joanna's untimely death. (Print, detail, by Henry Cook, 1821.)

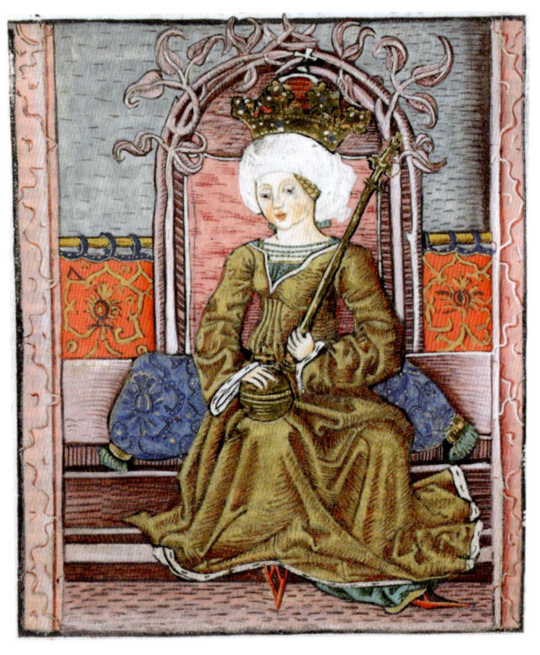

MARY, QUEEN OF HUNGARY AND CROATIA (*r.* 1382–1385; 1386–1395). Her throne was temporarily overthrown, but her mother had the usurper assassinated. (Manuscript miniature, detail, 1488.)

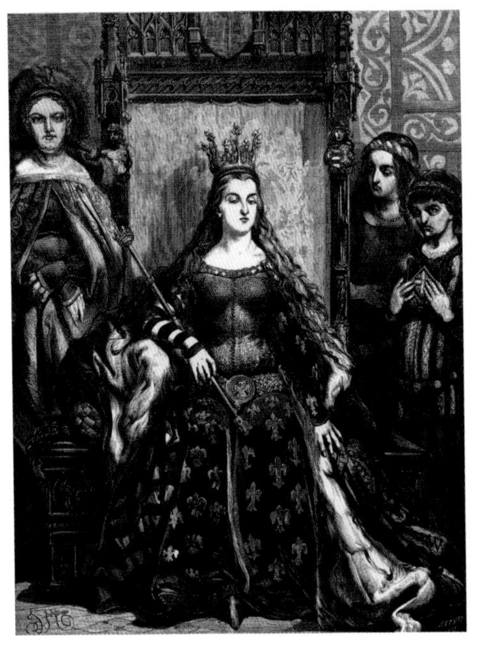

Jadwiga, or Hedwig, queen (coruler) of Poland (*r.* 1384–1399). She set out with an army to win back land for Poland, which she accomplished through peaceful negotiations. (Illustration by Jan Matejko, 1876.)

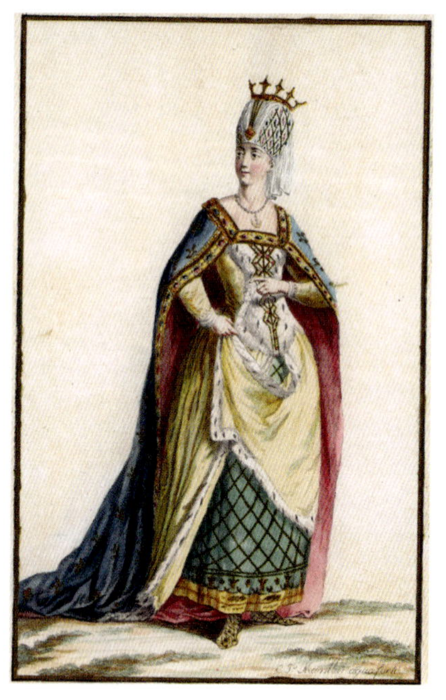

Isabeau of Bavaria, queen consort (de facto regent) of France (*r.* 1385–1422). Ruled for her mentally ill husband and was a fierce protector of the throne. (Print, detail, by Clément Pierre Marillier, 1750–1808.)

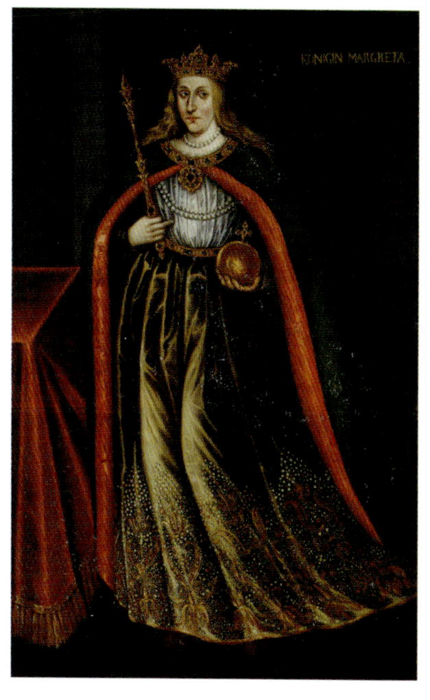

MARGARET I, QUEEN OF DENMARK, NORWAY, AND SWEDEN (*r.* 1387–1412). Founded the Kalmar Union, which unified the Scandinavian kingdoms for over a century. (Painting.)

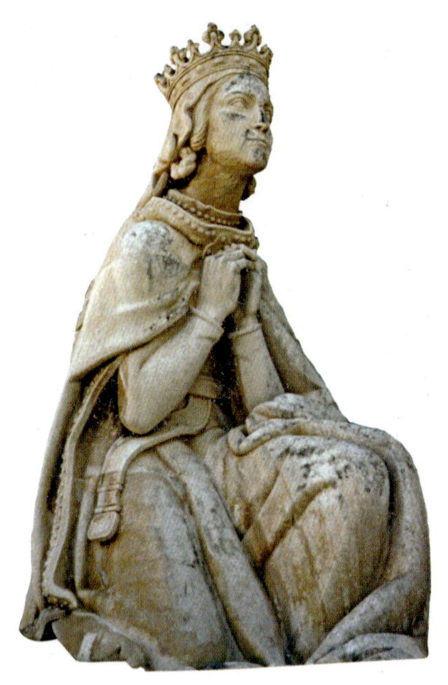

Philippa of Lancaster, queen consort of Portugal (*r.* 1387–1415). Geoffrey Chaucer is believed to have helped teach a young Philippa how to read and how to use an astrolabe. (Designed by Cottinelli Telmo and sculpted by Leopoldo de Almeida, 1958.)

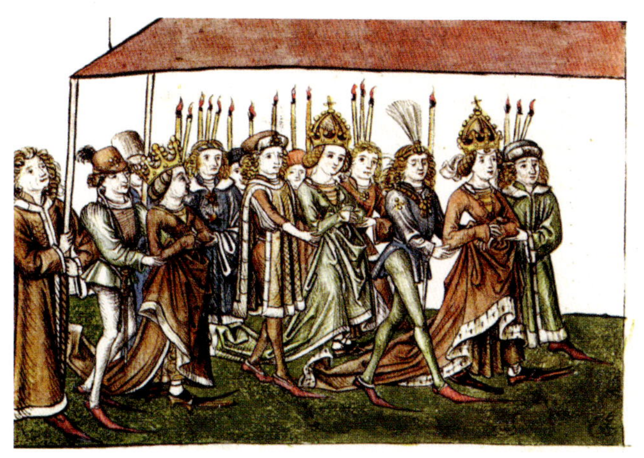

Barbara of Cilli, queen consort (*r.* 1405–1437) and regent of Hungary, Germany, and the Holy Roman Empire (*r.* 1412–1418, intermittently). Helped create the chivalric Order of the Dragon. (Far right, in brown; manuscript illustration, detail, c. 1440.)

Making History

Helen and her husband, King Dabisa, had designated King Sigismund of Hungary as their successor. However, the nobles wanted Helen to succeed her husband. After Dabisa's death, Sigismund led an army to claim the throne but ultimately withdrew. Though Helen was arguably a regent rather than sole ruler, she remains the only woman to have reigned in Bosnia and Herzegovina's history.

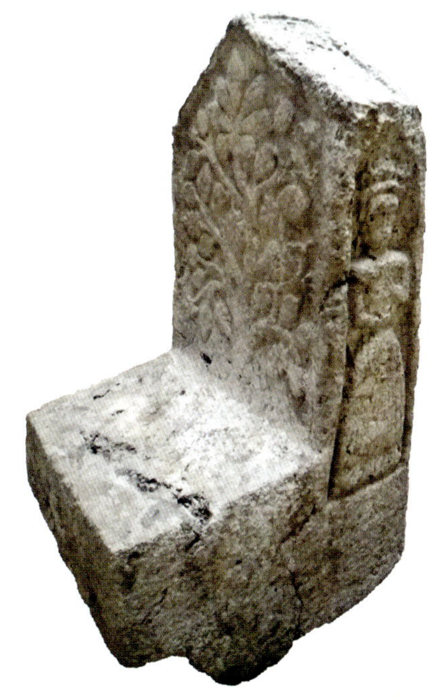

Helen, or Gruba, consort (*r.* 1391–1395)
and queen of Bosnia (*r.* 1395–1398).
(Pictured in the relief on the side of her judge's seat, c. 1391.)

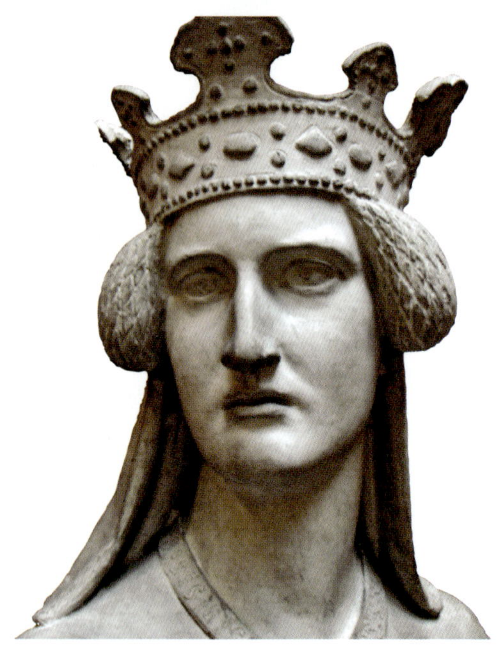

Philippa of England, queen consort (*r.* 1406–1430) and regent of Denmark, Sweden, and Norway (*r.* 1423–1425). Became a hero in Copenhagen for arranging the city's defense during the Dano-Hanseatic War. (Statue, detail, by H. W. Bissen, 1856).

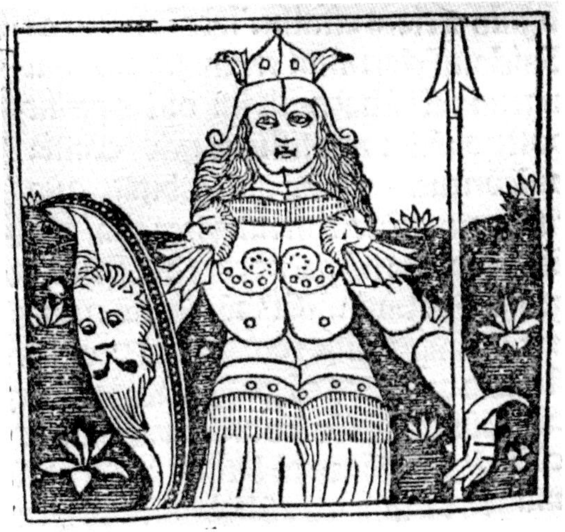

Joanna II, queen of Naples (*r.* 1414–1435). She was known for appointing her lovers to positions of power. (Print, detail, 1497.)

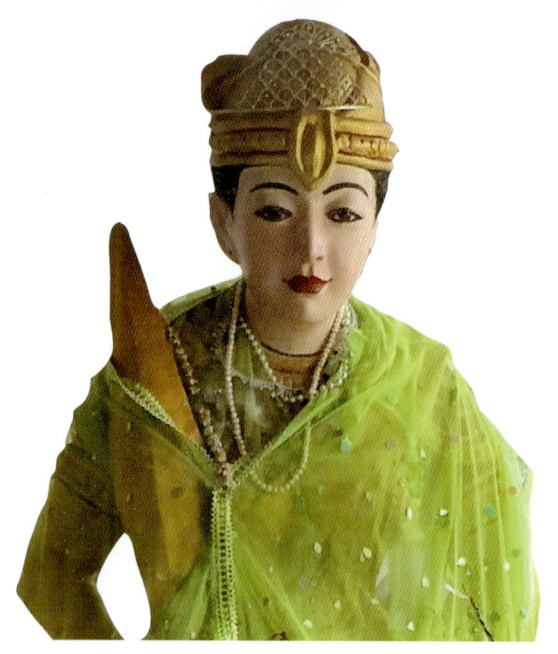

Shin Sawbu, consort of the Central Palace of Ava (*r.* 1423–1429), and queen of Hanthawaddy (Myanmar) (*r.* 1454–1471). Abdicated in order to devote herself to a religious life, settling near the Buddhist Shwedagon Pagoda. (Statue, detail.)

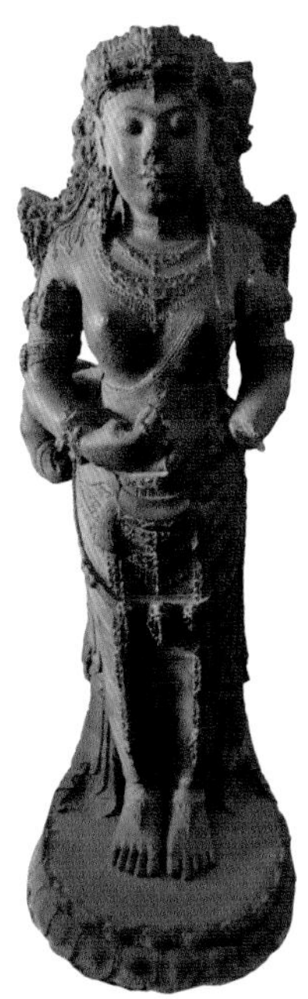

Suhita, queen of the Majapahit Empire (Java, Indonesia) (*r.* 1429–1447).
Reigned in her own right, though it was rare for women to rule in Java. (Statue, fifteenth century.)

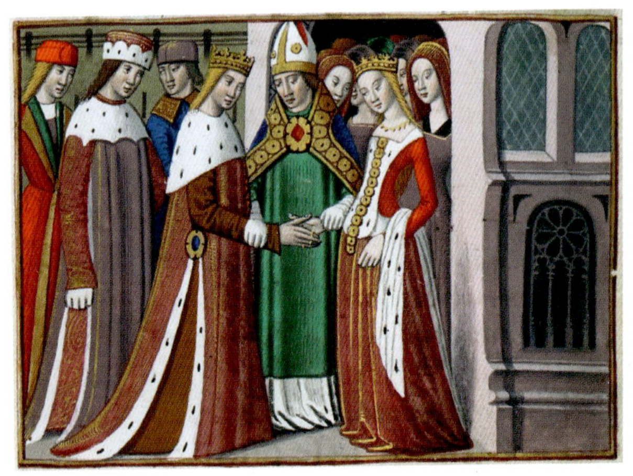

MARGARET OF ANJOU, QUEEN CONSORT OF ENGLAND (*r.* 1445–1461). Governed on behalf of her mentally unstable husband and led the house of Lancaster during the War of the Roses; her attempts to become sole ruler, though, were unsuccessful. (Right, in crown; manuscript miniature, c. 1484.)

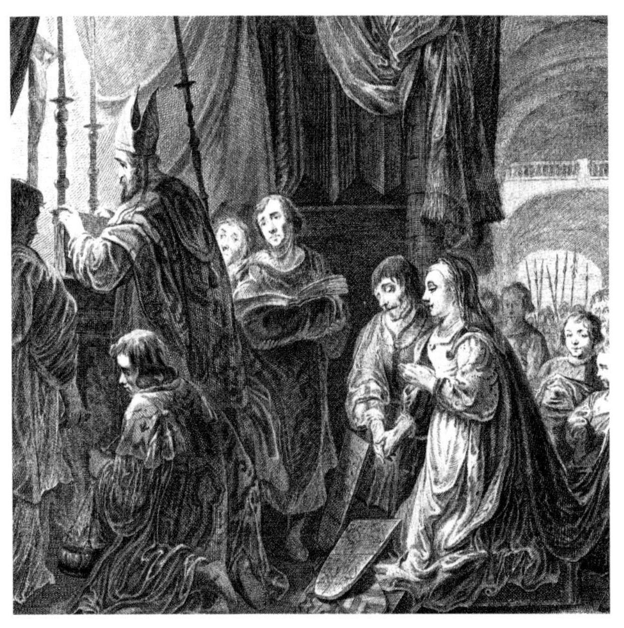

Mary of Guelders, queen consort (*r.* 1449–1460)
and regent of Scotland (*r.* 1460–1463).
Sheltered Queen Margaret (p. 138) during the
War of the Roses in exchange for the town of Berwick.
(Right; print, detail, by Jan Wildens, 1642.)

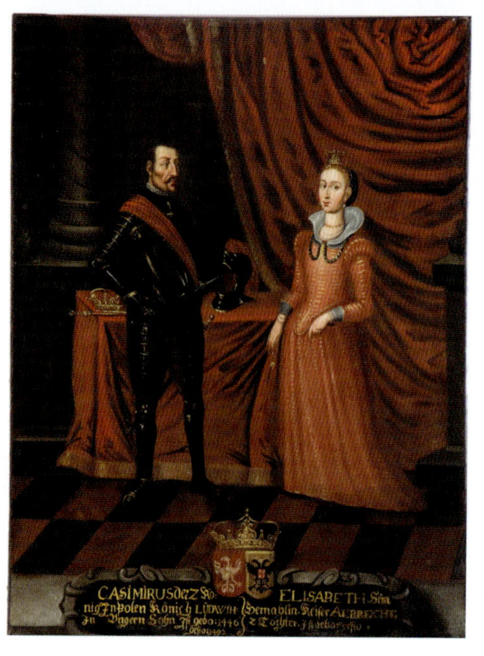

Elizabeth of Austria, queen consort of Poland (*r.* 1454–1492). Though many Renaissance marriages were fraught, Elizabeth was happily married and always traveled with her husband, Casimir IV (pictured). (Painting.)

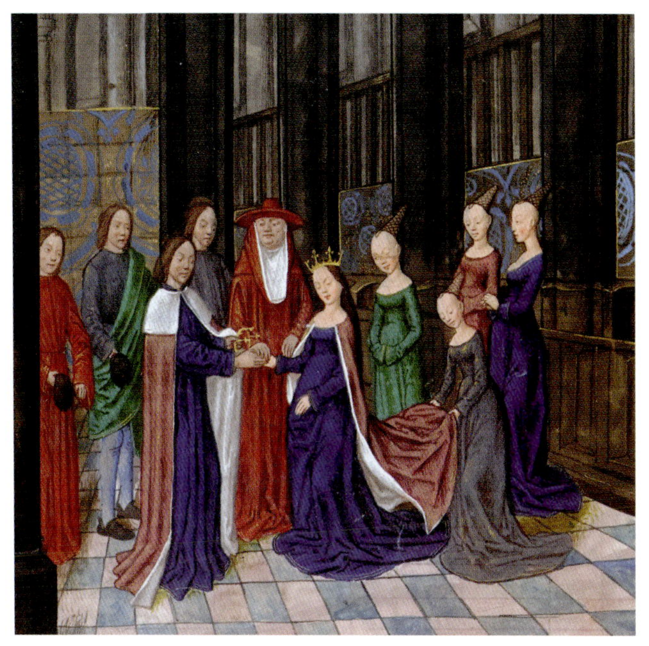

Elizabeth Woodville, queen consort of England (*r.* 1464–1470).
She became queen despite not being royal,
and used her position to elevate her relatives.
(Center; manuscript miniature, detail, fifteenth century.)

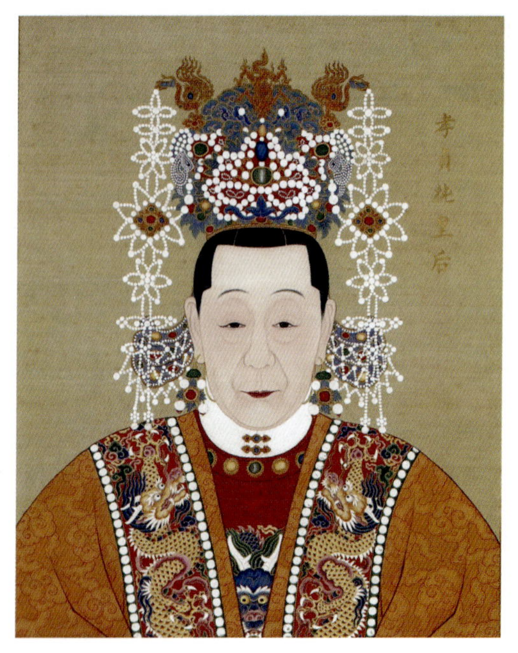

Wang, or Xiaozhenchun, empress consort (*r.* 1464–1487) and dowager of Ming China (*r.* 1487–1518). Artfully avoided conflict with the emperor's favorite concubine, who had deposed Wang's predecessor. (Painting.)

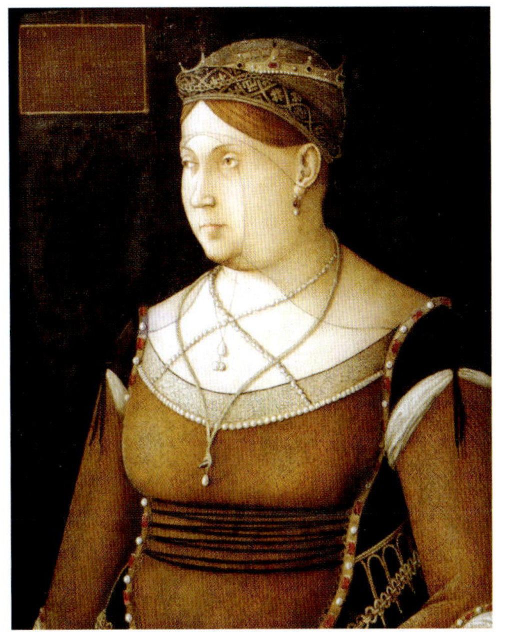

Catherine Cornaro, consort (*r.* 1472–1473), regent (*r.* 1473–1474), and queen of Cyprus (*r.* 1474–1489). Venice's government officials forced her to abdicate and cede power to the doge. (Painting, c. 1500.)

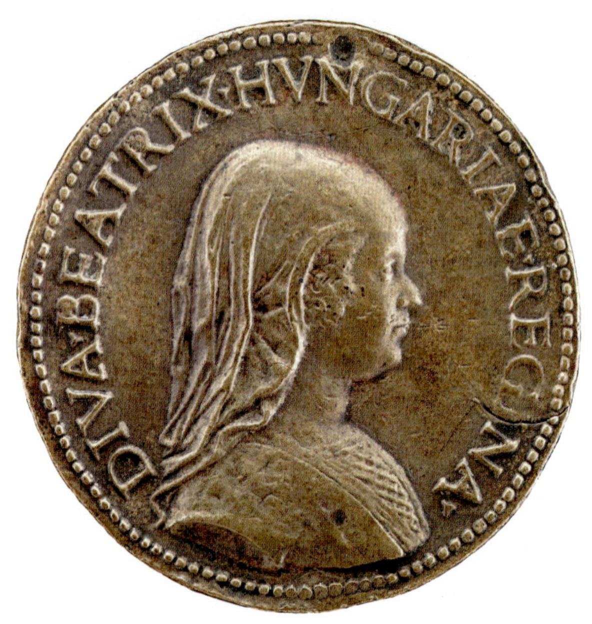

Beatrice of Naples, queen consort of Hungary and Bohemia (*r.* 1476–1490; 1491–1502).
Credited with bringing the Renaissance to Hungary, she supported the building of the Bibliotheca Corviniana.
(Coin by Circle of Giancristoforo Romano, 1491/1505.)

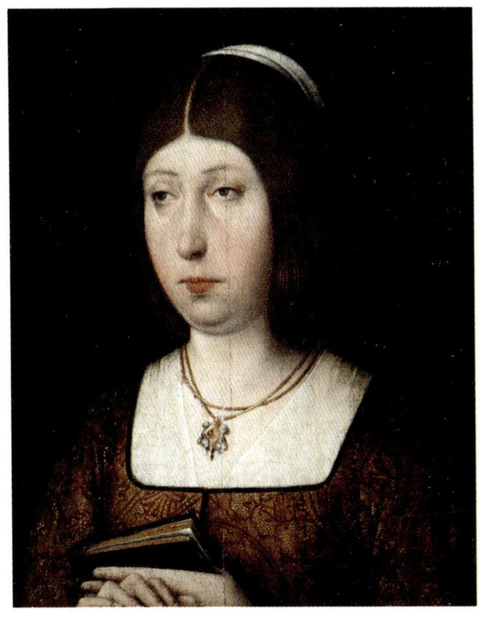

Isabella I, queen (coruler) of Castile and León and consort of Aragon (Spain) (*r.* 1479–1504). With her husband, Ferdinand II, Isabella financed Christopher Columbus's voyage to the New World. (Painting, c. 1490.)

The Harmonious Chief

Anacaona was a moderate and peaceful chief of Xaragua, the last independent province in Hispaniola during the Spanish conquest, and oversaw a congenial assimilation of Spanish settlers with her people. Despite this, the island's governor suspected an insurrection and ordered the execution of Anacaona and other Taino chiefs. Our image of her is one of defeat, as it appears in a colonialist record, and does not capture her courage and spirit.

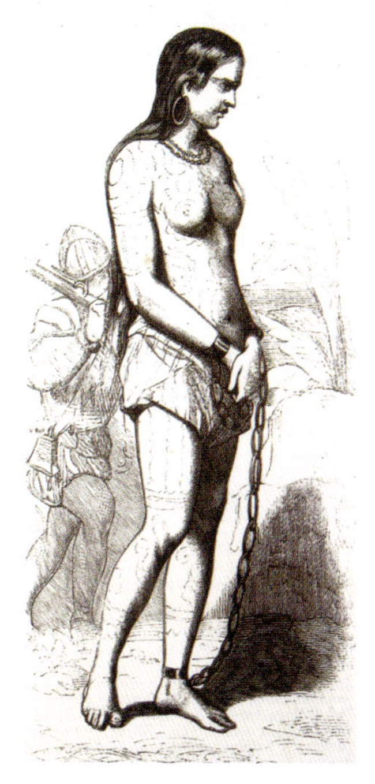

Anacaona, chief of Xaragua (Hispaniola) (*r.* c. 1480s–1504). (Illustration, 1851.)

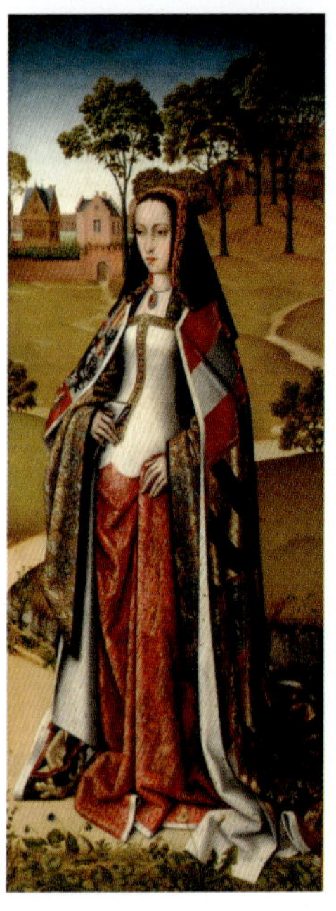

Joanna, queen of Castile and Aragon (Spain) (*r.* 1504–1555). Known as "Joanna the Mad," she spent most of her life unjustly imprisoned by her husband and father. (Painting, right triptych panel, by Master of Affligem, 1495–1506.)

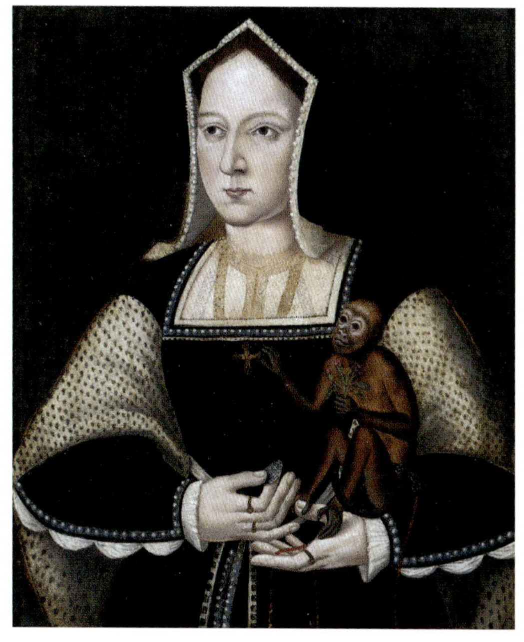

Catherine of Aragon, queen consort (*r.* 1509–1533) and regent of England (*r.* 1530).
As regent, her artful strategizing contributed to the English triumph at the Battle of Flodden. (Painting after Lucas Horenbout, c. 1525.)

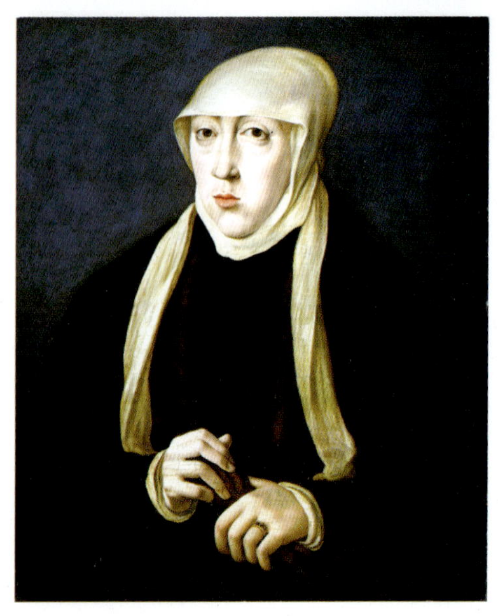

Mary of Austria, queen consort of Hungary and Bohemia (*r.* 1515–1526), regent of Hungary (*r.* 1526–1527), and regent of the Netherlands (*r.* 1531–1555). Decided to govern as sole regent of the Netherlands rather than remarry and become a consort elsewhere. (Painting after Jan Cornelisz Vermeyen.)

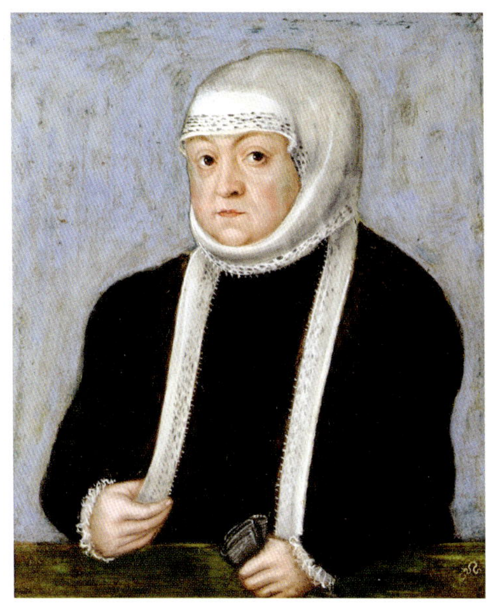

BONA SFORZA, QUEEN CONSORT OF POLAND (*r.* 1518–1548).
She helped initate the Renaissance in Poland,
overseeing numerous architectural projects.
(Painting by Lucas Cranach the Younger, c. 1565.)

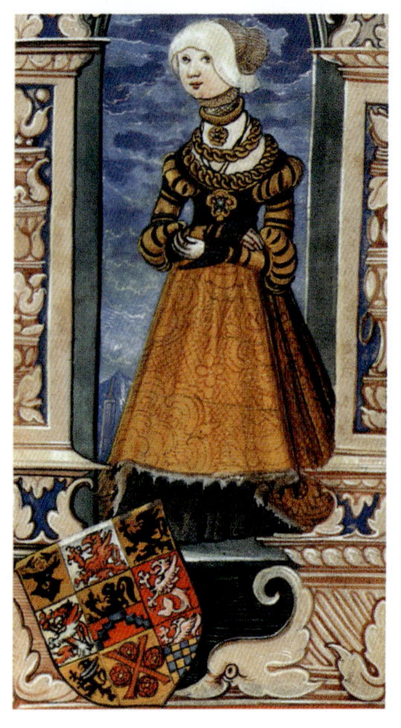

SOPHIE OF POMERANIA, QUEEN CONSORT OF DENMARK AND NORWAY (*r.* 1523–1533). Independently governed her fiefs for many years but was forced to relinquish her rule to the king. (Illustration attributed to Erhard Altdorfer, 1526.)

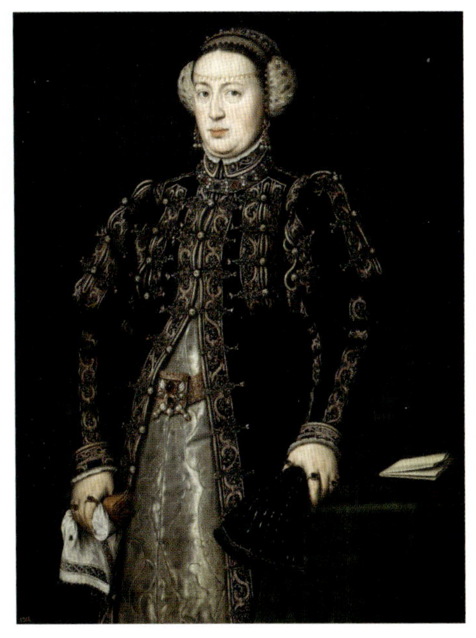

Catherine of Austria, queen consort (*r.* 1525–1557) and regent of Portugal (*r.* 1557–1562). Emphasized education in her family, amassing a library and inviting female scholars to her home. (Painting by Anthonis Mor, c. 1552–53.)

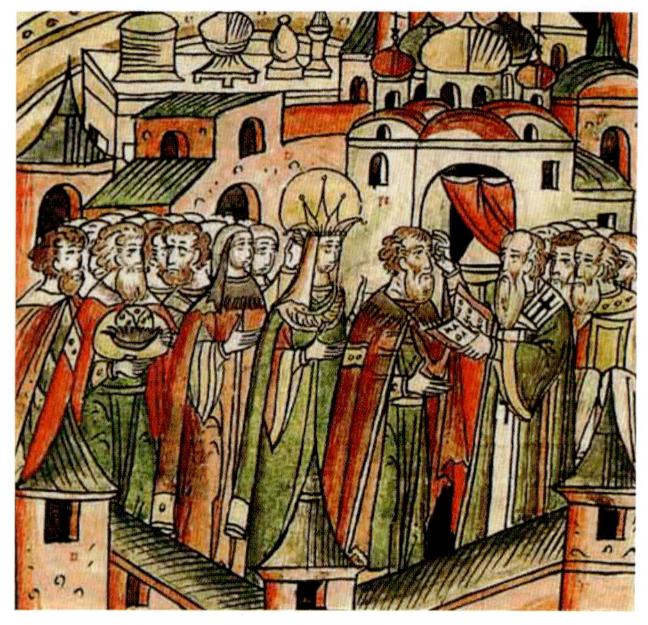

Elena Glinskaya, empress consort (*r.* 1526–1538) and regent of Russia (*r.* 1533–1538).
Signed an armistice with Lithuania and introduced a unified monetary system. (Center; manuscript miniature, detail, sixteenth century.)

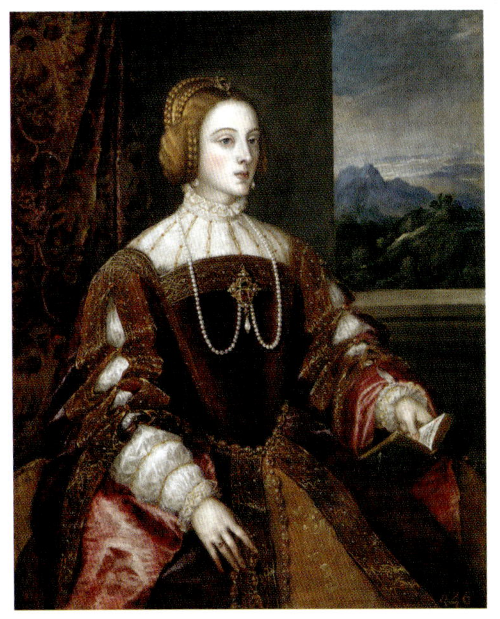

Isabella of Portugal, queen consort of Spain, Germany, the Netherlands, and the Holy Roman Empire (*r.* 1526–1539), and regent of Spain (*r.* 1529–1539, intermittently). She ensured Spain's independence and economic well-being during her regency. (Painting by Titian, 1548.)

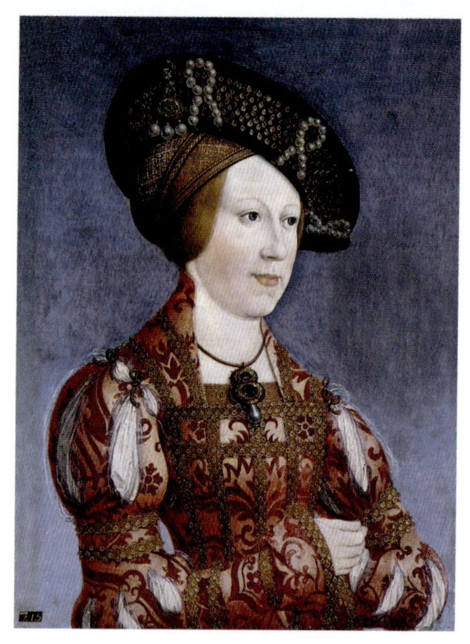

Anne, queen consort of the Romans,
Bohemia, and Hungary (*r.* 1526–1547).
Prague's magnificent Belvedere Castle was built for this devoted mother of fifteen children.
(Painting by Hans Maler, c. 1519.)

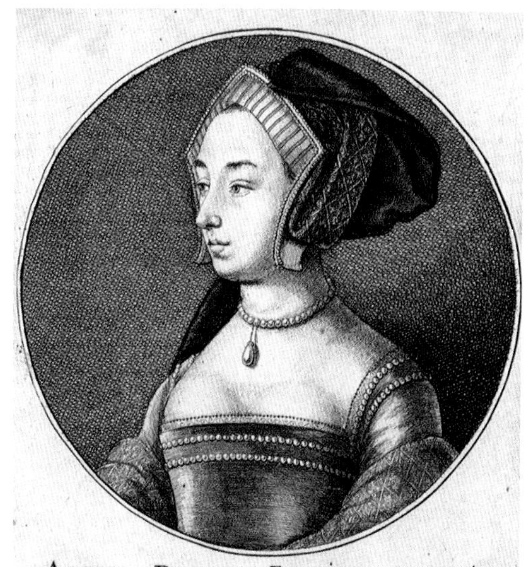

ANNE BOLEYN, QUEEN CONSORT OF ENGLAND (*r.* 1533–1536). The Church of England broke with Rome upon her controversial marriage to Henry VIII. (Print by Wenceslaus Hollar, 1659.)

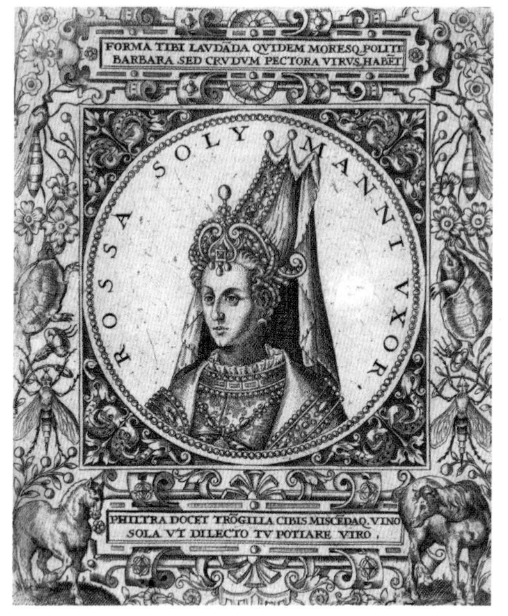

Hürrem, or Roxelana, empress consort of the Ottoman Empire (*r.* 1534–1558).
She was the first woman in the Ottoman Empire to receive the title of *haseki sultan*, or primary consort, as the sultan's wife and closest adviser. (Illustration by Johann Theodor de Bry, 1596.)

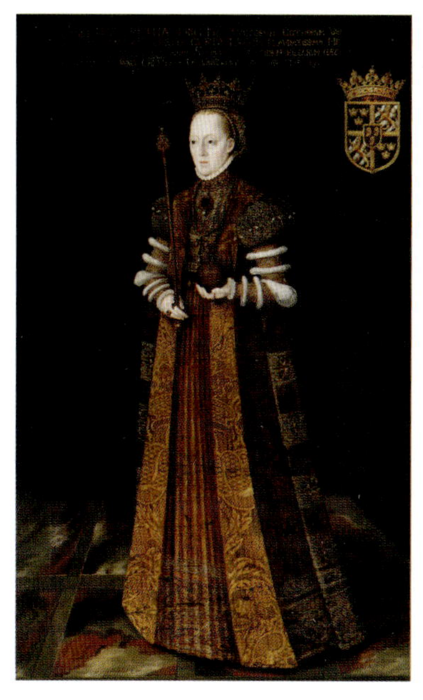

MARGARET LEIJONHUFVUD, QUEEN CONSORT OF SWEDEN (*r.* 1536–1551). Women approached her directly, rather than the king, because of her strong advocacy for their welfare. (Painting attributed to Johan Baptista van Uther, sixteenth century.)

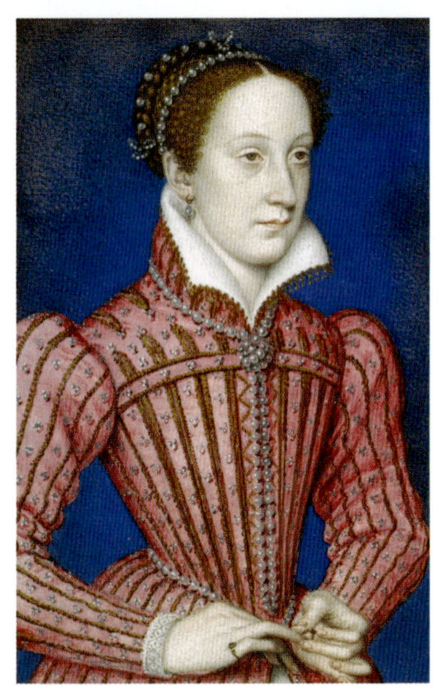

Mary, "Queen of Scots," queen of Scotland (*r.* 1542–1567), and consort of France (*r.* 1559–1560).
Considered a threat to Elizabeth I's throne, she was executed, though she was never directly involved in treasonous plotting.
(Painting by François Clouet, 1558–60.)

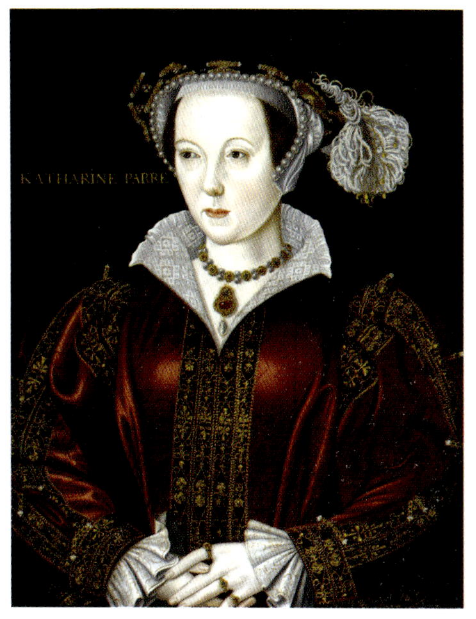

Catherine Parr, queen consort (*r.* 1543–1547) and regent of England (*r.* 1544).
The first woman in England to publish a book, *Prayers or Meditations*, in her name. (Painting, late sixteenth century.)

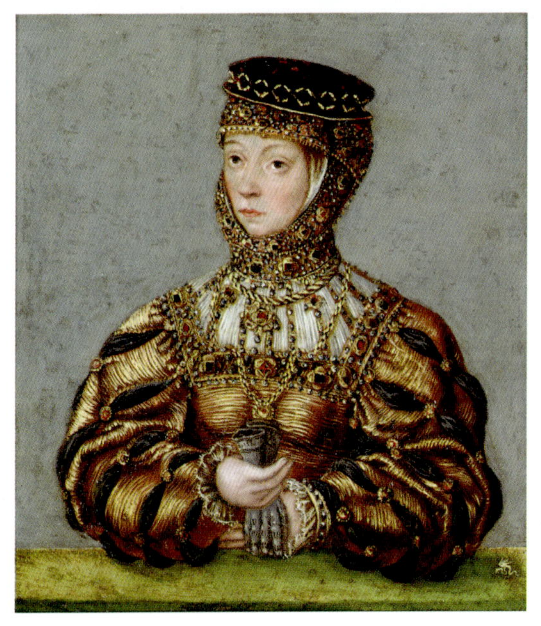

BARBARA RADZIWILL, QUEEN CONSORT OF POLAND (*r.* 1547–1551). Reputedly the Polish king, at the time Barbara's lover, built a tunnel connecting their palaces so they could meet in secret. (Painting by Lucas Cranach the Younger, c. 1565.)

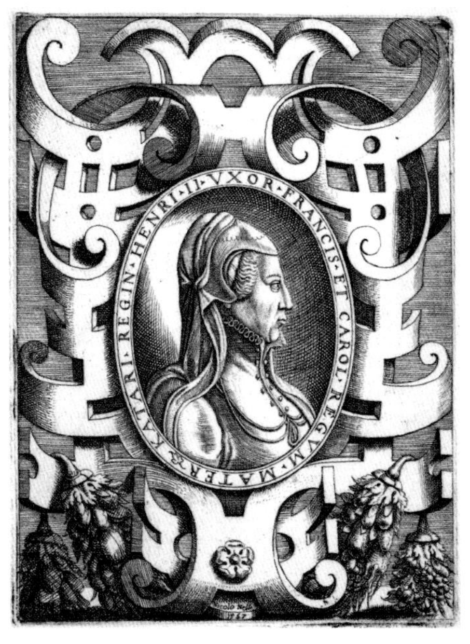

Catherine de Médicis, queen consort (*r.* 1547–1559) and regent of France (*r.* 1560–1563).
She is traditionally held responsible for instigating the Saint Bartholomew's Day Massacre of Huguenots by Catholics.
(Engraving by Nicolò Nelli, 1567.)

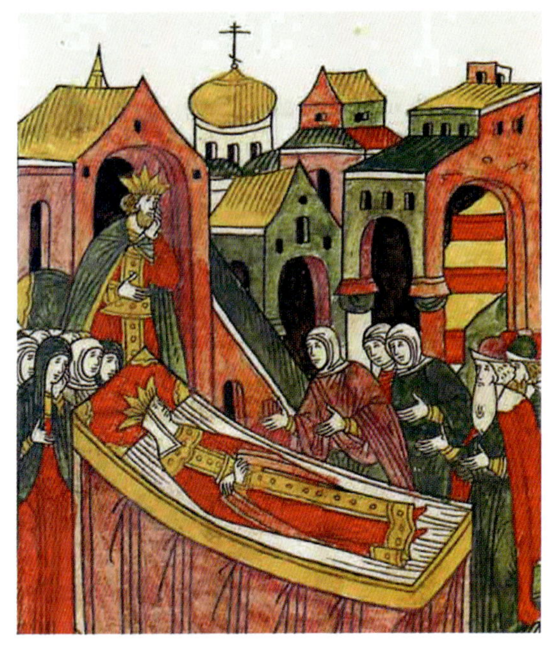

Anastasia Romanovna, empress consort of Russia (*r.* 1547–1560). She tempered the erratic behavior of her husband, Ivan the Terrible. (Pictured on her deathbed; manuscript miniature, detail, sixteenth century.)

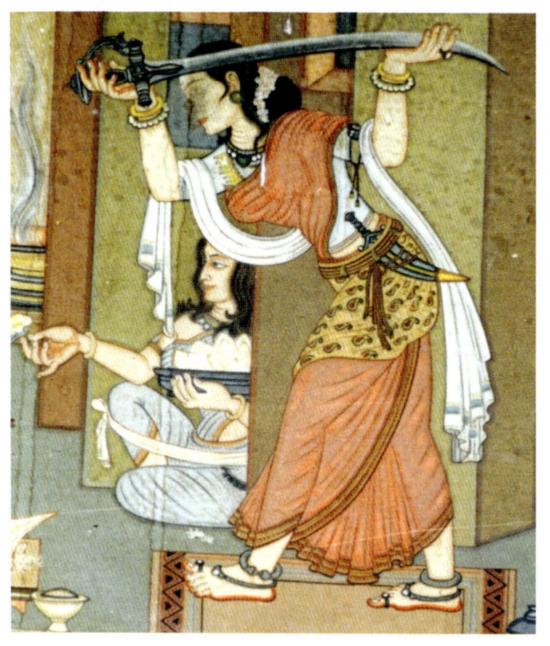

DURGAVATI, REGENT OF GONDWANA (INDIA) (*r.* 1550–1564). Rode into battle on an elephant to defend her kingdom. (Standing; fresco, detail, by Beohar Rammanohar Sinha, 1954.)

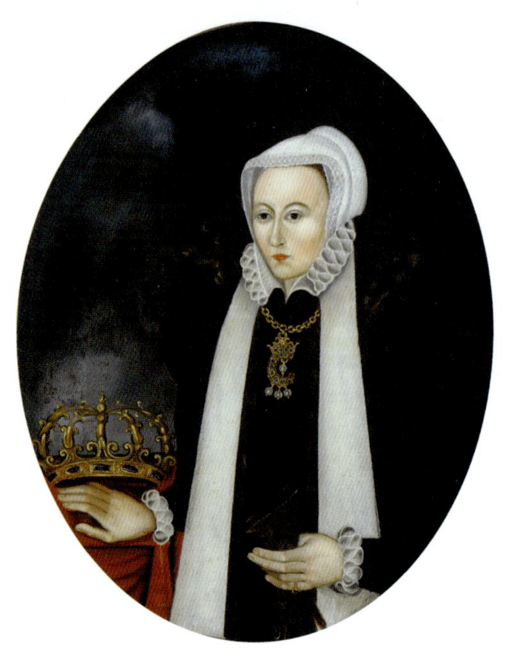

Catherine Stenbock, queen consort of Sweden (*r.* 1552–1560). Managed to keep the estate of Strömsholm, her seat as dowager queen, despite hostile threats from one Duke Karl. (Painting, c. sixteenth–seventeenth century.)

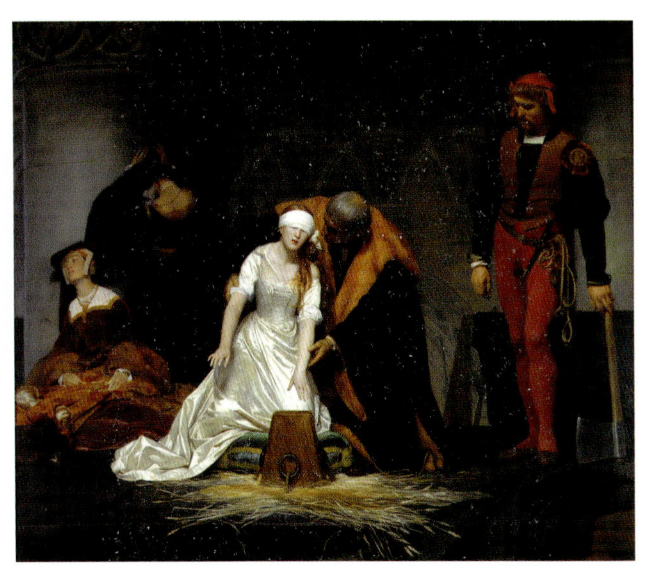

Lady Jane Grey, queen of England (*r.* 1553).
Queen for nine days and later executed, quite wrongfully,
for treason. (Painting by Paul Delaroche, 1833.)

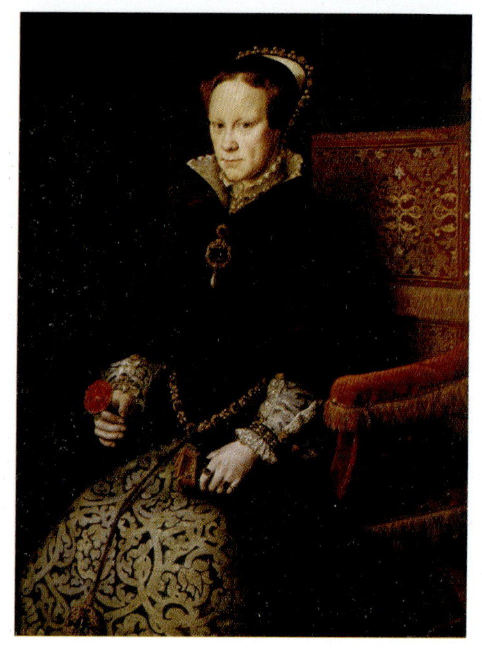

MARY I, QUEEN OF ENGLAND (*r.* 1553–1558).
Called "Bloody Mary" for her persecution of Protestant dissenters as she tried to revive Roman Catholicism in England. (Painting by Anthonis Mor, 1554.)

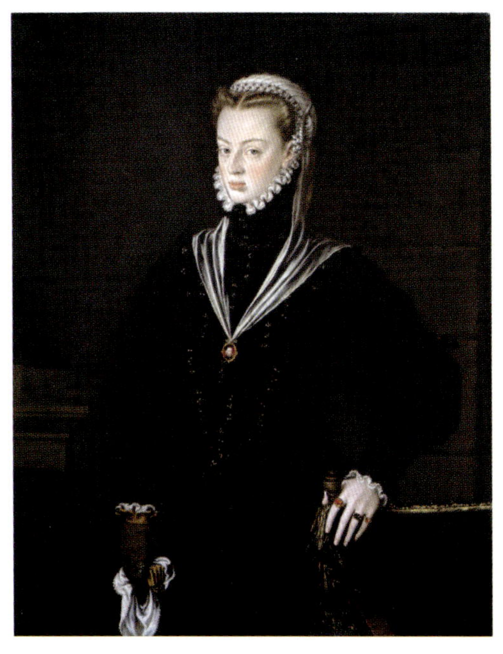

Joanna of Austria, regent of Spain (*r.* 1554–1559).
A Venetian ambassador described this astute regent as having "the sentiments of a man."
(Painting by Alonso Sánchez Coello, c. 1557.)

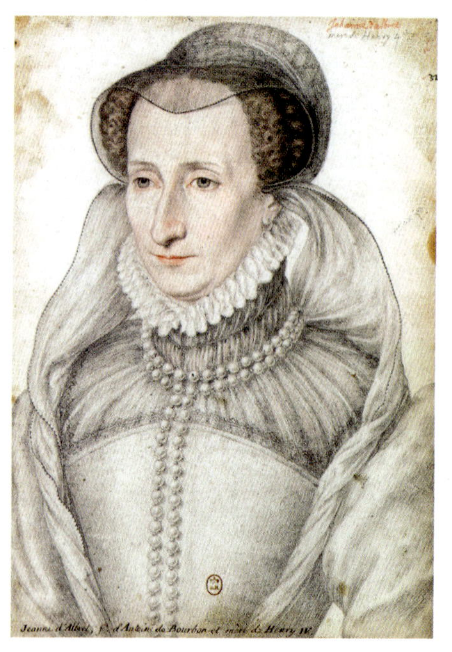

JEANNE D'ALBRET, OR JEANNE III, QUEEN OF NAVARRE (FRANCE) (*r.* 1555–1572).
Considered the leader of the French Huguenot movement.
(Drawing by School of François Clouet, c. 1560.)

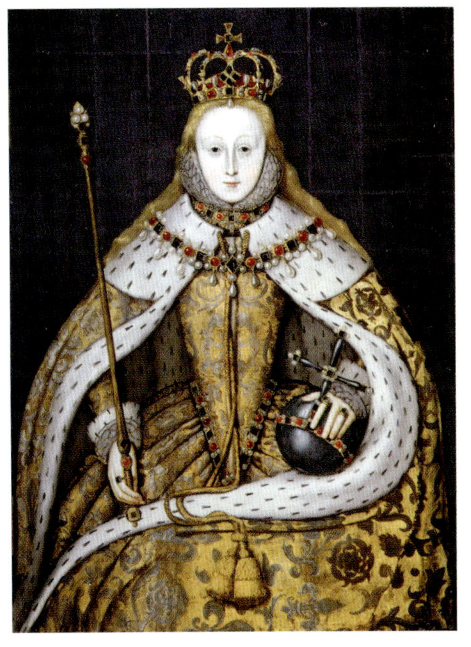

Elizabeth I, queen of England (*r.* 1558–1603). She said: "I know I have the body of a weak and feeble woman, but I have the heart and stomach of a king, and of a king of England too." (Painting, c. 1600–1610.)

A Fearless Warrior

Chand Bibi was a scholarly queen and close advisor to her husband, Sultan Ali Adil Shah I. After his death, she began to rule as a wise and capable regent. She is known for bravely defending her home city, Ahmednagar, against the Mughal forces of Emperor Akbar. In this illustration she is shown hawking, a particularly masculine activity, emphasizing her role as warrior queen. The bottom half of her horse is red to denote the queen's courageous ride into a bloody battle.

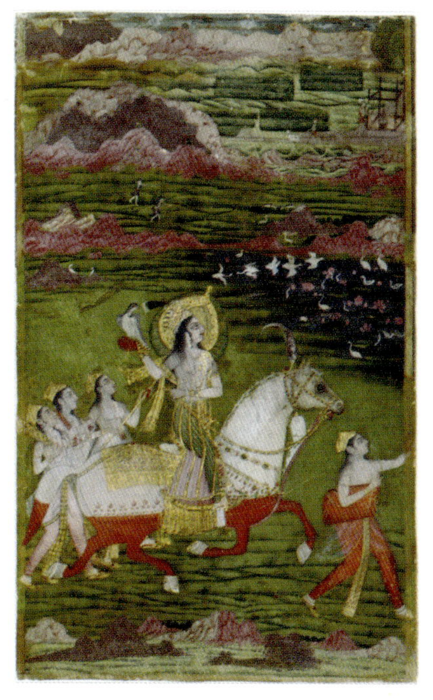

Chand Bibi, queen consort (*r.* 1565–1580) and regent of Bijapur, India (*r.* c. 1580–1585). (Painting, c. 1700.)

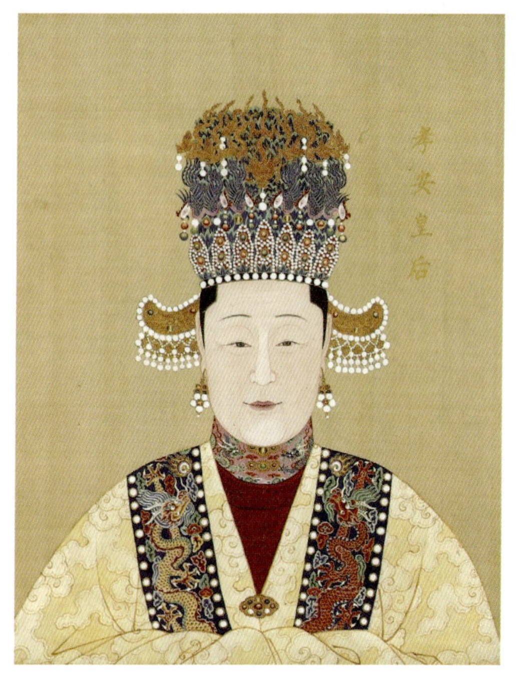

CHEN, EMPRESS CONSORT OF MING CHINA (*r.* 1567–1572). The emperor allegedly removed Chen from the palace because she critiqued his love of women and music. (Painting.)

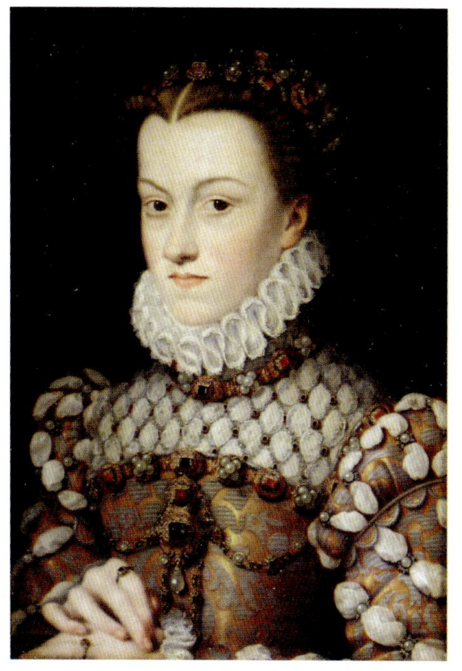

Elisabeth of Austria, queen consort of France (*r.* 1570–1574). Founded a monastery and devoted her life to helping the poor. (Painting by François Clouet, c. 1571.)

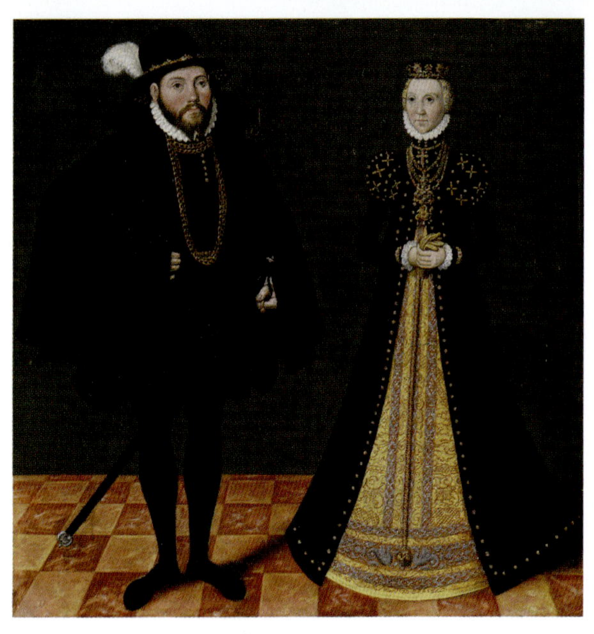

Sophie of Mecklenburg-Güstrow, queen consort (*r.* 1572–1588) and regent of Denmark and Norway (*r.* 1590–1594).
Managed to arrange her daughters' dowries and her own allowance, despite strong opposition from her council. (Right, with Frederick II; painting by Lucas Cranach the Younger, sixteenth century.)

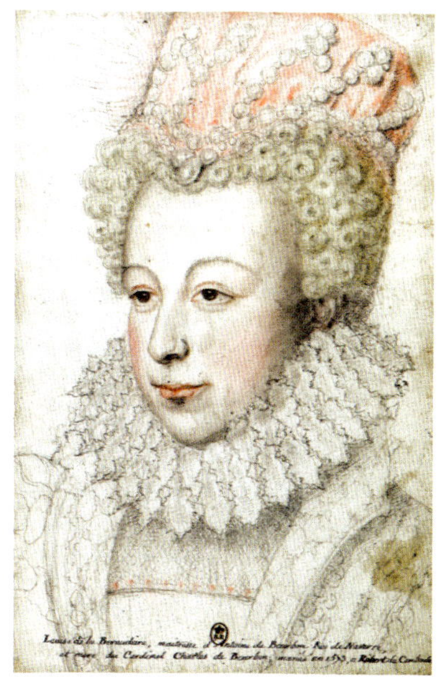

Margaret of Valois, Queen Consort of Navarre (*r.* 1572–1599) and France (*r.* 1589–1599). The first woman to have published her memoirs, which record the life of an independent, spirited queen. (Drawing, 1574.)

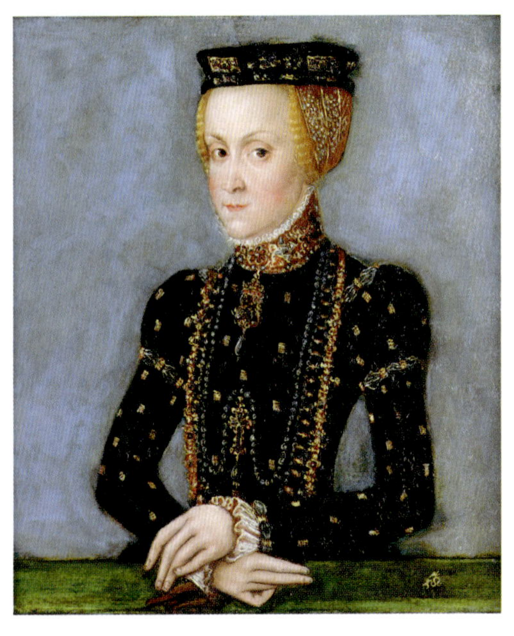

ANNA JAGIELLON, QUEEN (CORULER) OF POLAND (*r.* 1575–1586).
Orchestrated numerous building projects, including
the longest wooden bridge in Europe at the time.
(Painting by Lucas Cranach the Younger, c. 1565.)

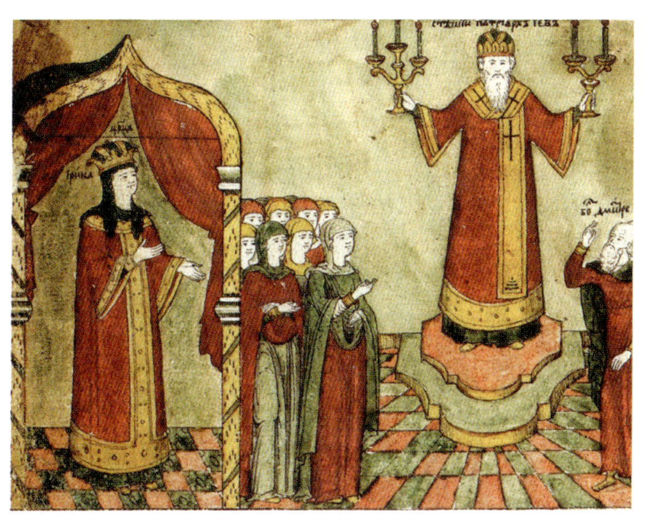

Irina Godunova, consort (*r.* 1584–1598)
and empress of Russia (*r.* 1598).
Entrusted with state affairs, Irina wrote her name on the emperor's decrees and corresponded with other rulers, including Elizabeth I. (Far left; manuscript illustration, detail, 1594.)

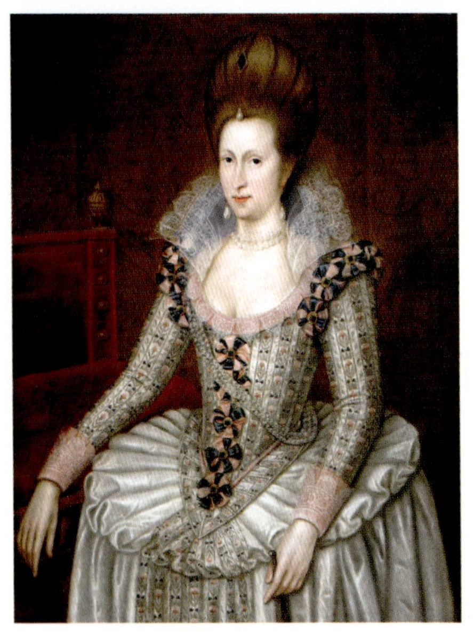

Anne of Denmark, queen consort of Scotland (*r.* 1589–1619), and England and Ireland (*r.* 1603–1619).
She participated in and helped popularize the court masque.
(Painting attributed to John de Critz the Elder, c. 1605.)

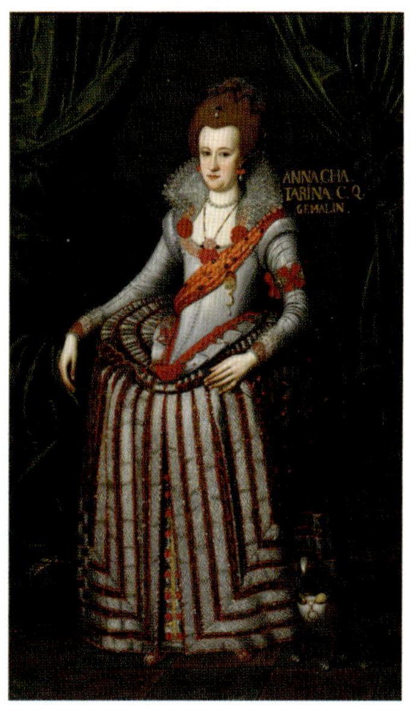

Anne Catherine of Brandenburg, Queen Consort of Denmark and Norway (*r.* 1597–1612).
She had expensive taste; the caps in her wedding trousseau cost more than the coronation tax of four Danish cities—and she spared no expense for her dog (pictured).
(Painting by Remmert Petersen after Pieter Isaacsz.)

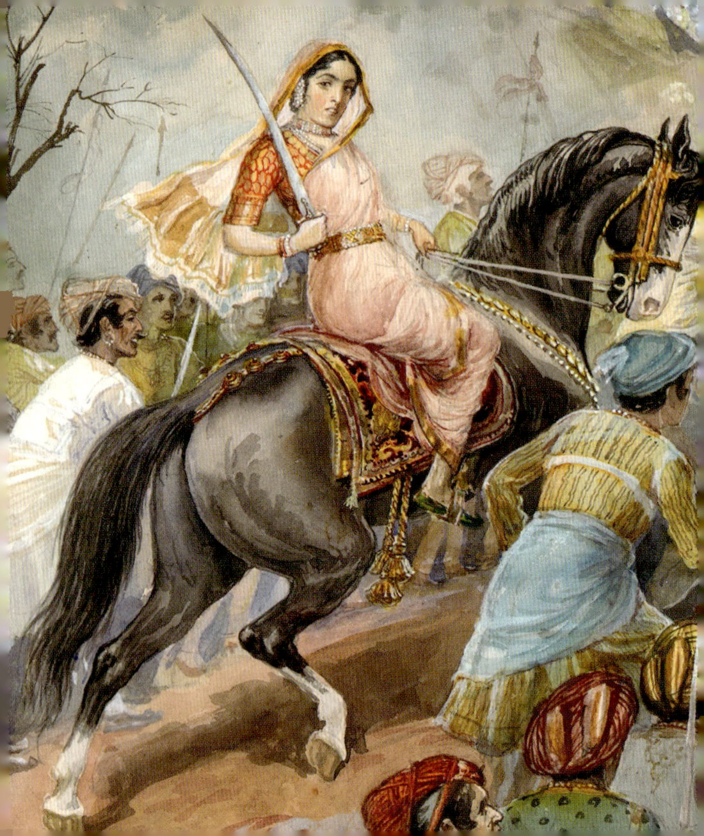

4. EARLY MODERN
1600–1799

Throwing a coup d'état isn't easy—you need political and military support and no small degree of savvy. Catherine the Great may be the most famous example, for ousting her husband, but she wasn't the first Russian empress to lead a coup. The regent Sophia Alekseyevna had attempted to seize the throne from Peter the Great but was stopped by his mother, Natalya Naryshkina, and Anna Leopoldovna lost power to the machinations of Elizabeth Petrovna. In the early modern era, usurpers were everywhere, from Russia to Angola to Denmark and Norway.

Though coups abounded during the early modern age, there were also queens consort and regents making the best of their role by wielding power over the king or their court. Power struggles persisted between a dowager queen, who still wanted to advise—that is, control—her son, and her daughter-in-law, who sought the same influence over her husband. Not every queen, though, wanted to dominate. Some were quick to cede control to their husbands; others had no choice: Ulrika Eleonora abdicated in favor of her husband because co-ruling was illegal in Sweden.

Queens were cultural stewards as well, ordering building projects and sponsoring artists; at this time print culture flourished, allowing women to create their own narratives.

Marriage was characteristically traditional, in a time of derogatory and conflicting perceptions of women, although it varied by place and culture. In China, for example, an emperor had numerous empresses consort—as many as three thousand—and would elevate one as empress. It was rare for a queen to choose not to marry, but some nevertheless did, such as Christina of Sweden. This period is exceptional for the rise of the mistress as an official position at the palace, and political conflicts between queens and mistresses abounded.

Despite the strides women made during this period, they were still shackled by the dominant perception that they belonged to the private sphere. As the Count-Duke de Olivares reputedly said to Elisabeth of France, queen consort of Spain and Portugal: "The mission of the friars is only to pray and that of women only to give birth." Sharply contrasting views of women were still ingrained. Juliana Maria of Denmark and Norway was compared to the biblical Esther and Deborah but called a devil by her opponents. Mary II of England was hailed as another Queen Elizabeth I but also as Cincinnatus, a Roman general who virtuously relinquished his power, because she had opted to share the throne with her husband, William III, who became the de facto king.

These perceptions do not resonate in depictions of queens, where the trappings of power prevail. Allegorical settings were in vogue—Marie de Médicis of France was pictured with classical figures and puffy clouds in an extensive work on her life she commissioned from Peter Paul Rubens (p. 188), and Catherine of Braganza, queen of Great Britain, appeared in a chariot floating through the clouds on a lavishly painted ceiling by Antonio Verrio (p. 210). These portraits exhibit queens in extravagant dresses and jewelry, accompanied by orbs, scepters, crowns (especially for queens regnant), fur-trimmed coronation robes, sashes, medals, and even a favorite pet (sometimes with their own accessories, as exhibited by Marie Leszczynska's dog on p. 229). However, not every artwork represented queens in an elaborate way. In Ethiopia, we see Mentewab positioned humbly at the bottom of a wall painting, in which the Virgin Mary stands at the center (p. 228). Other queens are dressed in more unassuming apparel as a way to subvert the expected royal portrayal. Queens weren't restricted to painted portraits; some appear in prints, such as Turhan of the Ottoman Empire (p. 205).

As part of globalization and colonization during this time, European records begin to include women from other cultures, albeit through a clearly biased lens. We begin to see female chiefs in the Americas, whose lives are known primarily in oral traditions, such as Aliquippa of the Seneca in Pennsylvania and Cockacoeskie of the Pamunkey in Virginia, both strong leaders who navigated complex political situations between the settlers and their people. Cockacoeskie is an example of a queen in a matrilineal society and was succeeded by her niece Betty. Though we do not have many illustrations of queens from Native American tribes, we know that they were not uncommon during this period, when women played an important role in their societies.

Though the perceptions of women from prior centuries prevailed during the early modern period, it was a time when queens could more easily justify their right to reign and get the vital backing they needed. This period was one of political, religious, and technological revolution, fomenting the perfect amount of chaos for queens to take charge.

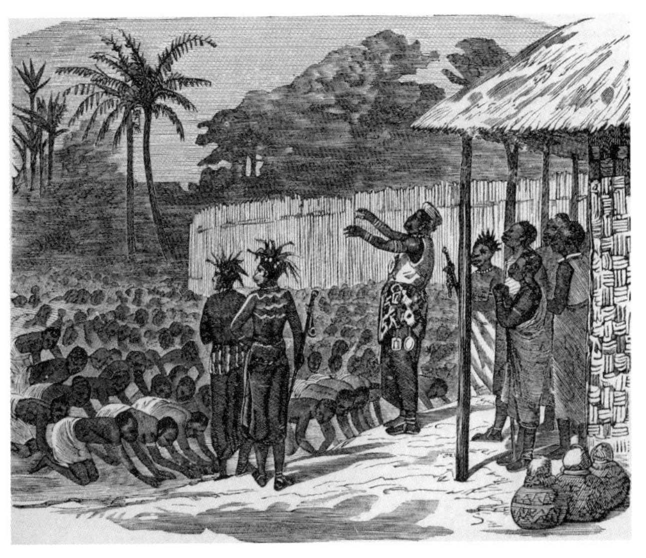

Tembandumba, queen of the Jaga (Angola)
(*r.* c. early seventeenth century).
Trained as a soldier, she led an army and usurped her mother as queen. (Standing, with arms outstretched; illustration, 1877.)

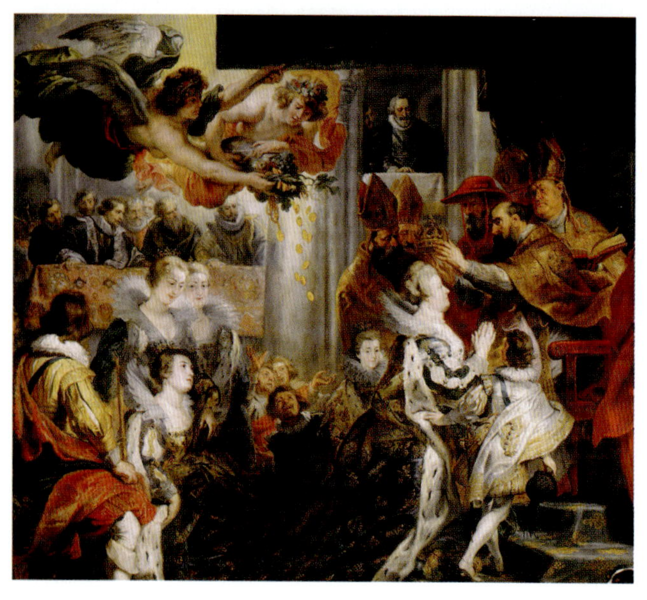

Marie de Médicis, queen consort (*r.* 1600–1610) and regent of France (*r.* 1610–1617).
Commissioned Peter Paul Rubens to create elaborate allegorical paintings of her life on the walls of Luxembourg Palace, such as her coronation (shown here).
(Painting, detail, by Peter Paul Rubens, c. 1622–25.)

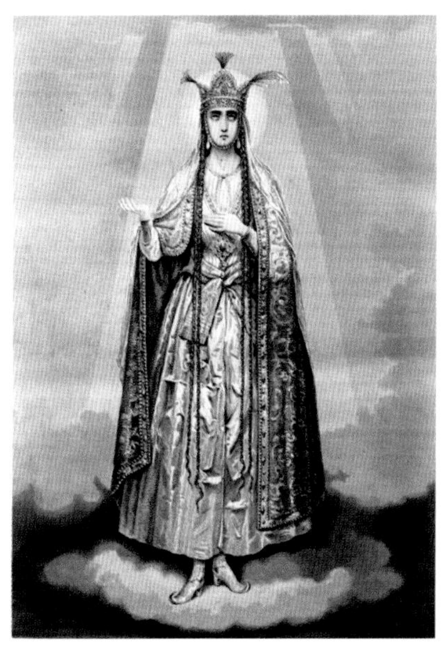

Saint Ketevan, consort (*r.* 1601–1602) and queen of Kakheti (Georgia) (*r.* 1605–1614). Martyred for refusing to give up her Christian faith. (Illustration, detail, 1882.)

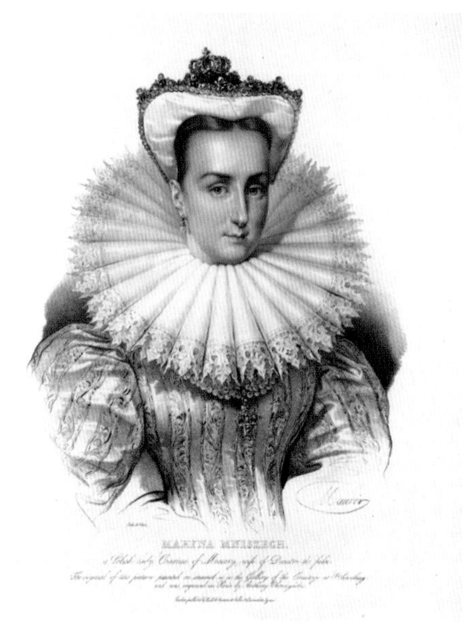

Marina Mniszech, empress consort of Russia (*r.* 1605–1606).
Married two pretenders to the Russian throne.
(Print, detail, by Nicolas Eustache Maurin, c. 1822–35.)

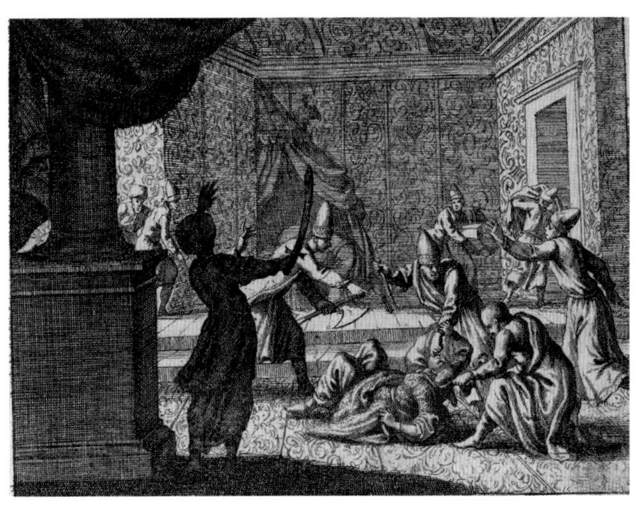

Kösem, empress consort (*r.* 1605–1617), dowager (*r.* 1623–1651), and regent of the Ottoman Empire (*r.* 1623–1632; 1648–1651). She overthrew her son, Sultan Ibrahim, and installed her grandson so she could exercise power as regent—her ambitious nature ultimately led to her assassination. (Center, on the ground; print attributed to Paul Rycaut, 1694.)

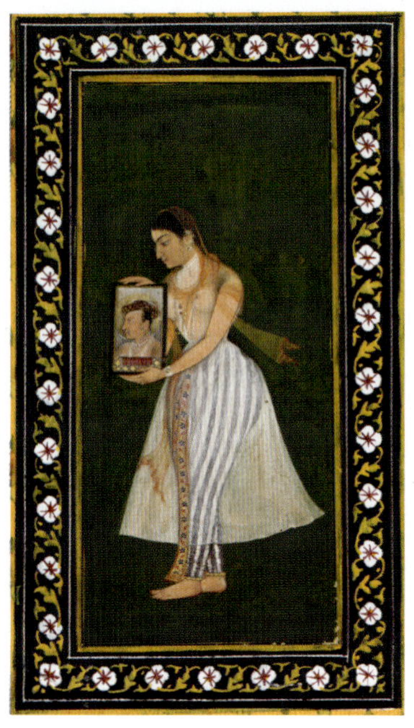

Nur Jahan, empress consort of the Mughal Empire (South Asia) (*r.* 1611–1627). The only Mughal empress with coins minted in her name. (Painting by Bishandas, c. 1627.)

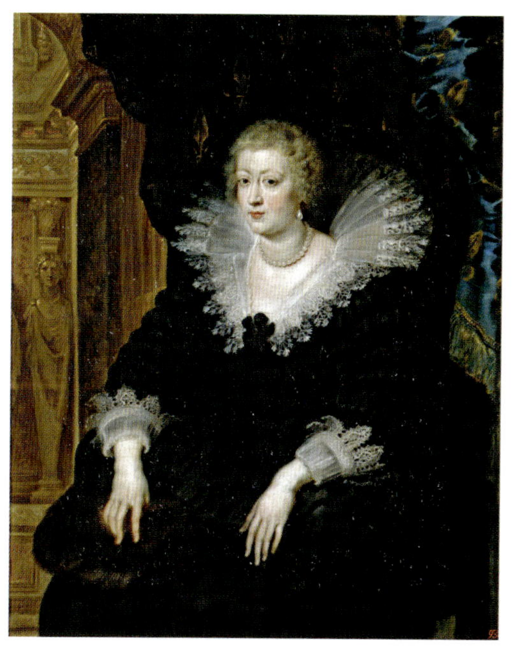

Anne of Austria, queen consort (*r.* 1615–1643) and regent of France (*r.* 1643–1651). Revoked the king's will that limited her authority as regent. (Painting by Peter Paul Rubens, c. 1622.)

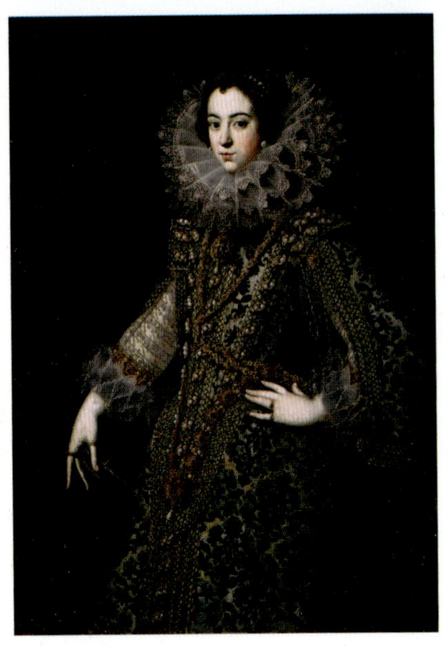

ELISABETH OF FRANCE, OR ISABEL OF BOURBON, QUEEN CONSORT OF PORTUGAL (*r.* 1621–1640) AND SPAIN (*r.* 1621–1644), AND REGENT OF SPAIN (*r.* 1640–1642; 1643–1644).
She may have participated in the "Women's Conspiracy," a plot by noble women to expel the Count-Duke de Olivares, Spain's prime minister, and restore her political status in court. (Painting, c. 1620.)

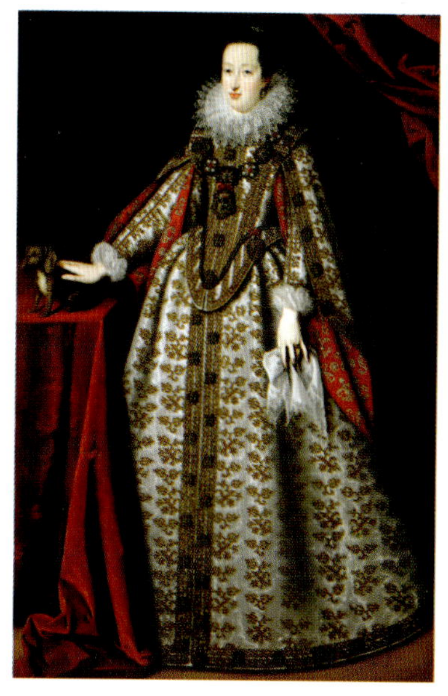

Eleonora Gonzaga, empress consort of the Holy Roman Empire, Germany, Hungary, and Bohemia (*r.* 1622–1655). The Vienna court became the epicenter for baroque music during her reign. (Painting by Justus Suttermans, 1621.)

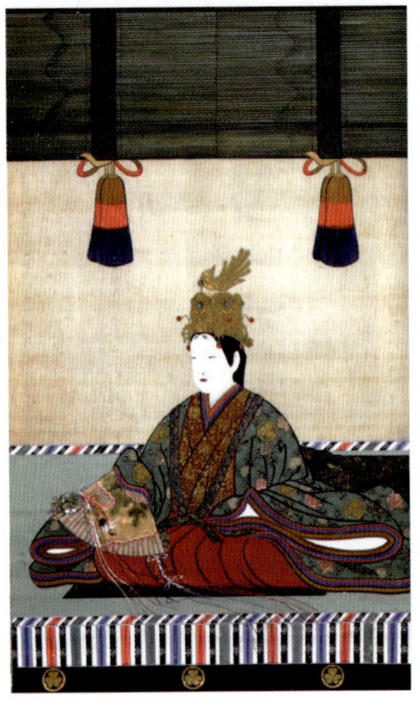

Tokugawa Masako, empress consort of Japan (*r.* 1624–1629). Though perceived as unsophisticated because she came from a warrior clan, she became a patron of the arts and a calligrapher. (Print by Yuan Xiufei, c. seventeenth–eighteenth century.)

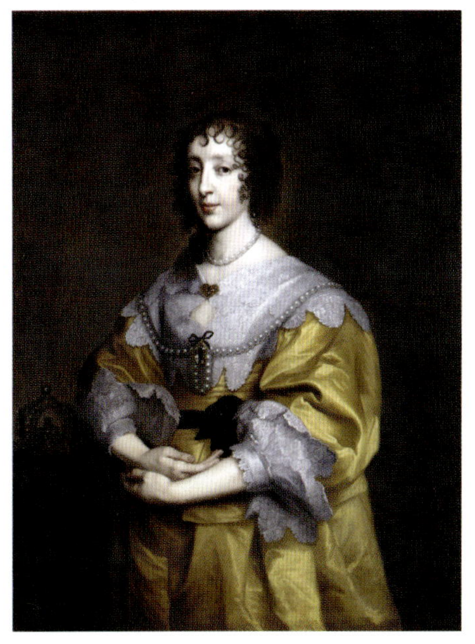

HENRIETTA MARIA, OR QUEEN MARY, QUEEN CONSORT OF ENGLAND, SCOTLAND, AND IRELAND (*r.* 1625–1649). The state of Maryland is named after her, though she preferred Henrietta and signed documents accordingly. (Painting by Anthony van Dyck, 1636.)

A Queen's Defiance

Portugal dominated numerous African countries during the early modern period. Portuguese diplomats, in a power move, would remain seated when visited by African leaders and refuse to offer their visitors a chair. Nzinga wouldn't have this. She had her female servant physically form a chair for her, showing her authority and maintaining her dignity. This incident quickly became famous. Nzinga consolidated her kingdom and secured it from Portuguese control. Her relationship with the Portuguese, always varying, soured when she offered asylum to escaped slaves. She remains one of the most famous African queens in history.

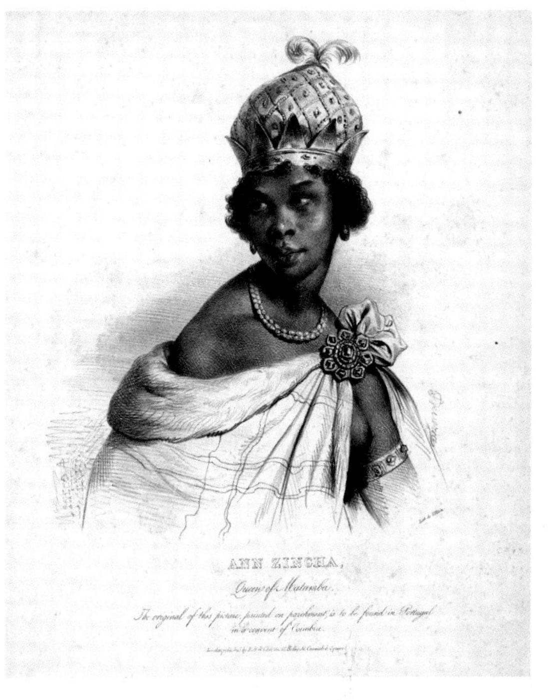

NZINGA, QUEEN OF NDONGO AND MATAMBA (ANGOLA) (*r.* 1624–1663).
(Print, detail, nineteenth century.)

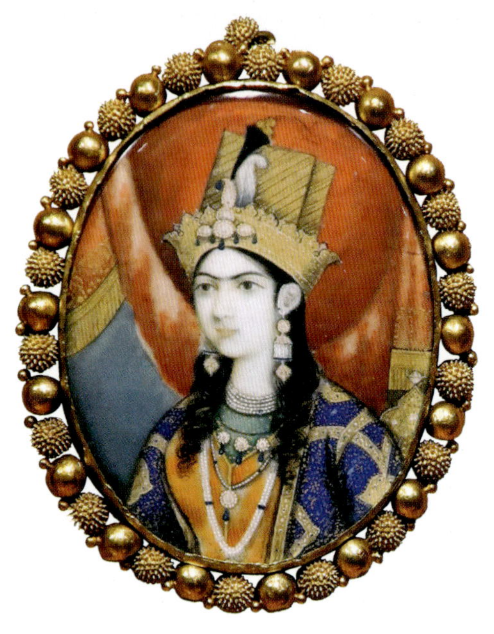

MUMTAZ MAHAL, EMPRESS CONSORT OF THE MUGHAL EMPIRE (SOUTH ASIA) (*r.* 1628–1631).
Her husband, Shah Jahan, commissioned the Taj Mahal as her final resting place. (Miniature painting, late nineteenth century.)

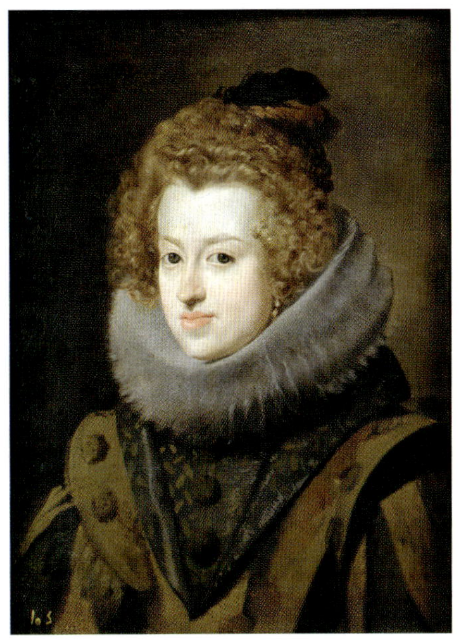

Maria Anna of Spain, empress consort (*r.* 1637–1646) and regent of the Holy Roman Empire, Hungary, and Bohemia (*r.* 1645). Interceded between the court of her husband, Emperor Ferdinand III of the Holy Roman Empire, and Spain, her homeland. (Painting attributed to Diego Velázquez, c. 1630.)

A Brilliant Mind

Christina is regarded as one of the most educated and culturally influential women of her time. She was taught philosophy by Descartes, established the first newspaper in Sweden, and was instrumental in ending the Thirty Years' War. She secretly converted to Catholicism (illegal in Sweden at the time) and moved to Paris, where she immersed herself in the arts and sciences. Regretting her decision to abdicate, she attempted to retake the throne of Sweden as well as the crowns of Naples and Poland. She also authored an autobiography.

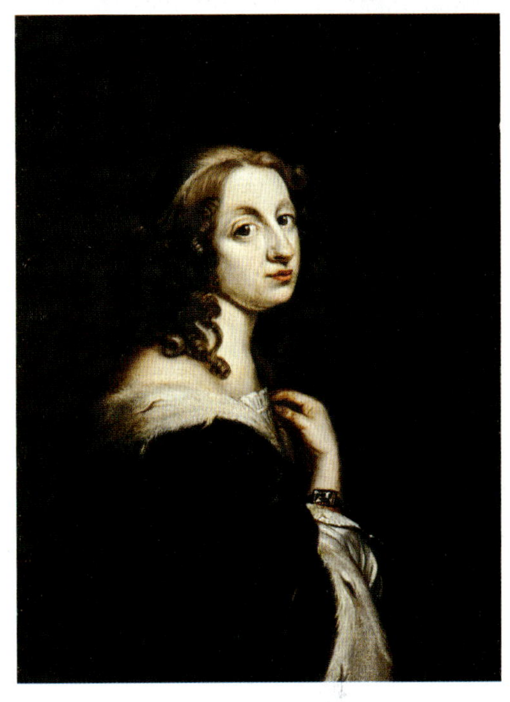

CHRISTINA, QUEEN OF SWEDEN (*r.* 1632–1654).
(Painting by David Beck, c. 1650.)

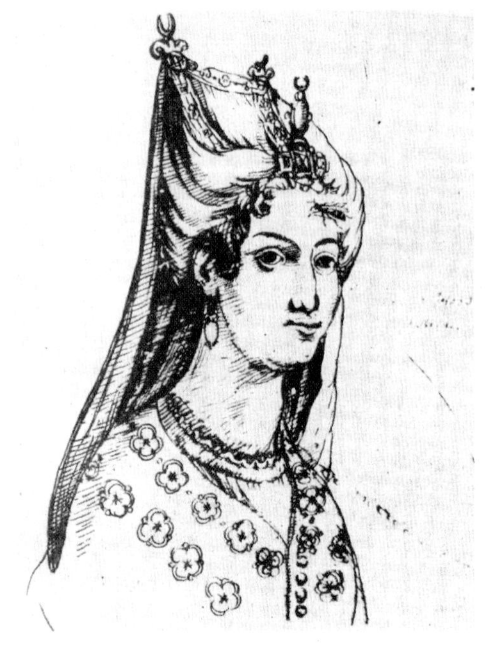

Mariam Dadiani, queen consort of Kartli
(Georgia) (*r.* 1638–1658; 1659–1675).
On the way to her wedding, her entourage of thousands fought off an opposing army. (Drawing by Teramo Castelli, c. 1630–49.)

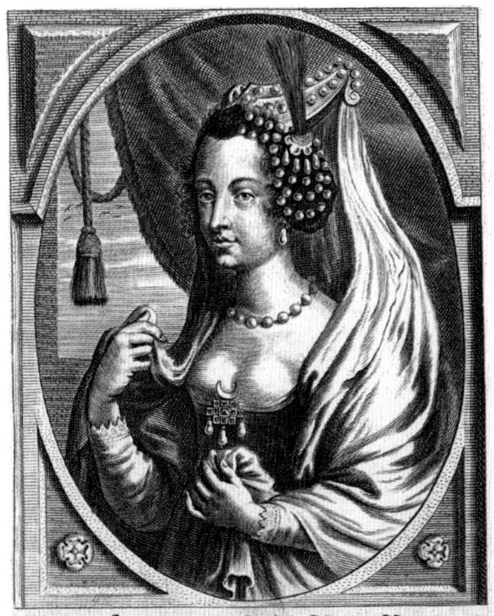

TURHAN, EMPRESS CONSORT (*r.* 1640–1648) AND REGENT OF THE OTTOMAN EMPIRE (*r.* 1651–1656). The only *valide sultan* (regent) in Ottoman history to co-rule equally with her son. (Print by Pietro de Jode II, c. 1640–60.)

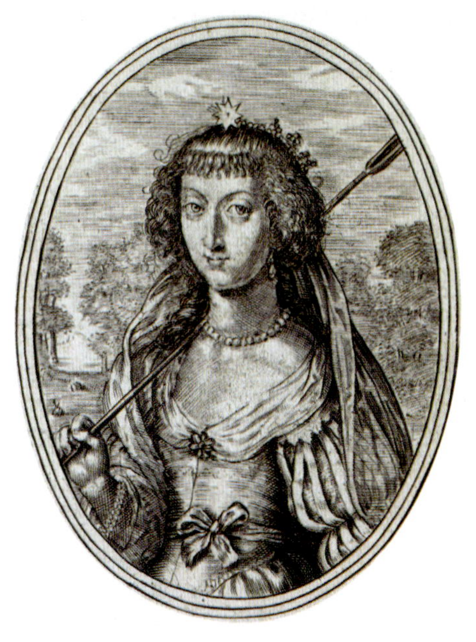

Luisa de Guzmán, queen consort (*r.* 1640–1656) and regent of Portugal (*r.* 1656–1662). Her leadership during the Portuguese Restoration War helped bring about the country's independence from Spain. (Print, detail, by Crispijn van de Passe the Younger, 1640.)

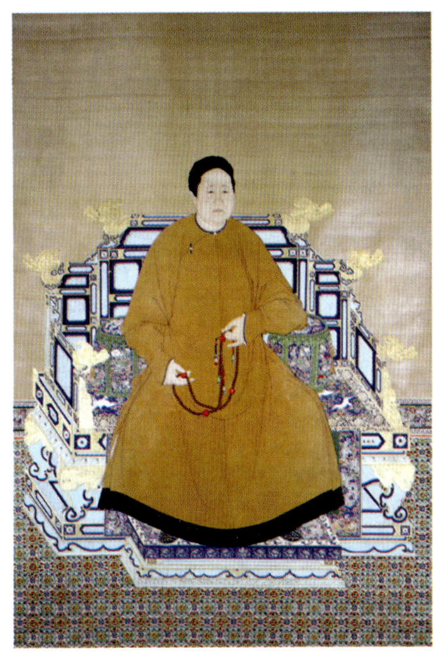

Xiaozhuang, or Lady Borjigit, empress dowager of Qing China (*r.* 1643–1688). Her political career earned her the title of empress posthumously. (Painting.)

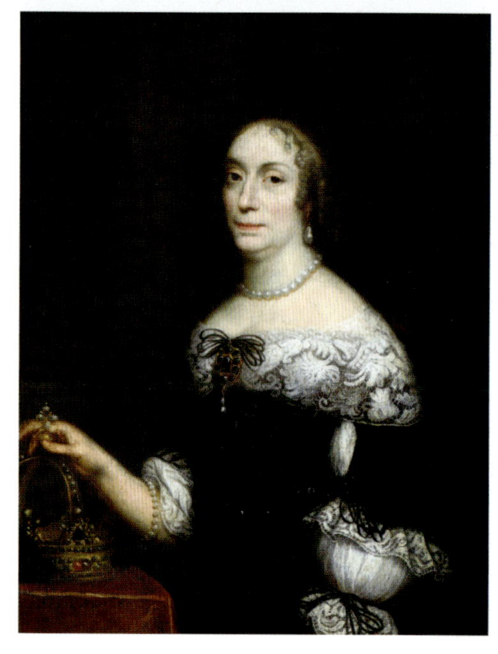

Marie Louise Gonzaga, queen consort of Poland (*r.* 1645–1648; 1649–1667). Founded the *Merkuriusz Polski* (*Polish Mercury*), the first Polish newspaper. (Painting by Daniel Schultz II, c. 1667.)

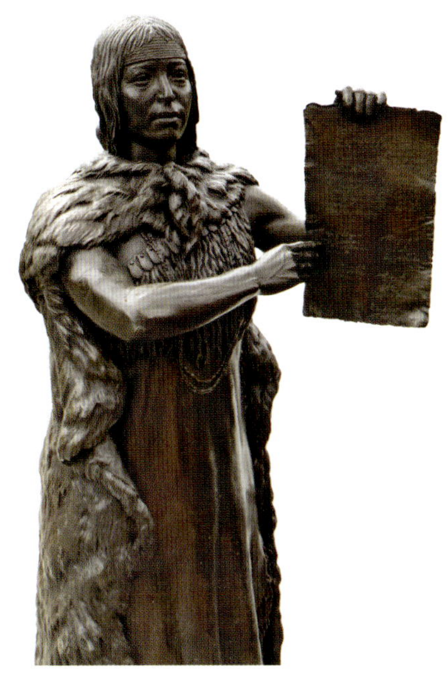

COCKACOESKIE, CHIEF OF THE PAMUNKEY (VIRGINIA) (*r.* 1656–1686). She was first to sign the Treaty of Middle Plantation, which offered protection for her tribe and established the first Native American reservation. (Statue, 2019.)

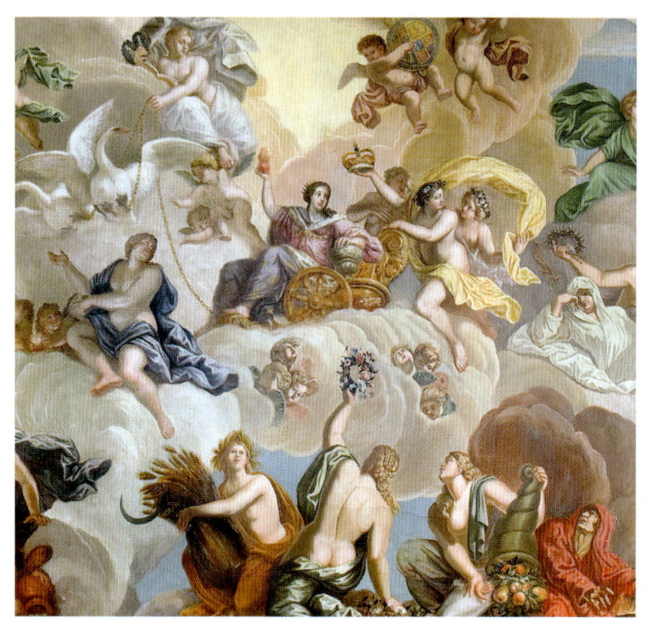

Catherine of Braganza, queen consort of England, Scotland, and Ireland (*r.* 1662–1685), and regent of Portugal (*r.* 1701; 1704–1705). She popularized tea drinking in England. (Center; painting, detail, by Antonio Verrio, 1675–c. 1684.)

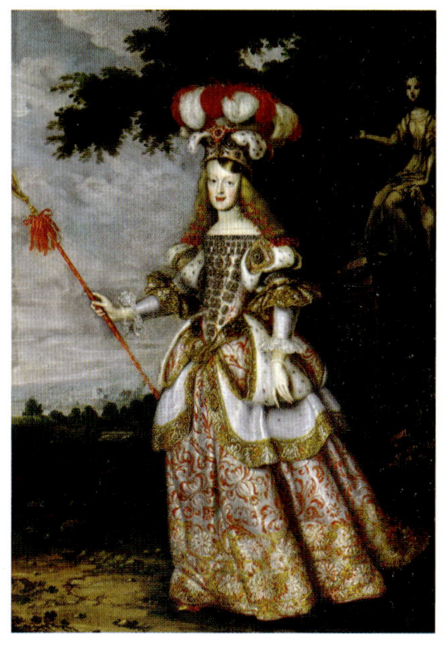

Margaret Theresa of Spain, empress consort of the Holy Roman Empire, Germany, Austria, Hungary, and Bohemia (*r.* 1666–1673). She and her husband, Leopold I, were great patrons of theater—she is seen here in costume. (Painting by Jan Thomas van Ieperen, 1667.)

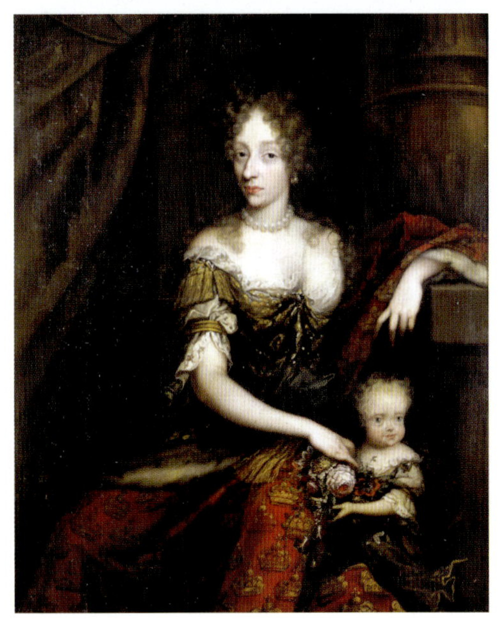

Charlotte Amalie of Hesse-Kassel, queen consort of Denmark and Norway (*r.* 1670–1699). Effectively arranged the defense of Copenhagen from Swedish invaders. (Painting by Jacques d'Agar, seventeenth century.)

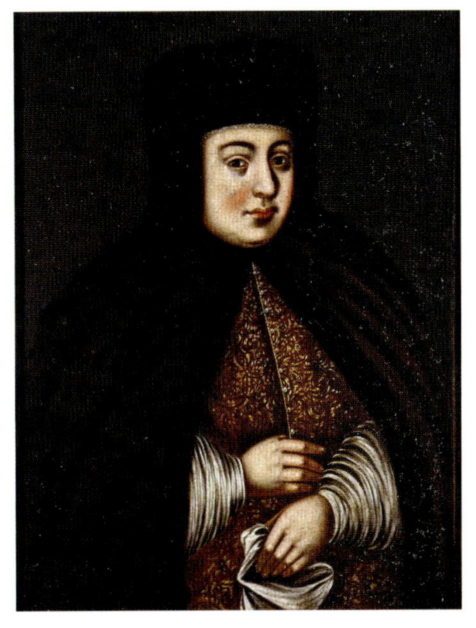

Natalya Naryshkina, empress consort (*r.* 1671–1676) and regent of Russia (*r.* 1682).
Helped place her son, Peter the Great, on the throne, despite riots instigated by rival Sophia Alekseyevna (p. 216).
(Painting, late seventeenth century.)

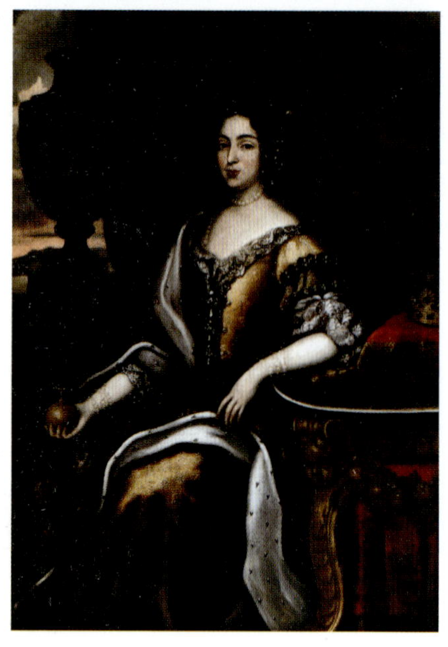

Marie Casimire, queen consort of Poland (*r.* 1676–1696). She used her political acumen to help her husband, John III Sobieski, ascend to the throne. (Painting by Jan Tricius, c. 1676.)

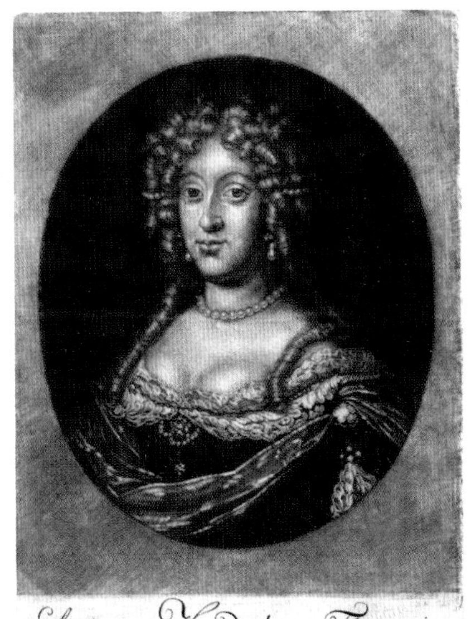

ELEONORE MAGDALENE OF NEUBURG, EMPRESS CONSORT (*r.* 1676–1705) AND REGENT OF THE HOLY ROMAN EMPIRE, GERMANY, AUSTRIA, HUNGARY, AND BOHEMIA (*r.* 1711). She translated the Bible from Latin into German. (Print, detail, 1676–1724.)

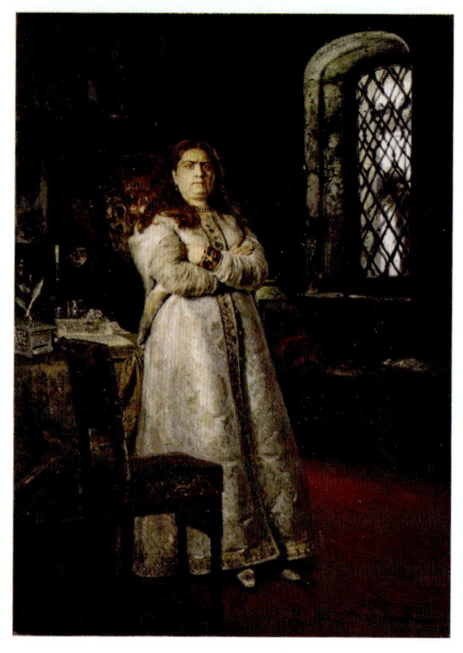

SOPHIA ALEKSEYEVNA, REGENT OF RUSSIA (*r.* 1682–1689). Seized the regency from Natalya Naryshkina (p. 213) in an unparalleled move for a female royal—and set a precedent for Russian empresses. (Painting by Ilya Repin, 1879.)

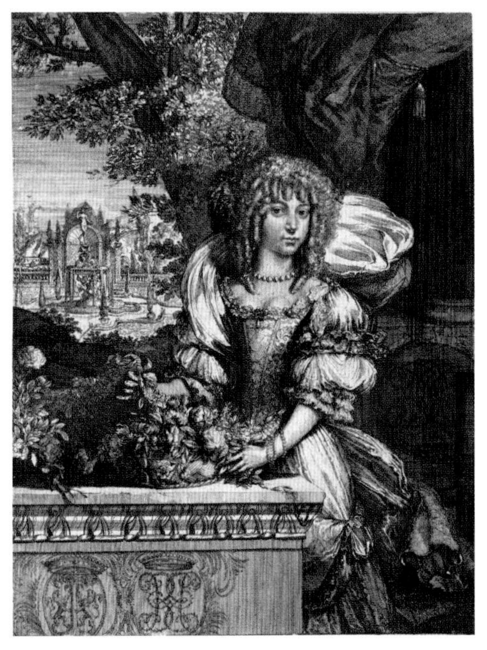

MARY II, QUEEN (CORULER) OF ENGLAND (*r.* 1689–1694). Persuaded by her husband, William III, to depose her father and take the throne. (Print by Romeyn de Hooghe.)

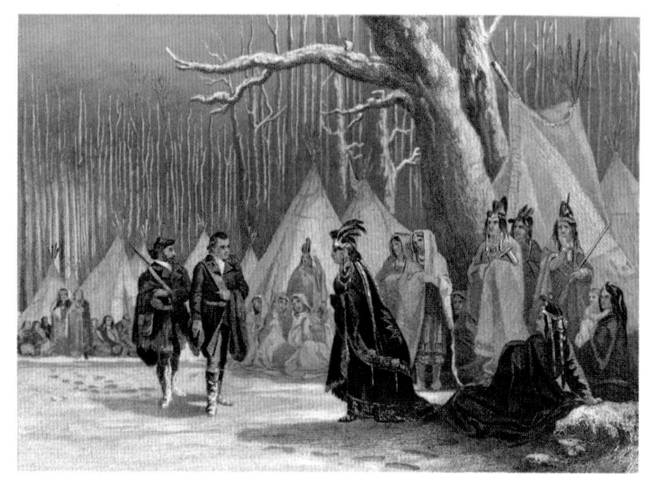

ALIQUIPPA, CHIEF OF THE SENECA (PENNSYLVANIA)
(*r.* c. eighteenth century).
A formidable leader who denied French colonizers the opportunity to influence her people; she is depicted here meeting General George Washington. (Illustration, detail, 1857.)

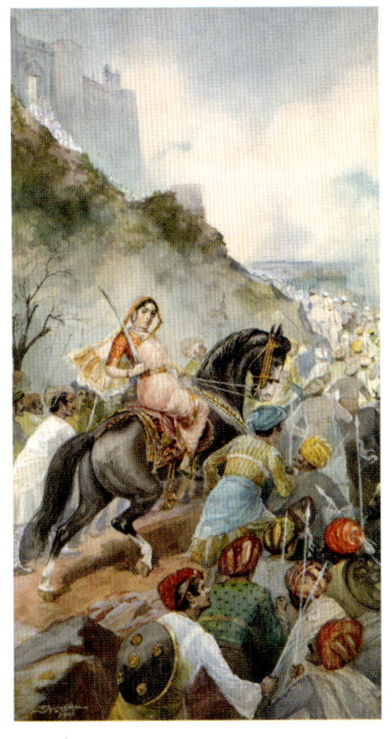

Tarabai, regent of the Maratha Empire (India) (*r.* 1700–1708).
Commanded Maratha forces against the Mughals.
(Painting by Mahadev Visvanath Dhurandhar, 1927.)

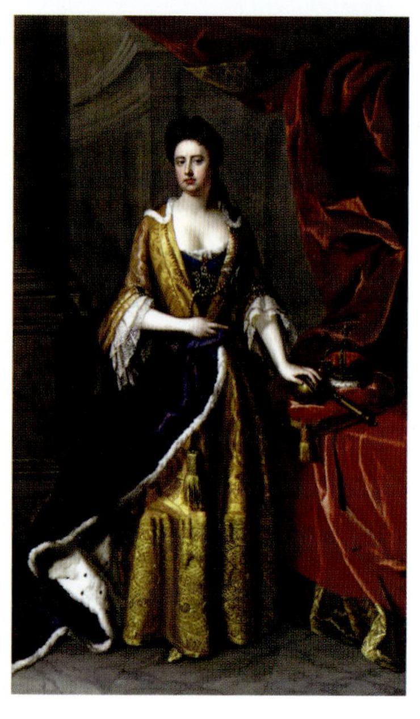

Anne, queen of England (*r.* 1702–1714). England and Scotland united during her reign, becoming Great Britain. (Painting by Michael Dahl, 1705.)

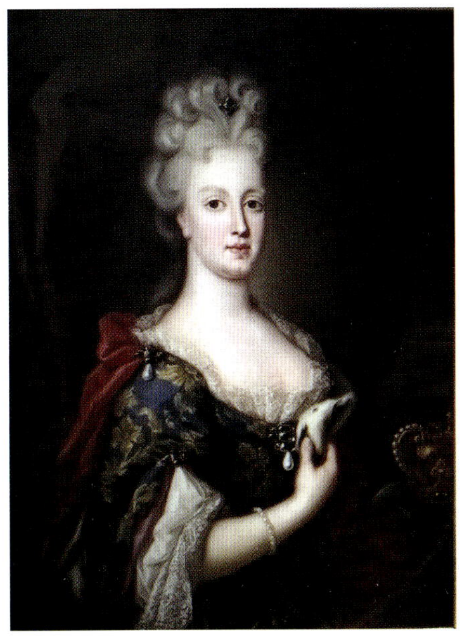

Maria Anna of Austria, queen consort (*r.* 1708–1750) and regent of Portugal (*r.* 1742–1750).
As regent, she removed the Marquis of Pombal, who had controlled her husband for many years. (Painting attributed to Pompeo Girolamo Batoni, eighteenth century.)

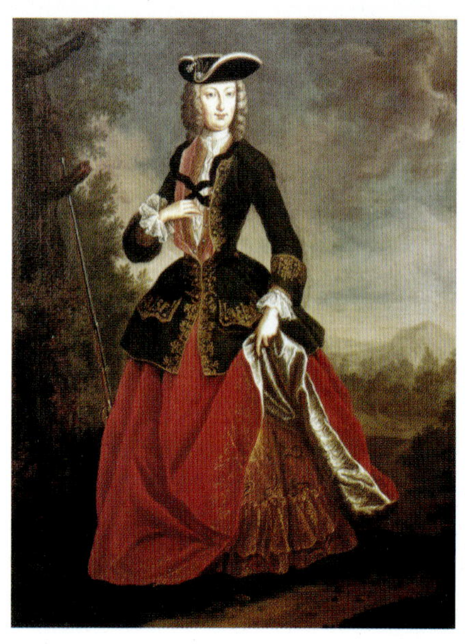

Elisabeth Christine of Brunswick-Wolfenbüttel, regent of Catalonia (Spain) (*r.* 1711–1713), and empress consort of the Holy Roman Empire (*r.* 1711–1740). Elisabeth, pressured to produce an heir, became unhealthily overweight after being prescribed a diet said to guarantee fertility. (Painting, eighteenth century.)

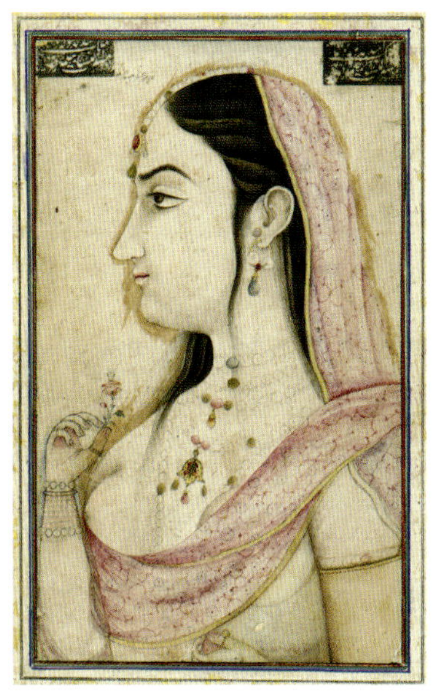

Lal Kunwar, empress consort of the Mughal Empire (South Asia) (*r.* 1712–1713).
She was a dancer before becoming empress and is known for her love of decadence. (Manuscript miniature, detail, eighteenth century.)

Consort in Name Only

Elisabeth's husband, Philip V, was known to be unstable and violent. Yet, she had the strength to overcome his behavior and establish her control over the court. She chose officials who would support her ambition to extend Spain's reach in Italy and secure Italian principalities for her children to inherit, since her stepchildren would be given the Spanish throne and lands. She also made reforms to the economy, military, and government during her reign as queen and regent.

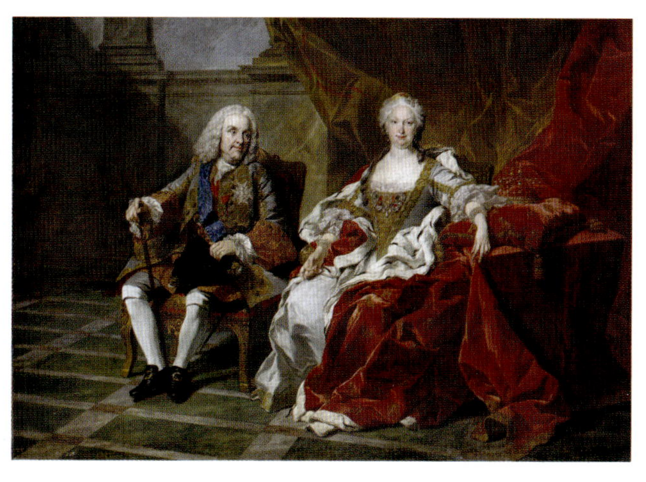

Elisabeth Farnese, queen consort (de facto regnant) (*r.* 1714–1746) and regent of Spain (*r.* 1759–1760).
(Right, with Philip V; painting by Louis-Michel van Loo, 1743.)

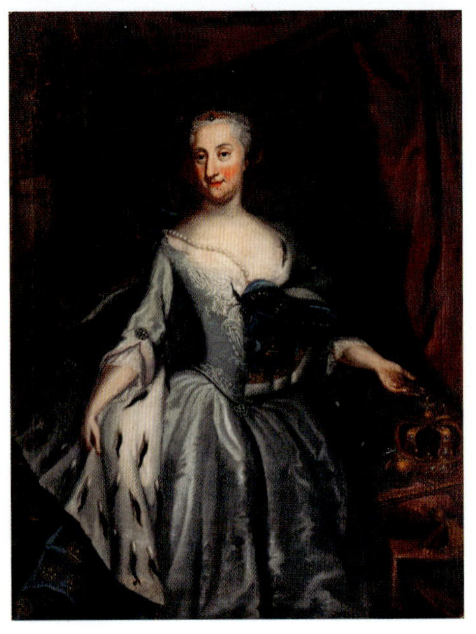

Ulrika Eleonora, queen (*r.* 1718–1720) and consort of Sweden (*r.* 1720–1751).
She and her husband initiated the Age of Freedom, a nearly fifty-year period of parliamentary rather than absolutist government. (Painting by Georg Engelhard Schröder, eighteenth century.)

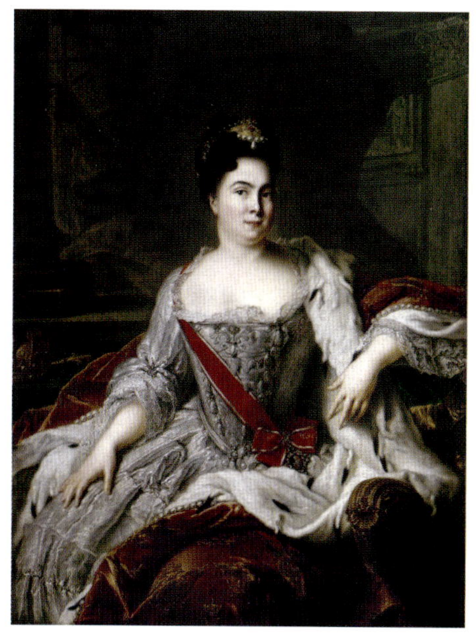

Catherine I, consort (*r.* 1721–1725) and
empress of Russia (*r.* 1725–1727).
She was a peasant before becoming Peter the Great's second wife and empress. (Painting by Jean Marc Nattier, 1717.)

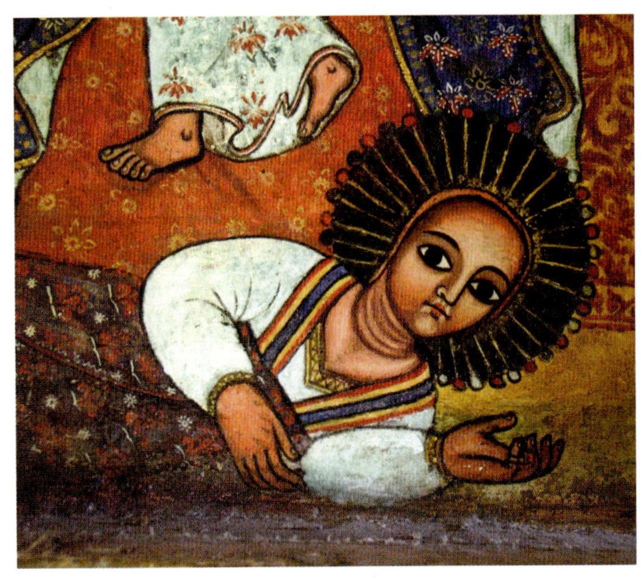

Mentewab, consort (*r.* 1723–1730) and empress (coruler) of Ethiopia (*r.* 1730–1755).
Went head-to-head with her daughter-in-law for the right to ascend the throne—neither won. (Painting, late eighteenth century.)

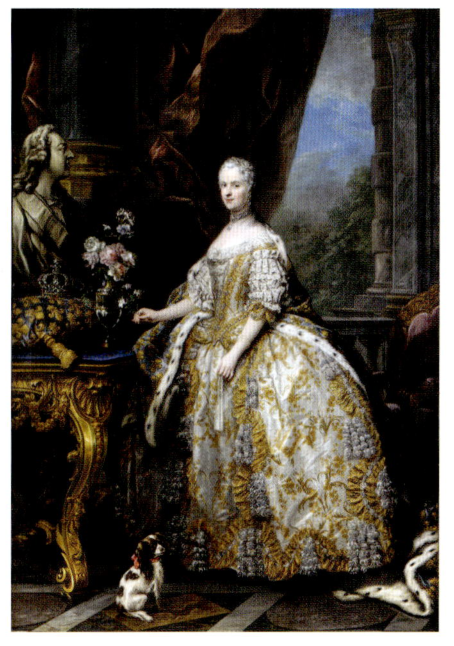

Marie Leszczynska, queen consort of France (*r.* 1725–1768). The longest-serving queen, by marriage to Louis XV, in the history of France. Banished Voltaire from Versailles. (Painting by Charles André van Loo, 1747.)

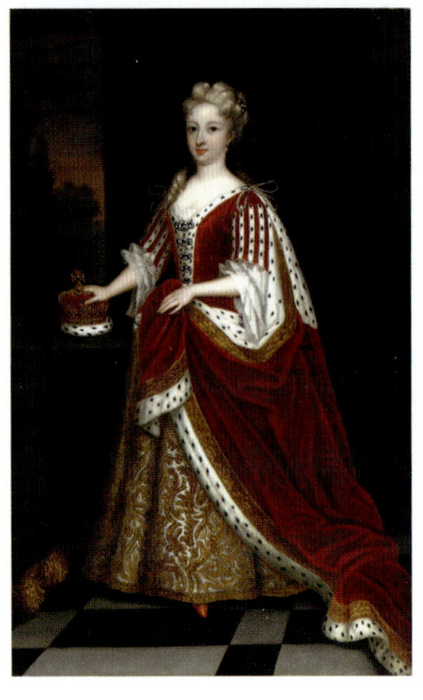

Caroline of Ansbach, queen consort (*r.* 1727–1737) and regent of England (*r.* 1729–1737, intermittently). One of England's leading patrons of the arts and sciences in her time, and the host of famous salons. (Painting by Godfrey Kneller, 1716.)

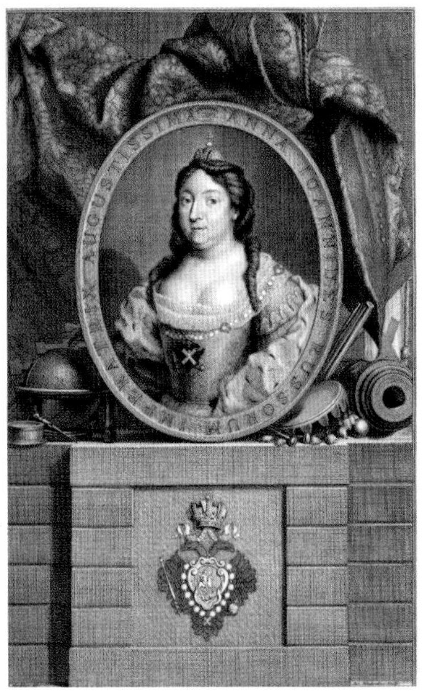

ANNA, EMPRESS OF RUSSIA (*r.* 1730–1740).
Accepted the throne with conditions that made her the council's puppet; she later tore up the conditions and abolished the council. (Print by Jacobus Houbraken after Jan Wandelaar, eighteenth century.)

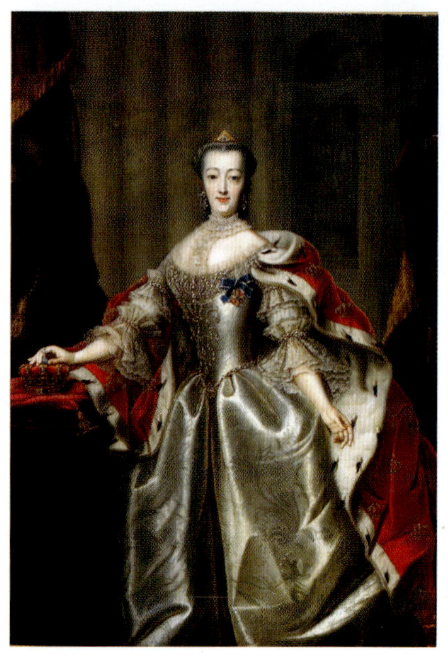

Sophie Magdalene of Brandenburg-Kulmbach, queen consort of Denmark and Norway (*r.* 1730–1746). Established the Ordre de l'Union Parfaite (see insignia pinned on her dress) for happily married couples, the first order in Denmark to include women. (Painting by Andreas Petersen Brünniche, eighteenth century.)

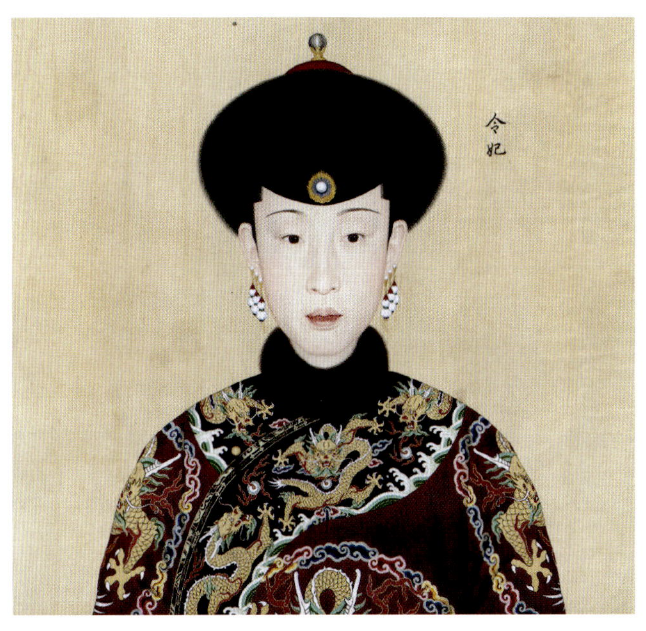

XIAOXIANCHUN, OR LADY FUCA, EMPRESS CONSORT OF QING CHINA (*r.* 1738–1748). The first empress to lead the consorts in the rites of sericulture, a ritual concerning the cultivation of silkworms. (Painting, detail, by Giuseppe Castiglione, c. 1738.)

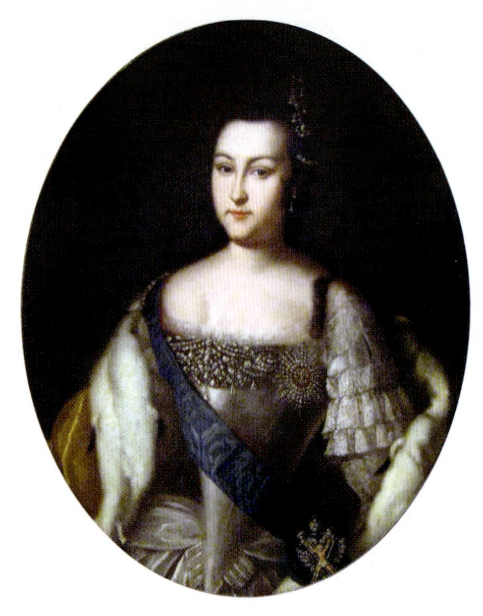

Anna Leopoldovna, regent of Russia (*r.* 1740–1741). Anna's rival, Elizabeth Petrovna (p. 237), revolted and exiled the empress and her family. (Painting by Workshop of Louis Caravaque, c. 1730.)

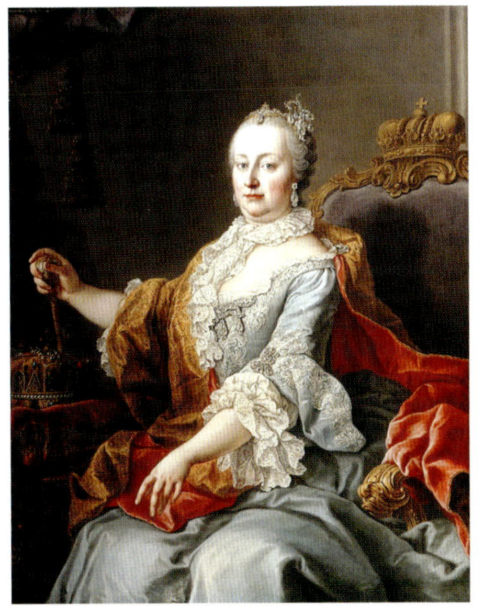

Maria Theresa, queen of Hungary and Croatia (*r.* 1740–1780) and Bohemia (*r.* 1743–1780), and empress consort of the Holy Roman Empire (*r.* 1745–1765). Defied all expectations by ruling as sovereign over her lands rather than ceding power to her husband and son. (Painting by Martin Mytens the Younger, 1759.)

A Determined Empress

After overthrowing Empress Anna Leopoldovna in a coup, Elizabeth would bring Russia through two significant conflicts of the time, the War of Austrian Succession and the Seven Years' War. She made many contributions to arts and culture, and oversaw the formation of the University of Moscow, the Imperial Academy of Arts, and the Winter Palace. She also fulfilled her own promise to not allow any executions during her reign.

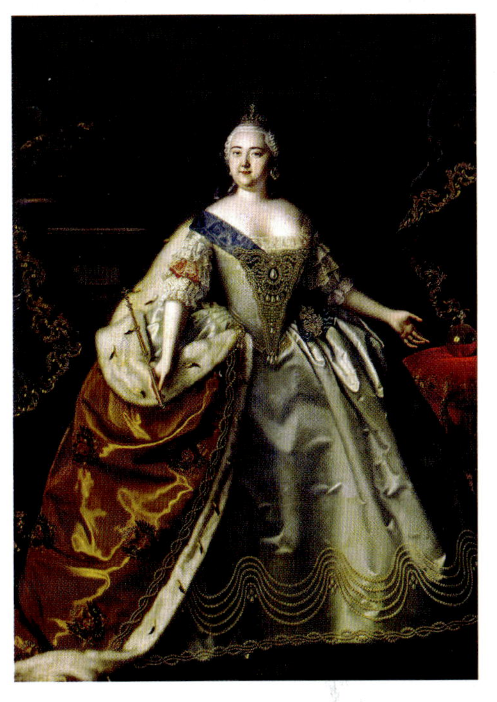

ELIZABETH PETROVNA, EMPRESS OF RUSSIA (*r.* 1741–1762).
(Painting by Louis Caravaque, 1750.)

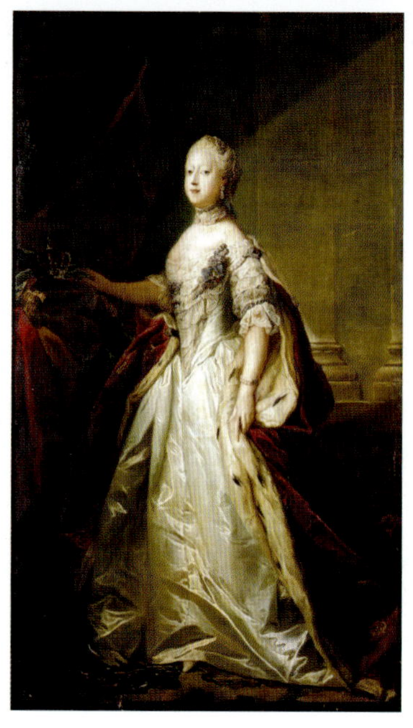

Louise of Great Britain, queen consort of Denmark and Norway (*r.* 1746–1751).
She was popular for bringing the arts to the Danish court.
(Painting by Carl Gustaf Pilo, c. 1745.)

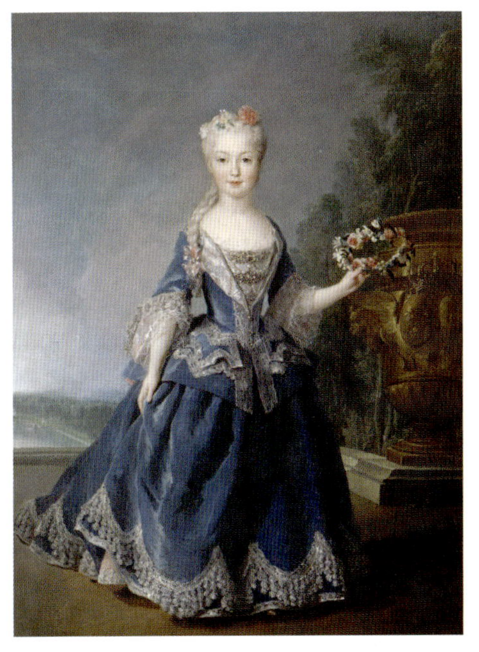

Mariana Victoria of Spain, queen consort (*r.* 1750–1777) and regent of Portugal (*r.* 1776–1777).
Restored good relations between Portugal and Spain.
(Painting by Alexis-Simon Belle, c. 1725–26.)

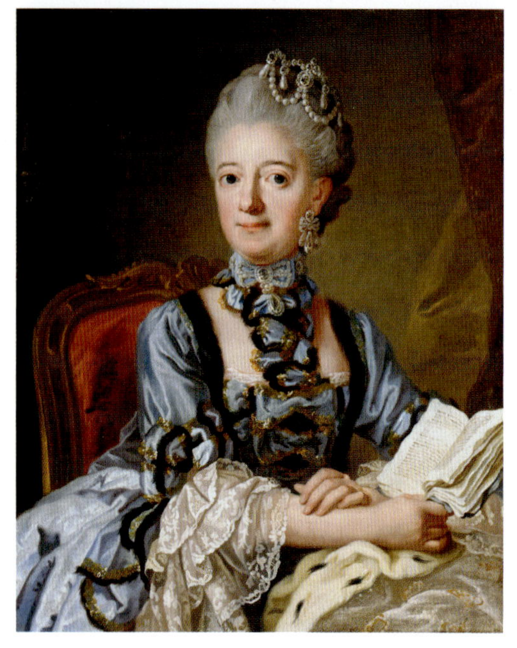

LOUISA ULRIKA OF PRUSSIA, QUEEN CONSORT OF SWEDEN (*r.* 1751–1771).
Attempted to reinstate an absolute monarchy in Sweden.
(Painting by Lorens Pasch the Younger, 1768.)

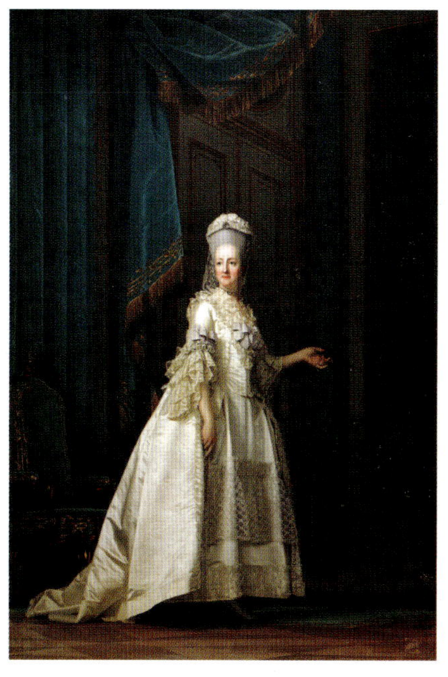

JULIANA MARIA, QUEEN CONSORT (*r.* 1752–1766) AND DE FACTO REGENT (*r.* 1772–1784) OF DENMARK AND NORWAY. Overthrew the queen consort, as well as the consort's lover, to gain the regency. (Painting by Vigilius Eriksen, 1776.)

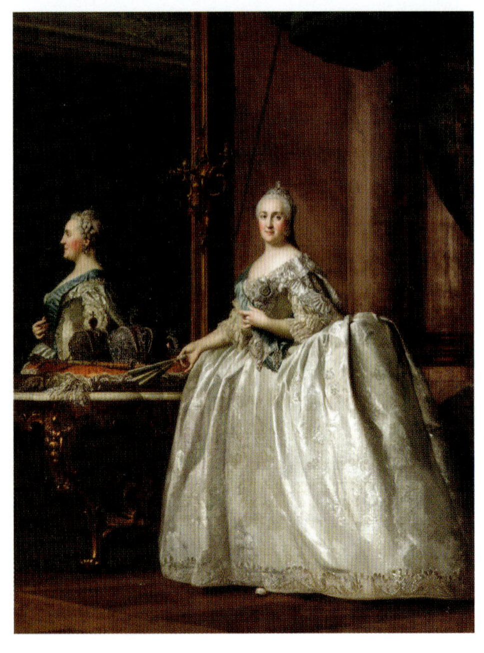

Catherine II, the Great, consort (*r.* 1762) and empress of Russia (*r.* 1762–1796).
She became Russia's longest-ruling female leader after ousting her husband in a coup d'état. (Painting by Vigilius Eriksen, 1792.)

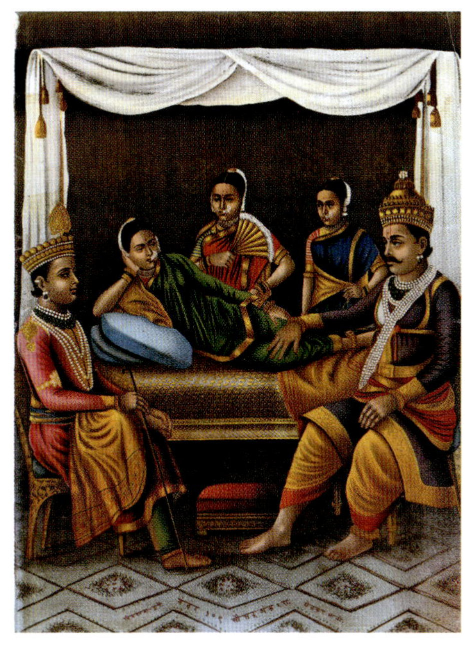

Ahilyabai Holkar, queen of the Malwa Kingdom (India) (*r.* 1767–1795). A shrewd political player, she also developed Indore from a village to a thriving city. (Lying down; chromolithograph.)

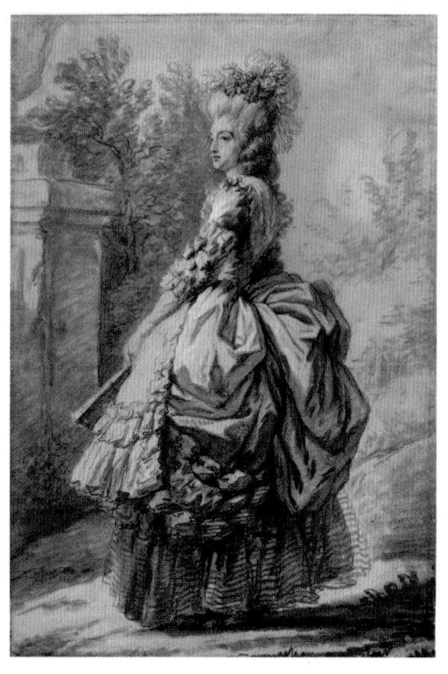

Marie Antoinette, queen consort of France (*r.* 1774–1792). French revolutionaries, repulsed by her lavish lifestyle, sentenced the queen and her husband, Louis XVI, to death by guillotine. (Drawing by Elisabeth Louise Vigée Le Brun, c. 1780–81.)

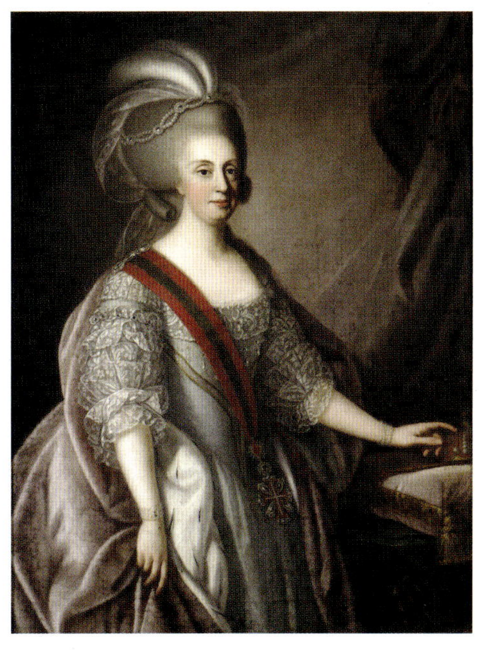

MARIA I, QUEEN OF PORTUGAL (*r.* 1777–1799) AND BRAZIL (*r.* 1815–1816). She was the first queen regnant of Portugal, but a mental collapse forced her to transfer power to her son. (Painting by Giuseppe Troni, 1783.)

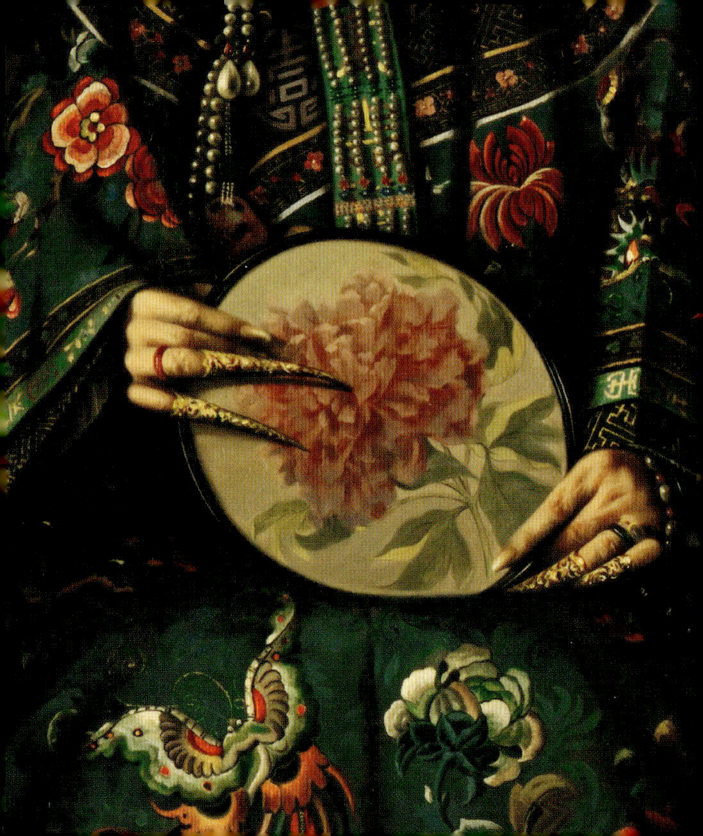

5. MODERN & CONTEMPORARY

1800–Present

For nearly five thousand years of recorded history, women have valiantly worked to secure the throne for themselves. At the start of the nineteenth century, the world was a more welcoming place for queens—and yet, change is slow. When Emma of Hawaii lobbied for sole possession of the throne, an opponent said, "I believe in beautiful women and fine horses, but no petticoat shall rule me." In 1972, Margrethe II of Denmark ascended the throne only because an amendment to the Danish Act of Succession positioned her before her male relatives. However, this law would have permitted a brother to take the throne before Margrethe, had there been one, and it was not until 2009 that an amendment allowed the Danish monarch's oldest child to inherit the throne, regardless of sex.

That the question of agnatic primogeniture, the law that allows only male heirs to inherit a throne, still exists in the twenty-first century is remarkable—in Japan it is still under debate. However, this does not mean the whole world struggles with the idea of female rule. Many societies have witnessed a rise in female power in the past couple hundred years, from the Polynesian chiefs to the rain queens, or Modjadji, of the Balobedu people in South Africa. Their title derives from the belief that these queens control the bringing of rain to the land; they remain the only matrilineal monarchy on the continent.

In many countries today, the closest parallels we have to traditional queens are prime ministers and presidents, with a shift from monarchical to constitutional and democratic governments. Leading women today include Prime Minister Jacinda Ardern of New Zealand and Chancellor Angela Merkel of Germany, among others. The queen's rule retracts from the concerns of previous centuries—violent coups, battles, assassinations—and expands to focus on social justice (particularly for women and children), health, education, and other initiatives. There have been exceptional leaders in these areas, such as Sirikit of Thailand and Rania of Jordan. Most queens today have a largely symbolic role, and as figureheads their responsibilities include such duties as attending charities and receiving foreign dignitaries. Some of these queens have the authority to make or veto political decisions, but they are for the most part meant to be apolitical.

Lineage, even to this day, remains important, and queens consort are still pressured to produce an heir. There are more instances of women taking the initiative and leaving unfaithful or cruel husbands and obtaining divorces. An unhappy marriage nowadays, in contrast to previous years, doesn't always have to end in exile—though that is not to say that divorce hasn't been messy for many royals.

The nineteenth century saw queens reigning around the world, and with the advent of photography and the proliferation of illustrations in books and newspapers, we now have more images of queens available than just their official portraits. Though we naturally observe the familiar trappings of wealth and power, we also begin to witness queens in more intimate settings, often with their families and wearing casual clothing. In some instances, we are observing the royal family for the first time. Photography provides a unique opportunity to glimpse the personality of a queen, though it should be noted that many of these images were not taken by someone from the queen's own culture and aren't without bias. With the proliferation of photography and social media, maintaining a public image is more complicated for queens than it has ever been.

From Hatshepsut to Elizabeth II, and all the women that came before and after, the role of queen has been and remains a position to drive change in the world. Queens have pushed boundaries and overcome barriers, and they will only continue to reign in remarkable ways.

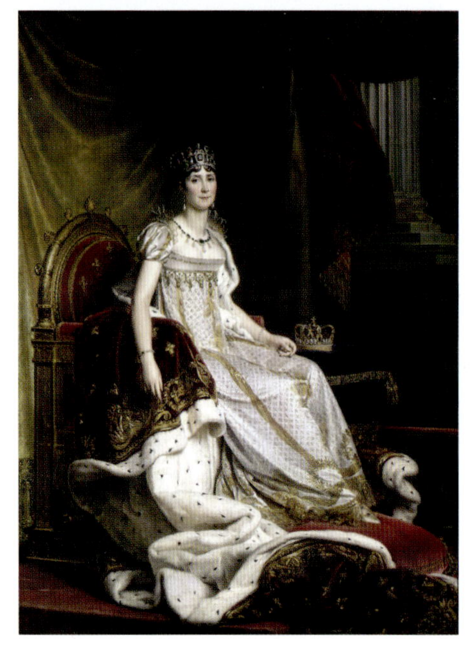

Joséphine Bonaparte, empress consort of France and Italy (*r.* 1804–1810). Transformed the perception of Napoleon from a general to a politician. (Painting by Baron François Gérard, 1807–8.)

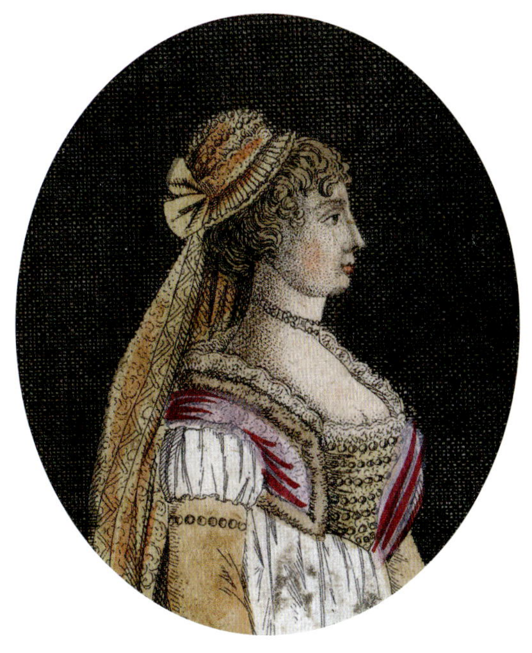

Maria Ludovika of Austria-Este, empress consort of Austria and Hungary (*r.* 1808–1816). A key member of a court-led war party that promoted fighting with France and defeating Napoleon. (Painting, detail, 1808.)

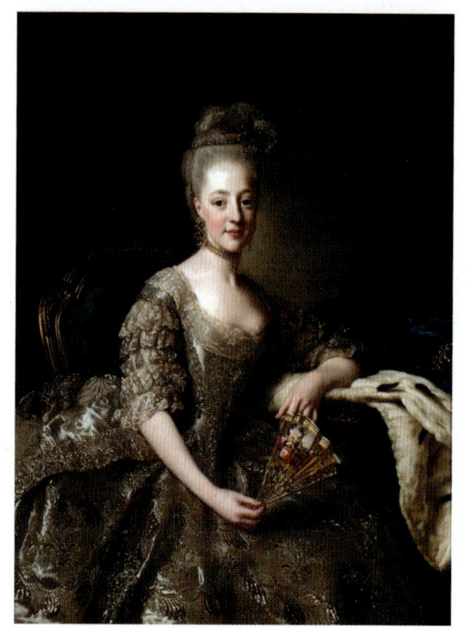

Hedvig Elisabeth Charlotte of Holstein-Gottorp, queen consort of Sweden (*r.* 1809–1818) and Norway (*r.* 1814–1818). Her witty and insightful diary, kept from 1775 to 1817, has become an invaluable historical record of her time. (Painting by Alexander Roslin, 1775.)

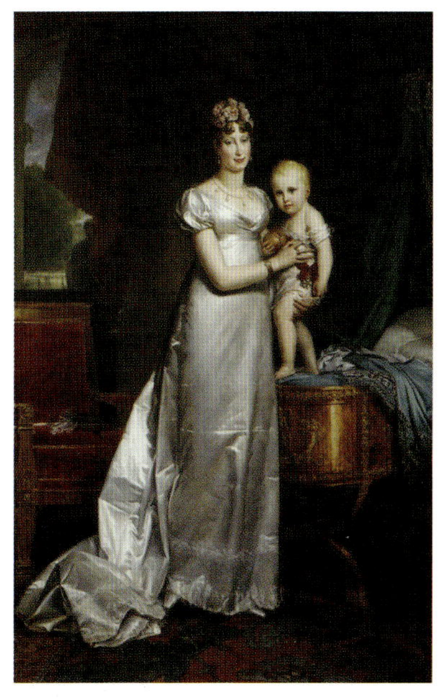

Marie Louise, empress consort (*r.* 1810–1814) and regent of France and Italy (*r.* 1812; 1814). Refused to join her husband, Napoleon, in exile and instead devoted herself to ruling her duchies. (Painting by Baron François Gérard, 1813.)

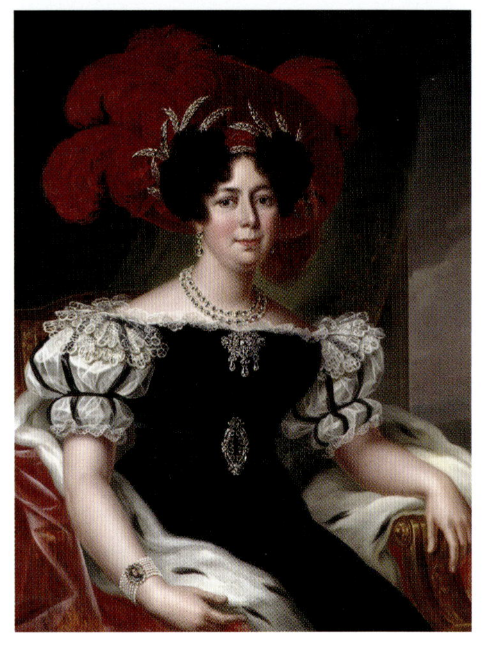

Désirée Clary, queen consort of Sweden and Norway (*r.* 1818–1844). Rose from common origins to become fiancée of Napoleon and later cofound the Bernadotte dynasty—Sweden's ruling house to this day. (Painting by Fredric Westin, 1830.)

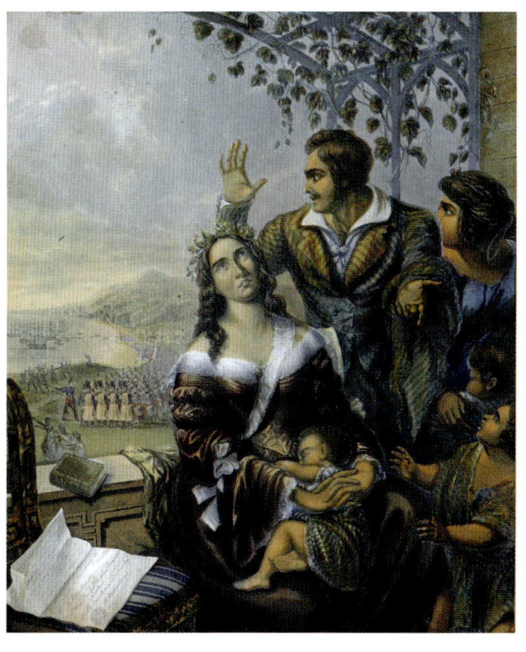

Pomare IV, queen of Tahiti (*r.* 1827–1877).
Despised French authority and the influence of its missionaries—she deported two Roman Catholic priests. (Seated, with child; print, detail, by George Baxter, 1845.)

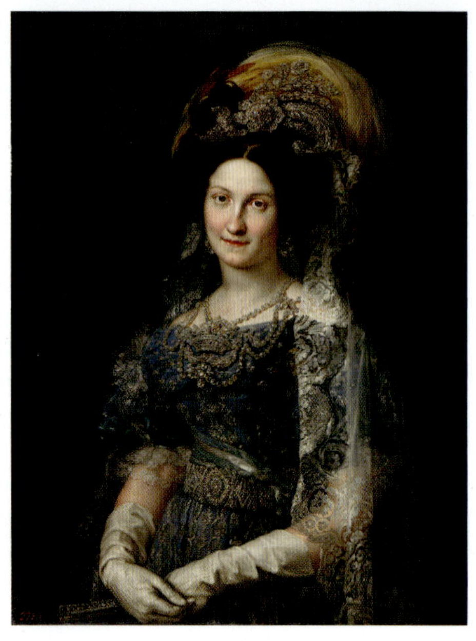

MARIA CRISTINA OF THE TWO SICILIES, QUEEN CONSORT (*r.* 1829–1833) AND REGENT OF SPAIN (*r.* 1833–1840). Influenced her husband to renounce Salic law, allowing their daughter, Isabella II, rather than the king's brother, to inherit the throne. (Painting by Vicente López y Portaña, 1830.)

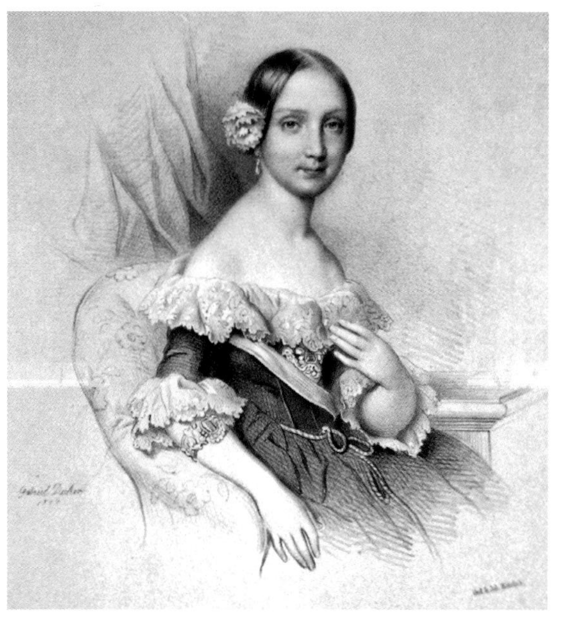

Isabella II, queen of Spain (*r.* 1833–1868).
Her rocky reign witnessed unending political trouble, ultimately leading to her deposition and exile.
(Lithograph, detail, by Gabriel Decker, 1844.)

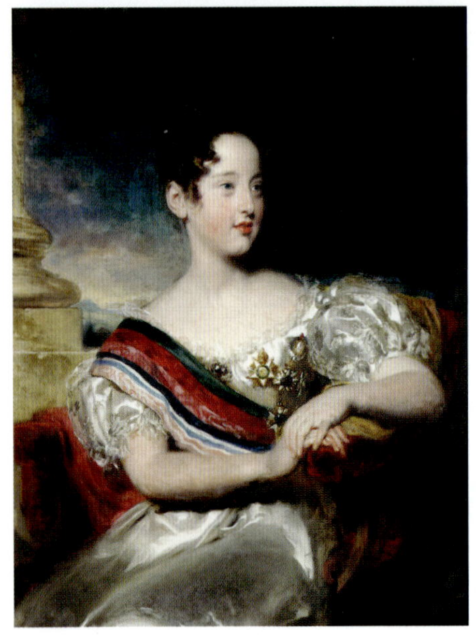

MARIA II, QUEEN OF PORTUGAL (*r.* 1834–1853). Oversaw Portugal's transition from an absolute to a constitutional monarchy. (Painting by Thomas Lawrence, 1829.)

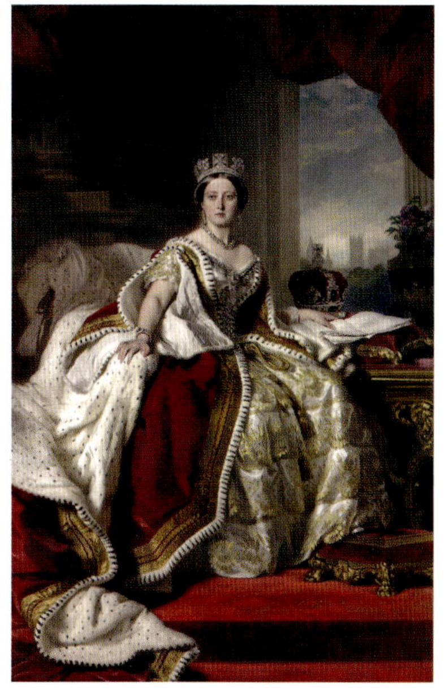

Victoria, queen of the United Kingdom (*r.* 1837–1901), and empress of India (*r.* 1876–1901).
She loved being an independent queen but reluctantly ceded many responsibilities to her husband, Prince Albert, during her nine pregnancies. (Painting by Franz Xaver Winterhalter, 1859.)

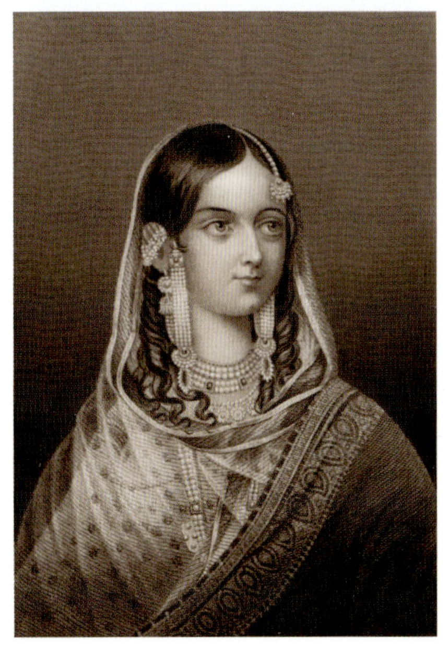

Zeenat Mahal, empress consort of the Mughal Empire (South Asia) (*r.* 1840–1857). Zeenat's efforts to place her son on the throne were thwarted by the British, who exiled her family and ended the monarchy. (Print, detail, c. 1830.)

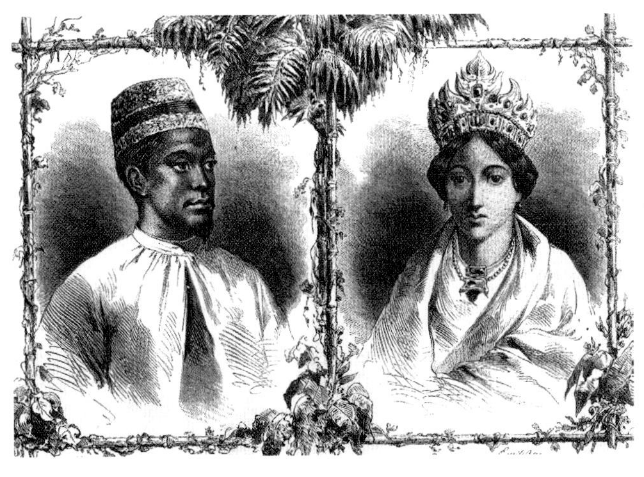

Djoumbé Fatima, queen of Mwali
(Comoro Islands) (*r.* 1842–1865; 1874–1878).
The queen, when she was only fourteen, dismissed the governess the French had installed, and chose her own husband, Said Muhammad bin Nassar Mkadara (pictured). (Newspaper illustration, 1861.)

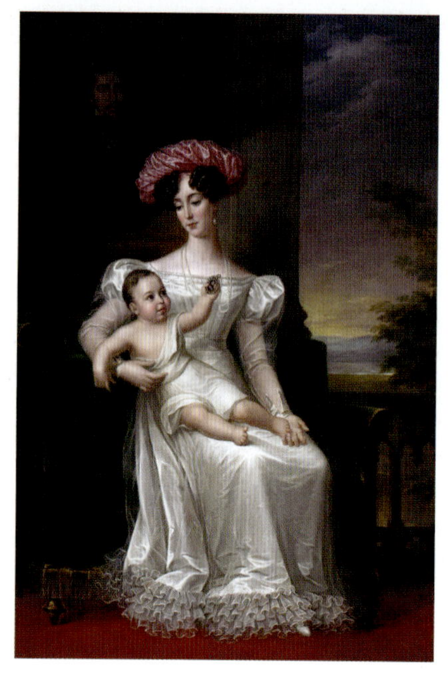

Josephine of Leuchtenberg, queen consort of Sweden and Norway (*r.* 1844–1859). Advocated for women's welfare and religious freedom for Catholics. (Painting by Fredric Westin, 1826.)

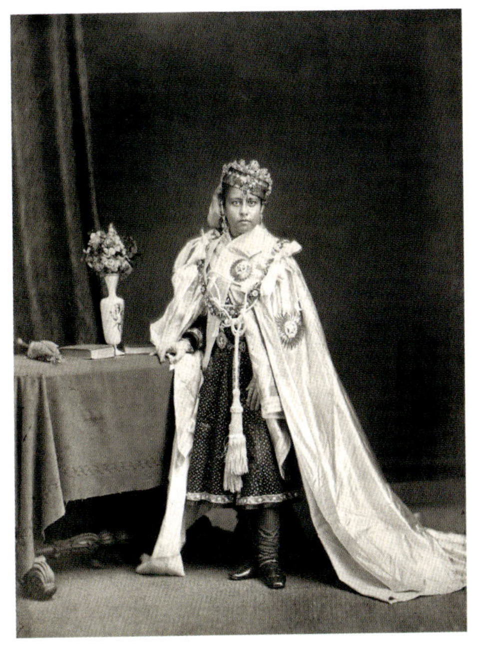

Shah Jahan Begum, queen of Bhopal (*r.* 1844–1860; 1868–1901). Supervised the construction of India's largest mosque, the Taj-ul-Masajid. (Photo by Bourne & Shepherd, 1872.)

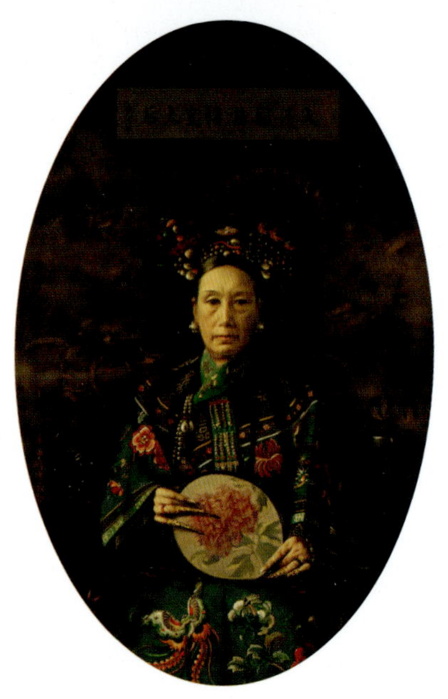

Cixi, empress consort (*r.* 1850–1861) and dowager (de facto empress) of Qing China (*r.* 1861–1908). Her control over the imperial house, and the empire, made her one of the most powerful women in China's history. (Painting by Hubert Vos, 1905–6.)

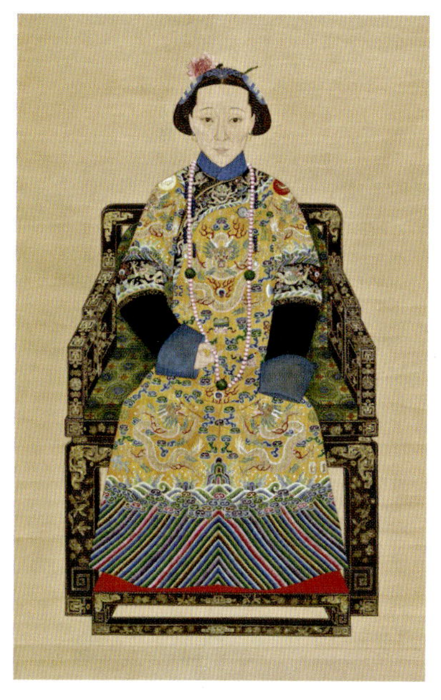

Xiaozhenxian, empress consort (*r.* 1852–1861) and dowager of Qing China (*r.* 1861–1881).
She ordered the execution of the dowager Cixi's eunuch for extorting payments from country peasants. (Painting, c. 1852–1912.)

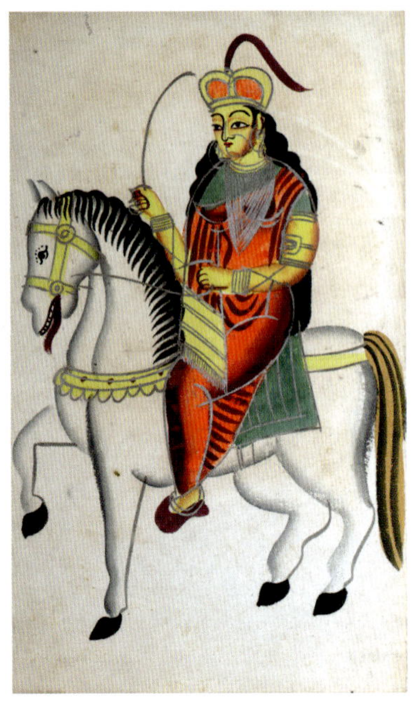

LAKSHMI BAI, QUEEN OF JHANSI (INDIA) (*r.* 1853–1858). Led troops, and lost her life, in the 1857–58 uprising against the British. (Painting, c. nineteenth century.)

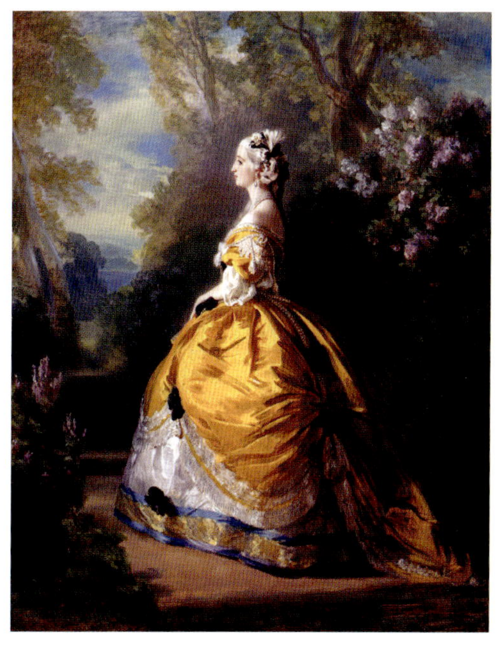

EUGÉNIE, EMPRESS CONSORT (*r.* 1853–1870) AND
REGENT OF FRANCE (*r.* 1859; 1865; 1870).
Politically shrewd adviser and last empress of the French Empire.
(Painting by Franz Xaver Winterhalter, 1854.)

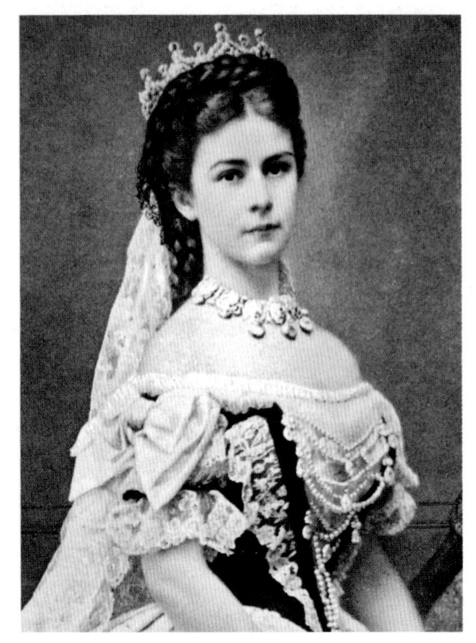

Elisabeth, empress consort of Austria, Hungary, Bohemia, Dalmatia, and Croatia (*r.* 1854–1866). Helped influence the Austro-Hungarian Compromise of 1867; tragically, she was assassinated by an Italian anarchist. (Photo, detail, by Emil Rabending, 1867.)

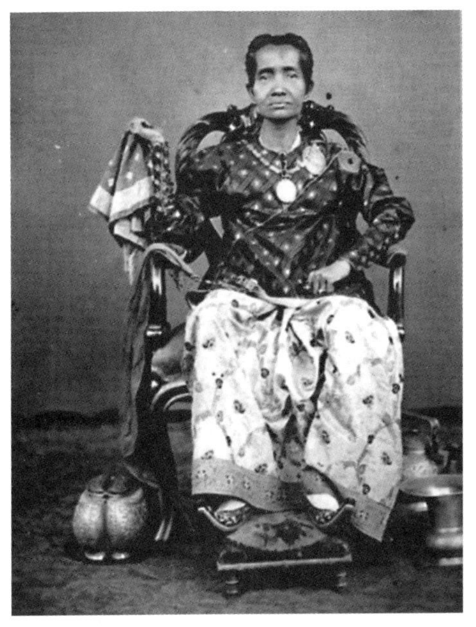

SITI AISYAH WE TENRIOLLE, REGENT OF TANETE,
SOUTH SULAWESI (INDONESIA) (*r.* 1855–1910).
She translated the epic *I La-Galigo* into modern
Buginese and championed gender equality in education.
(Photograph by Hendrik Veen, c. 1870.)

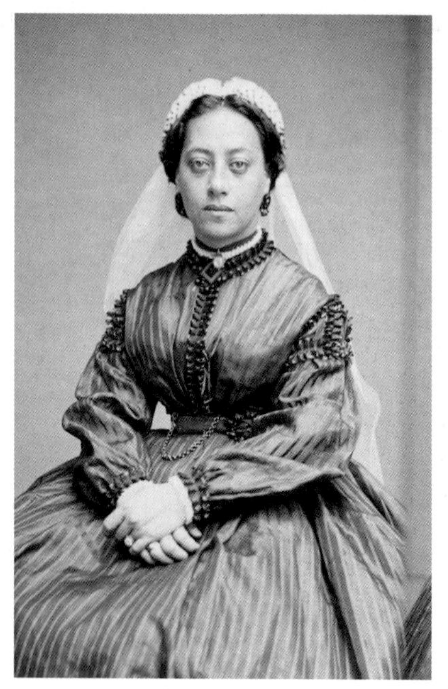

EMMA, QUEEN CONSORT OF THE HAWAIIAN ISLANDS (*r.* 1856–1863). She lost an election for sole rulership due to her British sympathies and anti-American sentiment. (Photo, detail, by Mathew B. Brady, 1855–65.)

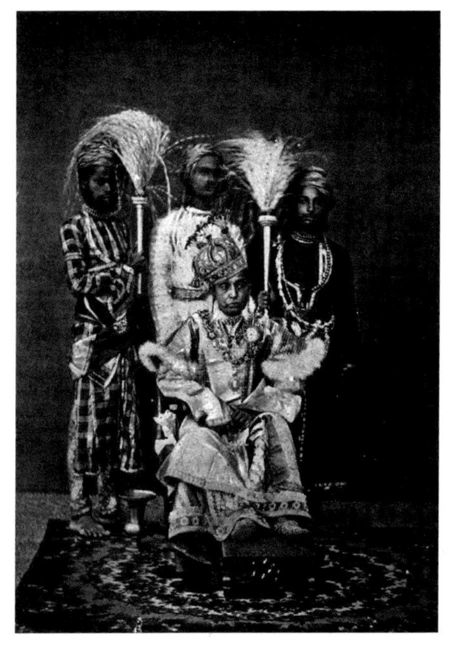

SIKANDAR BEGUM, QUEEN OF BHOPAL (*r.* 1860–1868). She was the first ruler of India to perform Hajj, the pilgrimage to Mecca. (Seated; photo, 1870).

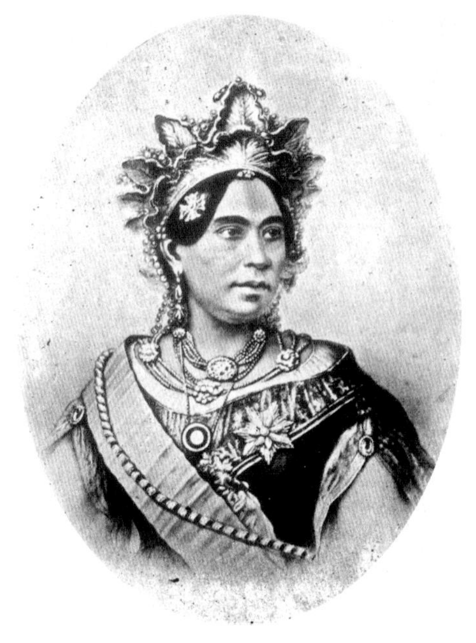

Rasoherina, consort (*r.* 1861–1863) and queen of Madagascar (*r.* 1863–1868). Ascended the throne after her husband's death—or disappearance—on the condition that she create a constitutional monarchy. (Photo, detail.)

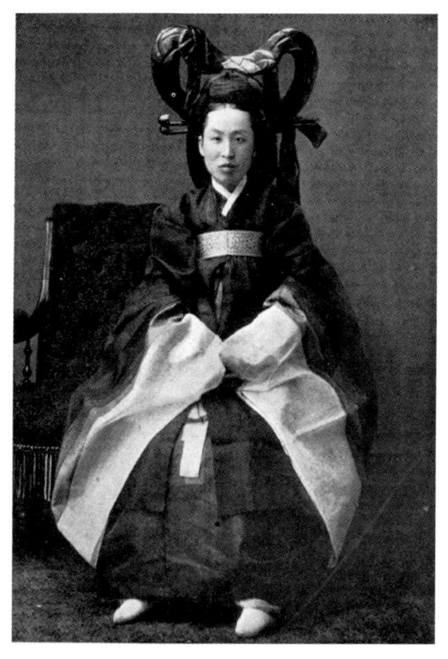

Myeongseong, empress consort (*r.* 1866–1895) and regent of Korea (*r.* 1895).
She was assassinated by Japanese-led troops for allegedly conspiring with Russia. (Photo, c. late nineteenth century.)

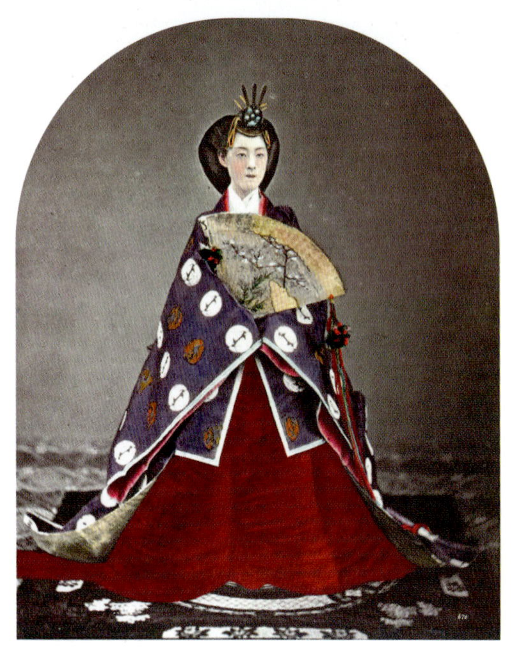

SHOKEN, EMPRESS CONSORT OF JAPAN (*r.* 1869–1912).
Brought sericulture to the imperial palace.
(Print, detail, by Kuichi Uchida, 1873.)

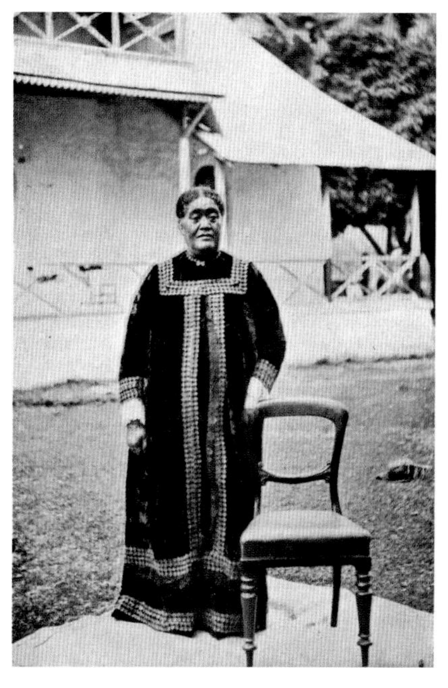

MAKEA TAKAU, QUEEN OF THE COOK ISLANDS (*r.* 1871–1911).
She enforced laws, though there was no centralized government, through a council dominated by women. (Photo, detail, by G. R. Crummer, c. 1906.)

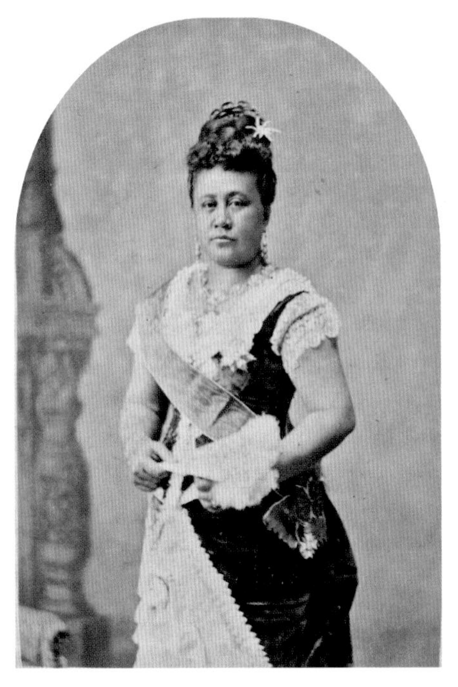

Kapiolani, queen consort of the Hawaiian Islands (*r.* 1874–1891). She founded a hospital for women and children. (Photo by Menzies Dickson, c. 1879.)

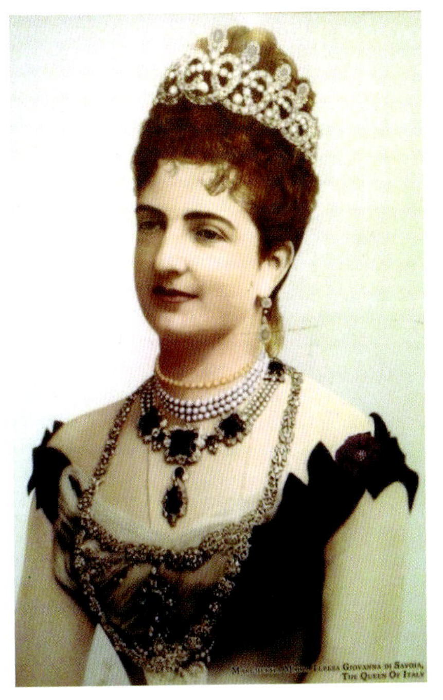

Margherita of Savoy, queen consort of Italy (*r.* 1878–1900).
Hosted a famed literary salon called the
"Queen's Thursdays." (Photo.)

Three's a Crowd

Deciding that she would marry Burma's King Thibaw, Supayalat initiated her plan to win him over by becoming his hairdresser. She overcame the boundaries of a gender-segregated palace by living with him, but some at the palace were upset with this arrangement and hoped to convince the king to marry other women to distract him from Supayalat. The king ultimately agreed to marry Supayalat and her sister in a joint ceremony. Supayalat forced her sister out of the palace and became chief consort, continuing to play an influential role at the side of the king and in her own right.

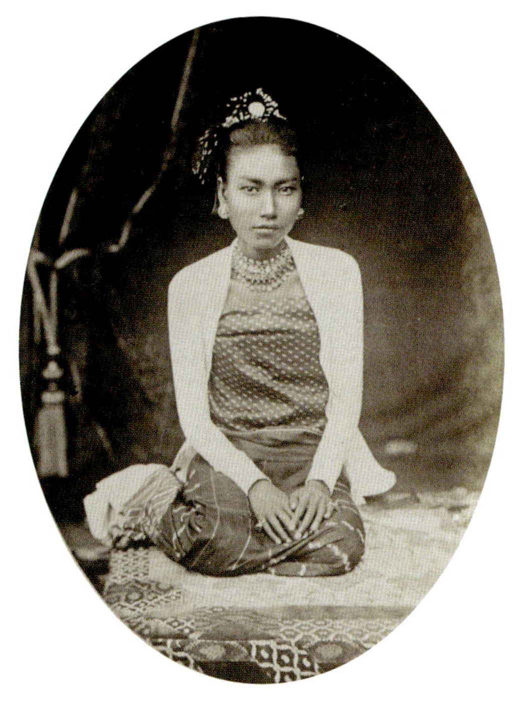

Supayalat, queen consort of Burma (Myanmar) (*r.* 1878–1885).
(Photo, detail, c. 1878–86.)

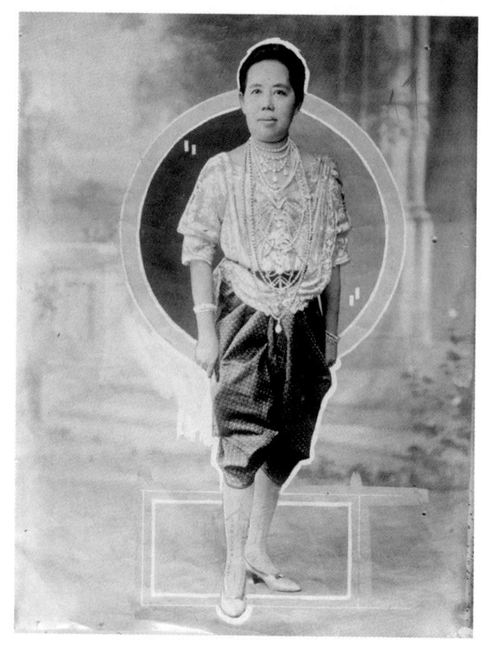

Sri Bajarindra, or Saovabha Phongsri, queen consort (*r.* 1878–1910) and regent of Siam (Thailand) (*r.* 1897). Founder of the Rajini School, one of the first schools for girls in Siam. (Photo, detail, c. 1870.)

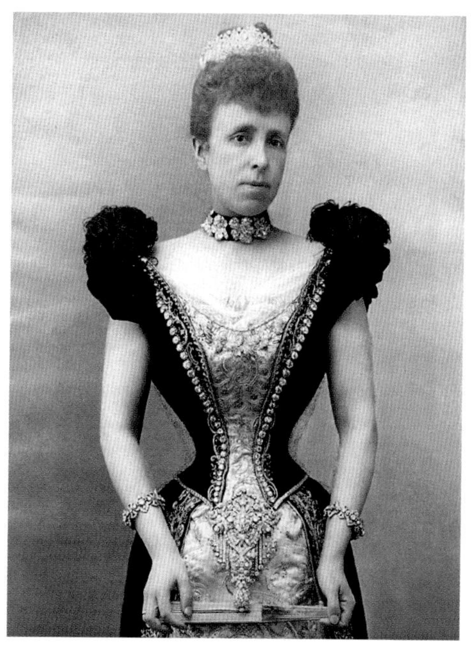

MARIA CHRISTINA OF AUSTRIA, QUEEN CONSORT (*r.* 1879–1885) AND REGENT OF SPAIN (*r.* 1885–1902). Reluctantly entered the Spanish-American War with the hopes of preserving the last traces of her empire. (Photo, c. 1880.)

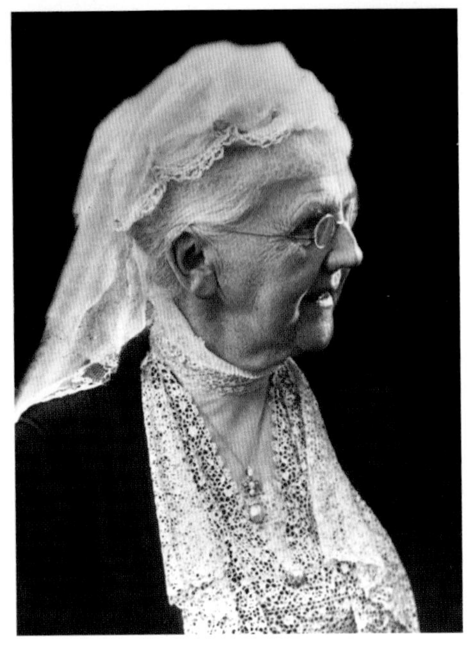

Emma of Waldeck and Pyrmont, queen consort (*r.* 1879–1890) and regent of the Netherlands (*r.* 1890–1898). Dispelled two revolts in the Dutch East Indies (Indonesia) during her regency. (Photo by Franz Ziegler, c. 1891–1933.)

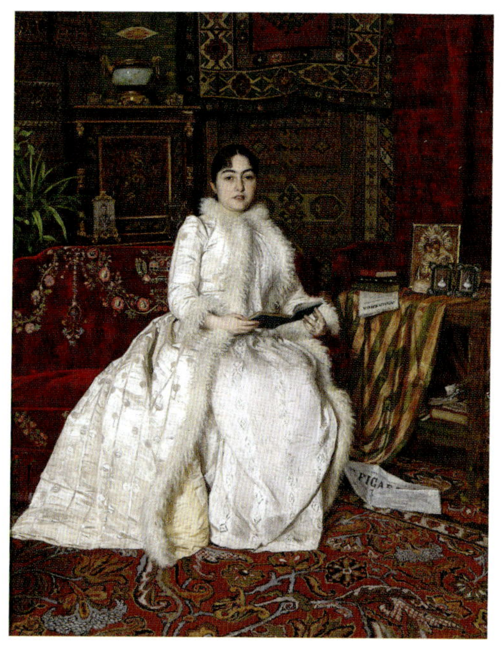

Natalija Obrenovic, or Natalie of Serbia,
queen consort of Serbia (*r.* 1882–1889).
Her pro-Russian sympathies caused a rift with her husband, and eventually led to their divorce. (Painting by Uros Predic, 1890.)

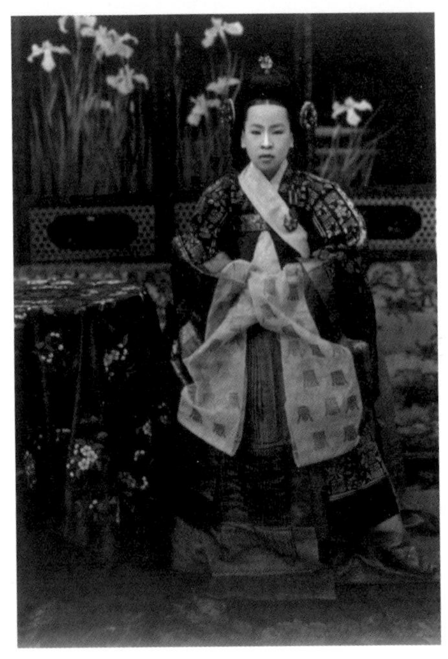

Sunmyeong, empress consort of Korea (*r.* 1882–1904). Suffered a serious back injury when attempting to protect her mother-in-law, Empress Myeongseong (p. 273), from assassination. (Photo, detail, 1890–1904.)

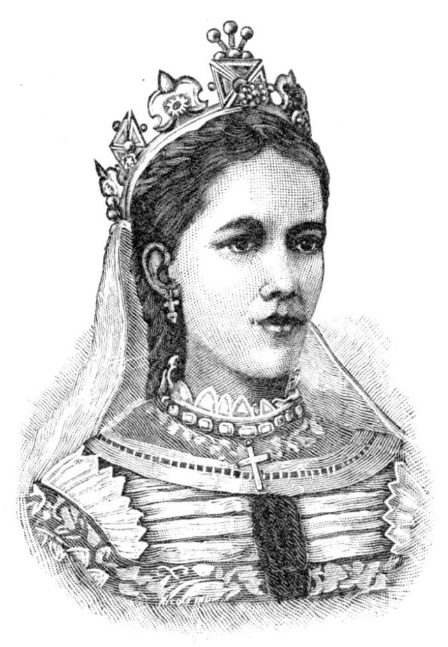

RANAVALONA III, QUEEN OF MADAGASCAR (*r.* 1883–1896). Forced into signing a treaty that united Madagascar with the French colonial empire. (Illustration, detail, 1893.)

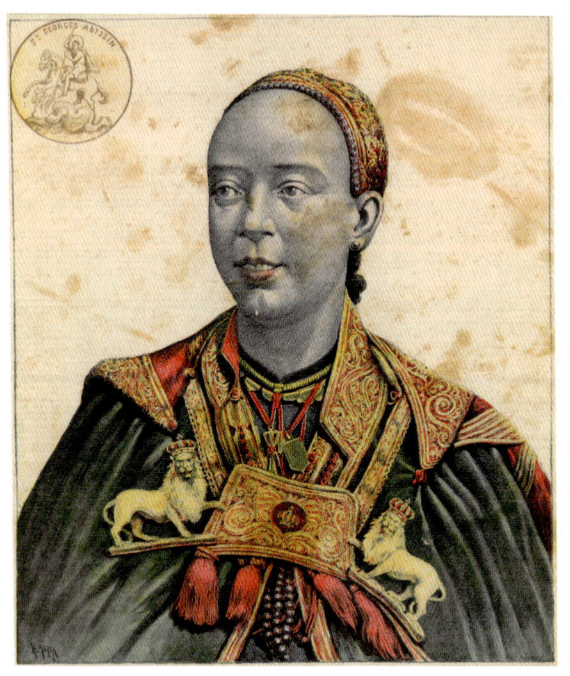

TAYTU BETUL, EMPRESS CONSORT OF ETHIOPIA (*r.* 1883–1913). She named Ethiopia's capital, Addis Ababa, and saw that women had access to education. (Newspaper illustration, 1896.)

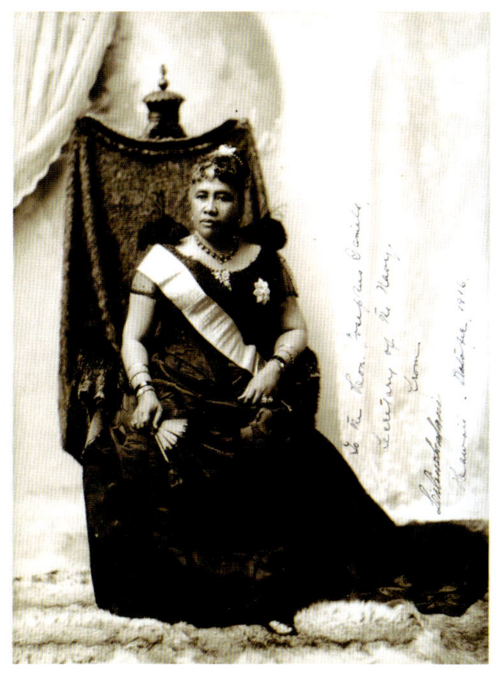

LILIUOKALANI, QUEEN OF THE HAWAIIAN ISLANDS (*r.* 1891–1893). Attempted to enact her own constitution that would reestablish monarchial authority in Hawaii. (Photo, c. 1891.)

Wartime Broadcasts

Wilhelmina instilled strength and unity in the Netherlands through two world wars. During World War II, she fled to England when Nazi Germany occupied the Netherlands. Her regular radio broadcasts from London, full of encouragement for her people, earned her a place in the hearts of her listeners. Her broadcast was illegal in the Netherlands, and her subjects had to find secretive ways to listen and avoid German retribution. Wilhelmina's image became a symbol of resistance.

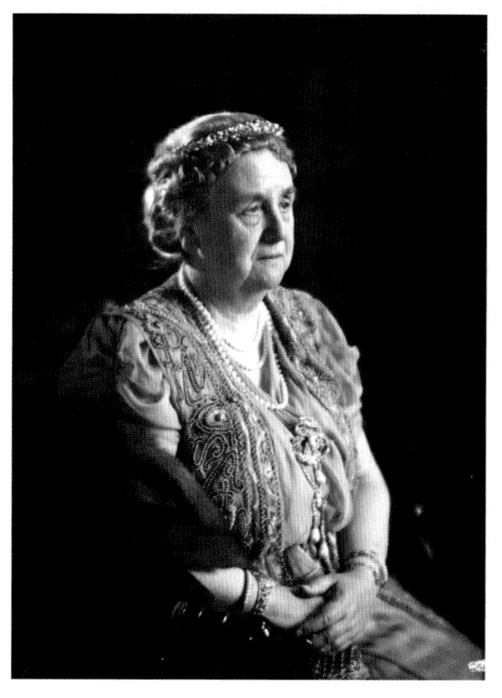

Wilhelmina, queen of the Netherlands (*r.* 1890–1948). (Photo by Atelier Jacob Merkelbach, c. 1948.)

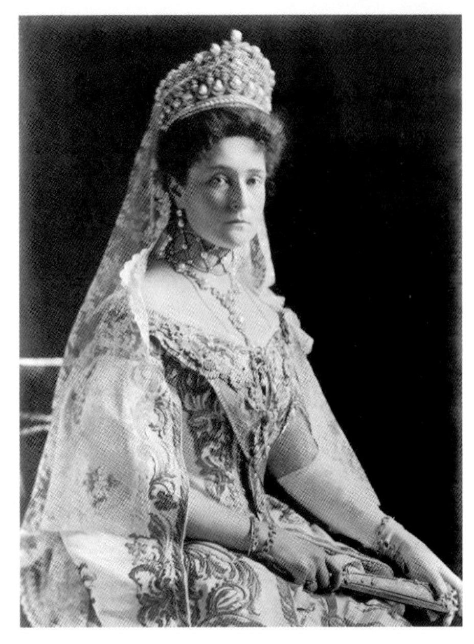

Saint Alexandra Feodorovna, empress consort of Russia (*r.* 1894–1917).
Her misplaced trust in the mystic Rasputin contributed to her family's downfall and eventual execution.
(Photo by Boasson and Eggler, 1908.)

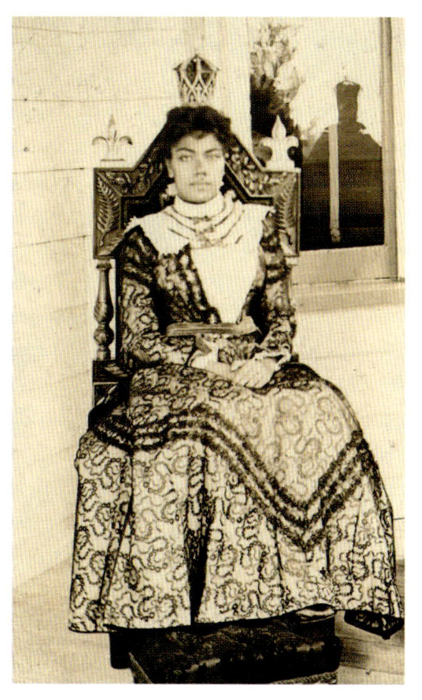

Lavinia Veiongo Fotu, queen consort of Tonga (Polynesia) (*r.* 1899–1902).
Became friends with her former rival, though their respective supporters once rioted against one another.
(Photographic print, detail, by Frederick Sears, 1900.)

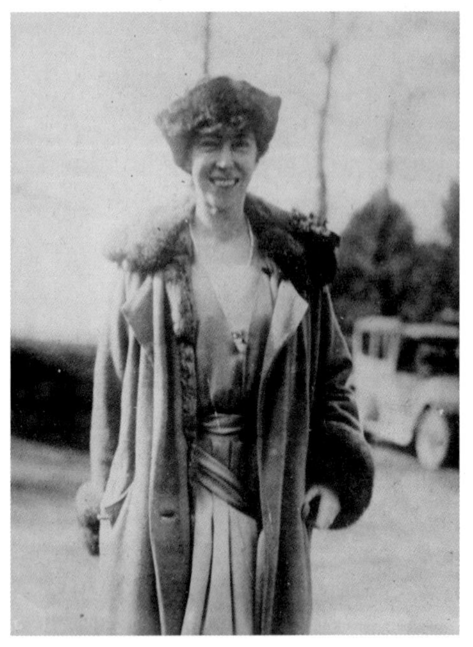

Elisabeth of Bavaria, queen consort of Belgium (*r.* 1909–1934). Financed and supervised the Queen Ambulance, a hospital for Belgian soldiers during World War I. (Photo, detail, c. 1915–20.)

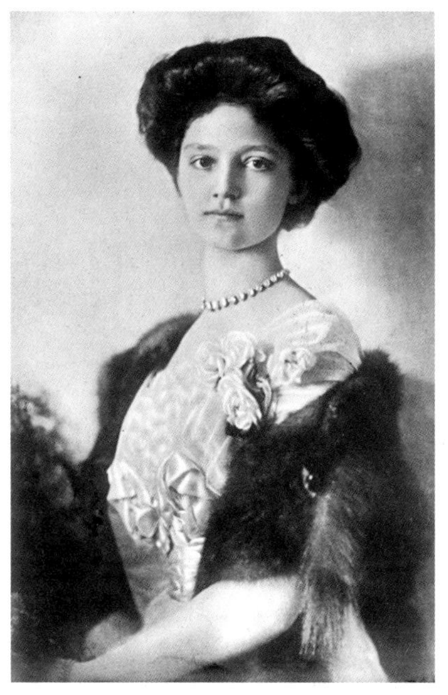

Zita of Bourbon-Parma, empress consort of Austria, Hungary, Bohemia, Dalmatia, and Croatia (*r.* 1916–1918). She mourned her husband's death by wearing black for the next sixty-seven years of her life. (Photo, 1914.)

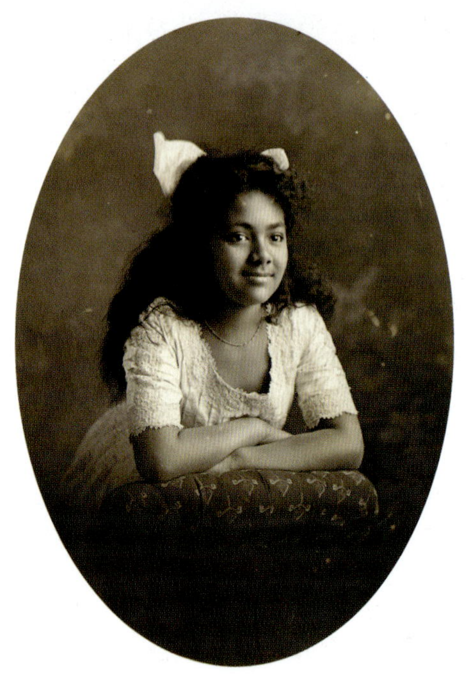

SALOTE TUPOU III, QUEEN OF TONGA (POLYNESIA) (*r.* 1918–1965). Secured her rule against opposition and unified her people with a strong sense of Tongan identity. (Photo, 1908.)

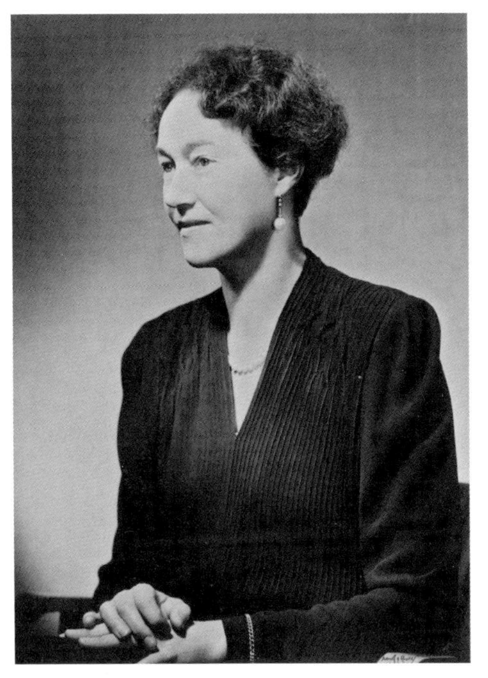

CHARLOTTE, GRAND DUCHESS OF LUXEMBOURG (*r.* 1919–1964).
Transformed Luxembourg into a democratic
modern state. (Photo, c. 1942.)

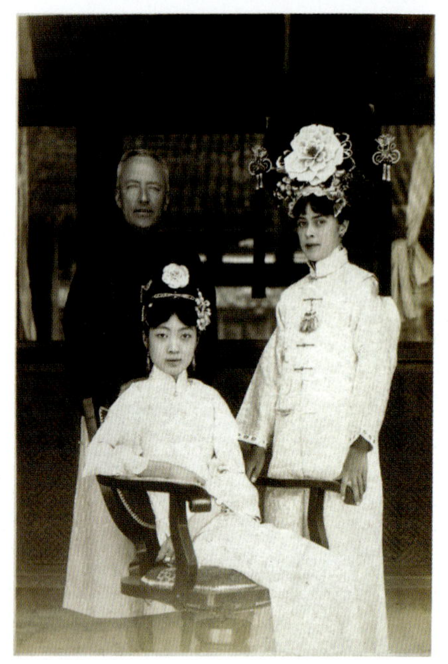

WANRONG, EMPRESS CONSORT OF QING CHINA (*r.* 1924–1946).
Oppressed by her husband's cruelty and stifling control,
she descended into mental illness and opium addiction.
(Seated; photo by Reginald Johnston, 1924.)

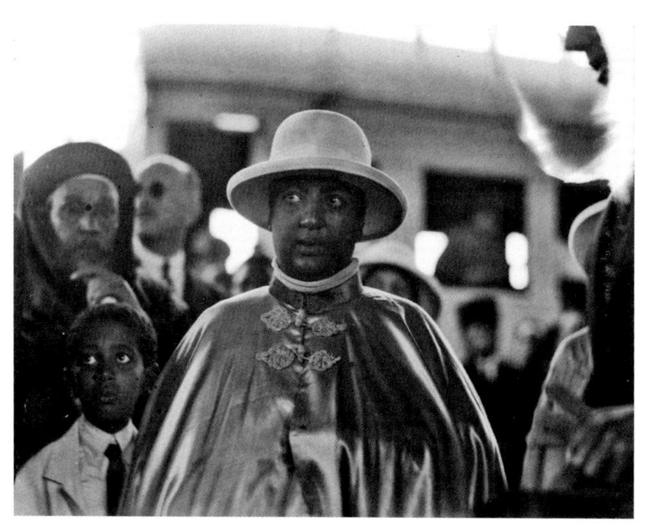

MENEN ASFAW, EMPRESS CONSORT OF ETHIOPIA (*r.* 1930–1962).
Ruled her own lands, where she had a coffee
production and trading business. (Photo, 1933.)

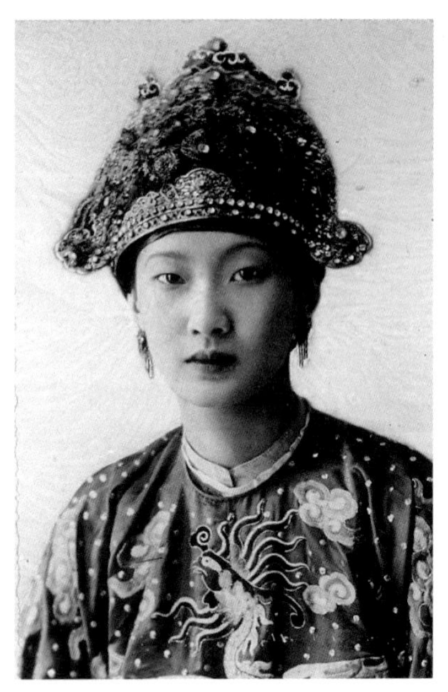

Nam Phuong, empress consort of Vietnam (*r.* 1934–1963). Kept her Catholic faith upon ascending the throne, despite strong opposition. (Photo, 1934.)

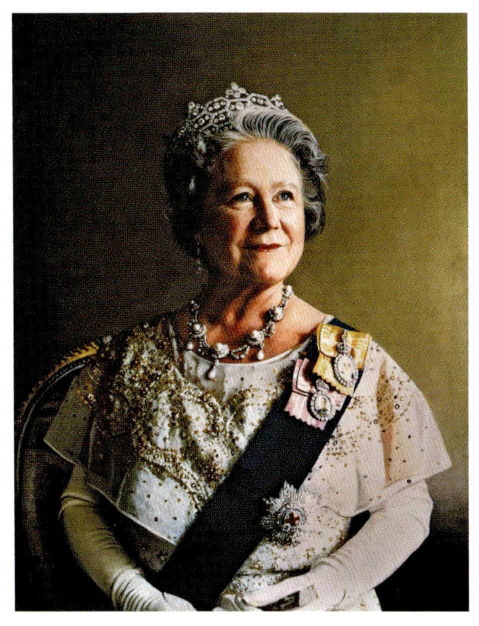

Elizabeth, the Queen Mother, queen consort of India (*r.* 1936–1947) and the United Kingdom (*r.* 1936–1952). She bravely remained in London during World War II, staying even after Buckingham Palace was bombed. (Painting by Richard Stone, 1986.)

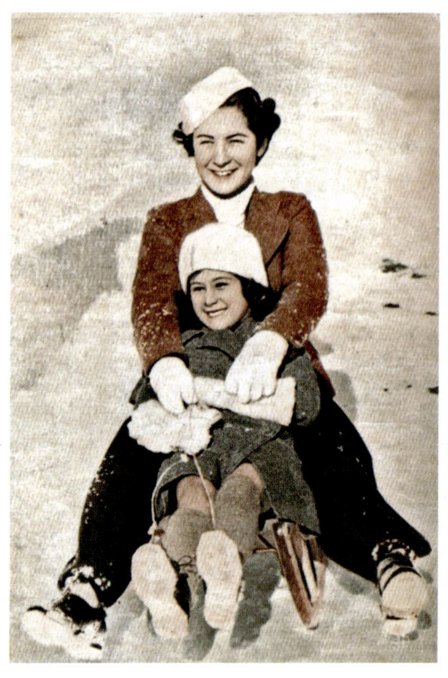

Farida, queen consort of Egypt (*r.* 1938–1948). After a difficult marriage and reign, she moved to Paris to practice art. (In red coat, with Princess Fathia; photo, 1937.)

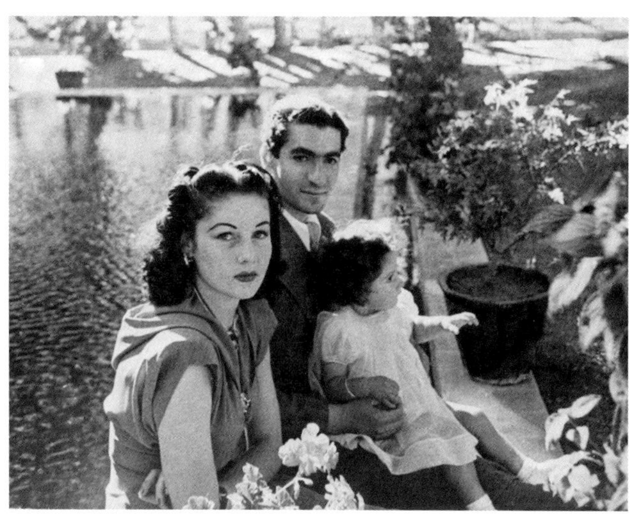

FAWZIA FUAD, QUEEN CONSORT OF IRAN (*r.* 1941–1948).
Neglected at the Iranian court and unhappily married to the Shah of Iran, Mohammad Reza Pahlavi (pictured), she obtained a divorce and remarried—this time for love. (Photo by Cecil Beaton, 1942.)

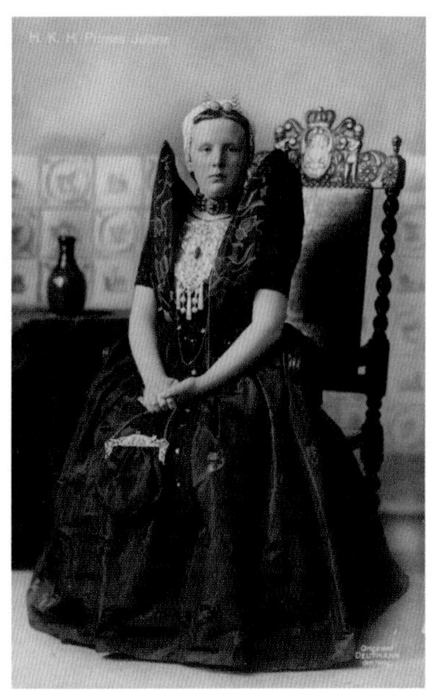

JULIANA, REGENT (*r.* 1947–1948) AND QUEEN OF THE NETHERLANDS (*r.* 1948–1980).
The "people's queen" abhorred formalities like the curtsy, shopped for her own groceries, and sometimes surprised her subjects for tea. (Photo by H. Deutmann, 1922.)

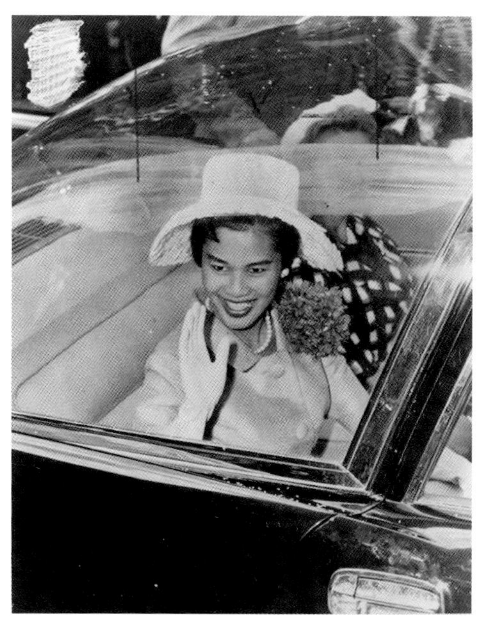

Sirikit Kitiyakara, queen consort (*r.* 1950–2016)
and regent of Thailand (*r.* 1956).
A onetime president of the Thai Red Cross, she was the recipient of prestigious awards for her humanitarian work.
(Photo by Phil Stanziola, 1960.)

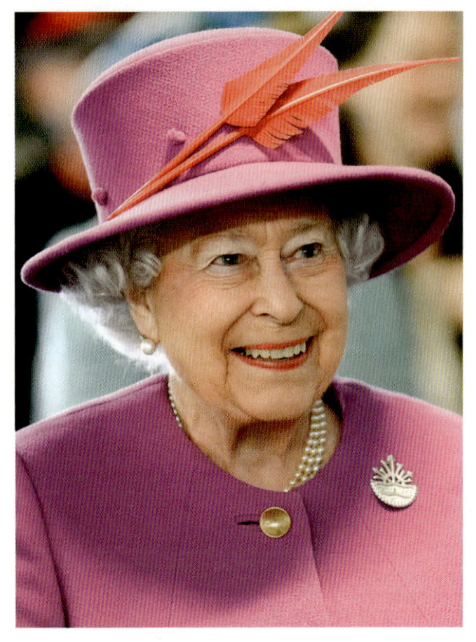

Elizabeth II, queen of the United Kingdom and Commonwealth Realms (*r.* 1952–).
The longest-reigning monarch in British history, she is known for her fortitude—and her fondness for corgis.
(Photo by Joel Rouse/Ministry of Defence, 2015.)

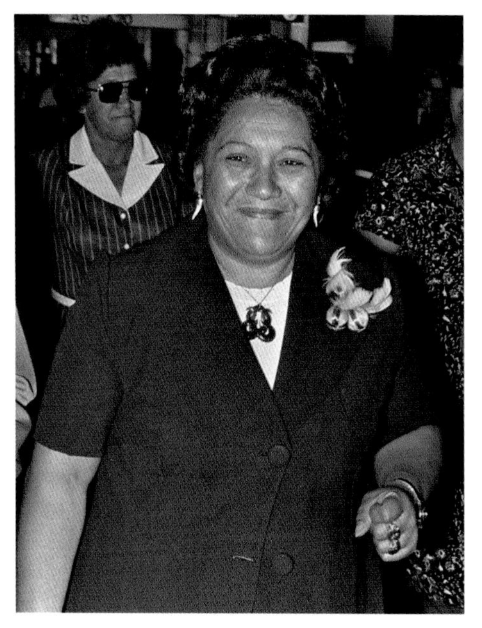

Te Atairangikaahu, queen of the Maori
(New Zealand) (*r.* 1966–2006).
She was the longest-reigning Maori monarch; her name
means "hawk of the morning sky."
(Photo, detail, by Rob Bogaerts/Anefo, 1975.)

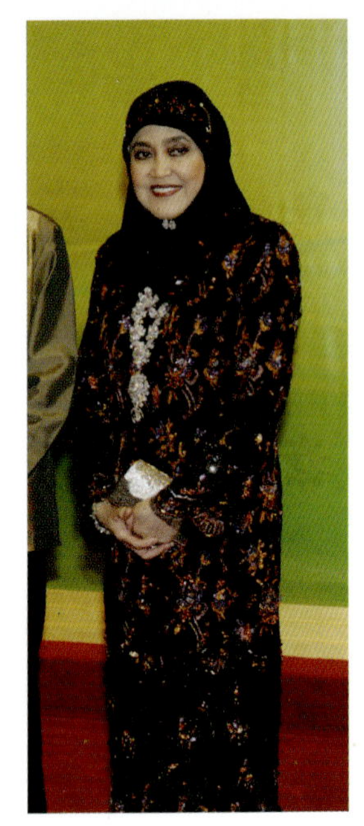

SALEHA, QUEEN CONSORT OF BRUNEI (BORNEO) (*r.* 1967–). An advocate for women's rights and welfare. (Photo, detail, by the Prime Minister's Office, Government of India, 2013.)

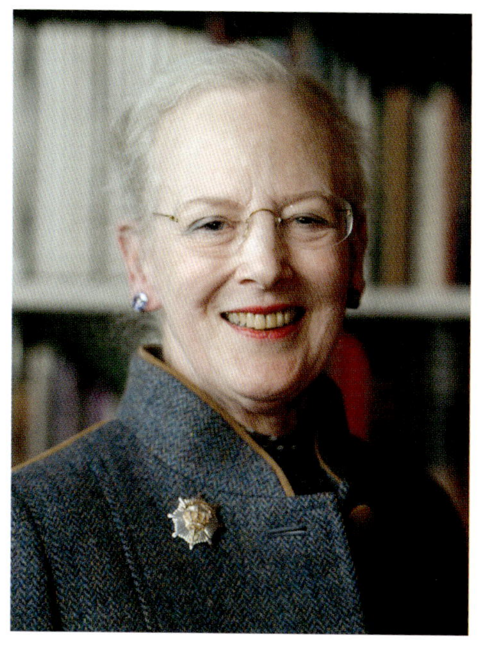

MARGRETHE II, QUEEN OF DENMARK (*r.* 1972–). Illustrated J. R. R. Tolkien's *Lord of the Rings* under the pseudonym Ingahild Grathmer; the author greatly admired her artwork. (Photo by Johannes Jansson, 2012.)

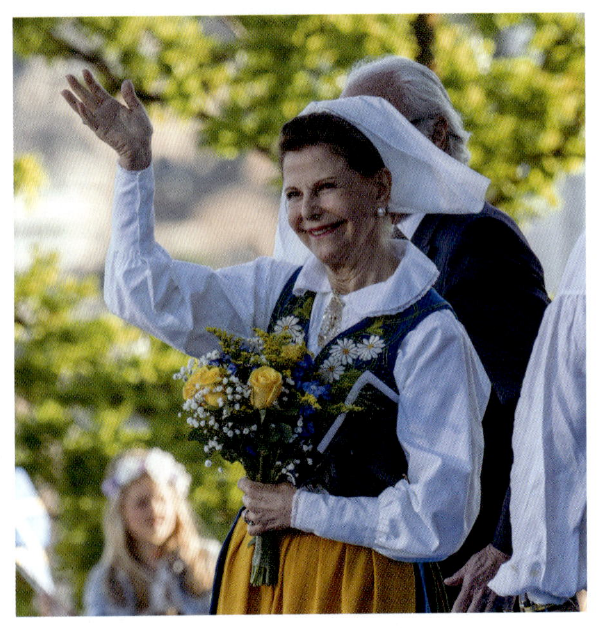

Silvia, queen consort of Sweden (*r.* 1976–).
Works tirelessly for the welfare of children.
(Photo, detail, by Bengt Nyman, 2017.)

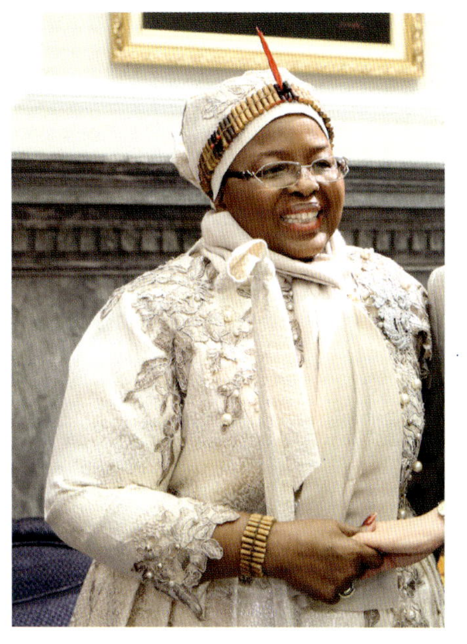

Ntfombi, regent (*r.* 1983–1986) and queen (coruler) of Eswatini (*r.* 1986–).
She is seen as the national and spiritual head of state, while her son functions as the administrative head of state.
(Photo, detail, by Presidential Palace, 2016.)

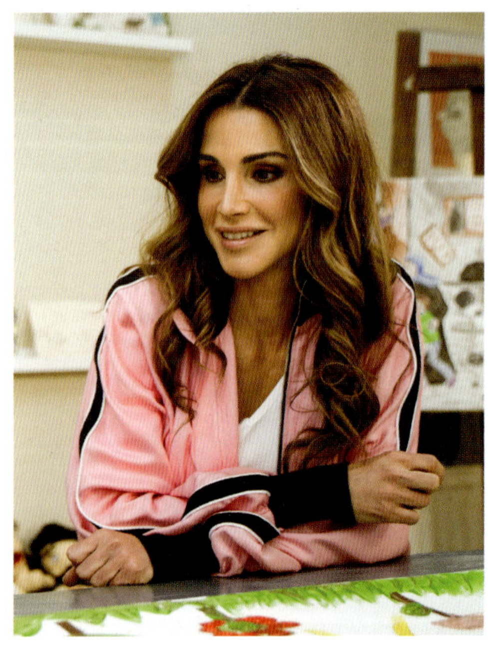

Rania Al-Abdullah, queen consort of Jordan (*r.* 1999–). A global activist for the rights of women and children, she also works to erode stereotypes of Arabs and Muslims. (Photo by Jordanian Royal Hashemite Court, 2018.)

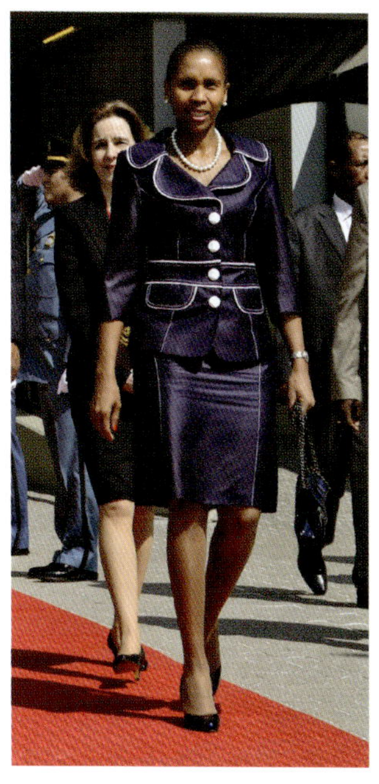

MASENATE MOHATO SEEISO, QUEEN CONSORT OF LESOTHO (*r.* 2000–). Made history by being the first commoner to marry into Lesotho's royal family. (Photo, detail, by IAEA Imagebank, 2013.)

SELECTED BIBLIOGRAPHY

Bauer, Susan Wise. *The History of the Medieval World: From the Conversion of Constantine to the First Crusade*. New York: W. W. Norton, 2010.

———. *The History of the Renaissance World: From the Rediscovery of Aristotle to the Conquest of Constantinople*. New York: W. W. Norton, 2013.

Castor, Helen. *She-Wolves: The Women Who Ruled England Before Elizabeth*. New York: Harper, 2011.

Cooney, Kara. *When Women Ruled the World: Six Queens of Egypt*. Washington, DC: National Geographic, 2018.

Craig, Robert D. *Historical Dictionary of Polynesia*, 3rd ed. Lanham, MD: Scarecrow Press, 2010.

Cruz, Anne J., and Mihoko Suzuki, eds. *The Rule of Women in Early Modern Europe*. Champaign, IL: University of Illinois Press, 2009.

Duggan, Anne, and Janet L. Nelson, eds. *Queens and Queenship in Medieval Europe*. New York: Red Globe Press, 2013.

Ehret, Christopher. *The Civilizations of Africa: A History to 1800*, 2nd ed. Charlottesville, VA: University of Virginia Press, 2016.

Freeman, Charles. *Egypt, Greece, and Rome: Civilizations of the Ancient Mediterranean*, 3rd ed. New York: Oxford University Press, 2014.

Haley, James L. *Captive Paradise: A History of Hawaii*. New York: St. Martin's Press, 2014.

Hoxie, Frederick E., ed. *The Oxford Handbook of American Indian History*. New York: Oxford University Press, 2016.

Jackson, Guida M. *Women Rulers Throughout the Ages: An Illustrated Guide*, 2nd ed. Santa Barbara, CA: ABC-CLIO, 1999.

Keay, John. *India: A History*. New York: Grove Press, 2011.

Lee, Lily Xiao Hong, and Sue Wiles, eds. *Biographical Dictionary of Chinese Women: Tang Through Ming, 618–1644*. Abingdon, UK: Routledge, 2014.

Levin, Carole, et al., eds. *Extraordinary Women of the Medieval and Renaissance World: A Biographical Dictionary*. Westport, CT: Greenwood Press, 2000.

McHugo, John. *A Concise History of the Arabs*. New York: The New Press, 2013.

Montefiore, Simon Sebag. *The Romanovs: 1613–1918*. New York: Alfred A. Knopf, 2016.

Mulhern, Chieko Irie, ed. *Heroic with Grace: Legendary Women of Japan*. New York: Taylor & Francis, 2015.

Schele, Linda, and David A. Freidel. *A Forest of Kings: The Untold Story of the Ancient Maya*. New York: William Morrow and Company, Inc., 1992.

Scott, Michael. *Ancient Worlds: An Epic History of East and West*. London: Windmill Books, 2017.

Tyldesley, Joyce A. *Chronicle of the Queens of Egypt: From Early Dynastic Times to the Death of Cleopatra*. New York: Thames & Hudson, 2006.

Wang, Daisy Yiyou, et al., eds. *Empresses of China's Forbidden City, 1644–1912*. Salem, MA: Peabody Essex Museum, 2018.

Waters, Matt. *Ancient Persia: A Concise History of the Achaemenid Empire, 550–330 BCE*. Cambridge, UK: Cambridge University Press, 2014.

INDEX OF NAMES AND PLACES

D

E

F

M

N

O

P

Q

R

S

T

U

V

W

X

Y

Z

PHOTO CREDITS

CLEVELAND MUSEUM OF ART: p. 233; HARVARD ART MUSEUMS, CAMBRIDGE, MA, PHOTOS © PRESIDENT AND FELLOWS OF HARVARD COLLEGE: Arthur M. Sackler Museum, Loan from the Trustees of the Arthur Stone Dewing Greek Numismatic Foundation: p. 34; Arthur M. Sackler Museum, Unspecified Collection, p. 50; Arthur M. Sackler Museum, Bequest of Thomas Whittemore, p. 74; Fogg Museum, Gift of William Gray from the collection of Francis Calley Gray: p. 231; Fogg Museum, Gift of Philip Hofer, p. 135; Fogg Museum, Bequest of Grenville L. Winthrop: pp. 246 (detail) and 264; LIBRARY OF CONGRESS, WASHINGTON, DC: pp. 133, 218, 280, 284, 292, 295, 297, 303 (Phil Stanziola); METROPOLITAN MUSEUM OF ART, NEW YORK: pp. 14 (detail) and 19, 30, 53, 84, 96, 150, 163, 173, 217, 244, 267; NEW YORK PUBLIC LIBRARY: pp. 199, 285; RIJKSMUSEUM, AMSTERDAM: pp. 24, 27, 43, 79, 128, 139; SOAS ARCHIVES, LONDON: p. 271; WALTERS ART MUSEUM, BALTIMORE: pp. 35, 93; WELLCOME COLLECTION: p. 110; WIKIMEDIA COMMONS: Adrian Michael, PD: p. 113; Anjou-Bijbel, PD: p. 123; anonimus, PD: p. 164; Anonymous, PD: pp. 134, 152, 154, 165, 179, 189, 191, 207, 252, 261, 265, 281, 286, 298; Art-catalog.ru, PD: p. 216; Parashamani Bara, CC-BY-SA 3.0: p. 277; Cecil Beaton, PD: p. 301; Biblioteca comunale di Trento, PD: p. 72; Biblioteca Nacional de España, PD: p. 101; Bibliotheca Corvina, PD: p. 126; Bibliothèque nationale de France, PD: pp. 119, 141; Boasson and Eggler, PD: p. 290; Rob Bogaerts/Anefo, PD: p. 305; Jeanne boleyn, PD: p. 118; Andreas F. Borchert, CC-BY-SA 3.0: p. 93; Mathew B. Brady, PD: p. 270; British Library, Bourne & Shepherd, PD: p. 263; Brown Digital Library, PD: p. 251; bruun-rasmussen.dk, PD: p. 78; Buchscan, PD: p. 235; Bukowskis, PD: p. 226; burusi, PD: p. 204; *A Chronicle of England: B.C. 55–A.D. 1485*, PD: p. 81; *Chronicle of the Romance of the Three Kingdoms*, PD: p. 47; Classical Numismatic Group (CNG), Inc., CC-BY-SA 3.0: p. 40; Cleveland Museum of Art, PD: pp. 192, 266; Collection Tropenmuseum, Hendrik Veen, PD: p. 269; Erik Cornelius/Nationalmuseum, PD: p. 159; G. R. Crummer, PD: p. 275; Czartoryski Museum, PD: pp. 151, 162, 178; Daderot, PD: p. 111; A. Davey, CC-BY-2.0: p. 228; Carlos Delgado, CC-BY-SA 3.0: p. 44; Diego Delso, CC-BY-SA 4.0: front endpapers; H. Deutmann, PD: p. 302; Menzies Dickson, PD: p. 276; Mikhail Dmitrievich, PD: p. 227; Dorotheum, PD: p. 283; *Dschingis Khan und seine Erben*, PD: p. 107; Duomo di Monza, PD: p. 64; Ealdgyth, CC-BY-SA 3.0: p. 99; Europeana, PD: p. 205; Flikr: pp. 147 (CC-BY-SA 4.0), 176, 187, 262 (PD); G41rn8, CC-BY-SA 4.0: p. 67; Gallica Digital Library, PD: pp. 138, 170, 177; Peter Geymayer, PD: p. 257; Giogo, CC-BY-SA 3.0: p. 62; Google Cultural Institute, PD: pp. 26, 104, 160, 169, 213–14, 229, 245, 250; Göttingen State and University Library, PD: p. 21; GualdimG, CC-BY-SA 4.0: p. 221; *Die Habsburger: Ein biographisches Lexikon*, PD: p. 222; © Ralph Hammann, CC-BY-SA 4.0: p. 76; HanTharWin, CC-BY-SA 4.0: p. 136; *Das Heilige Römische Reich*, PD: p. 88; Hermitage Museum, PD: pp. 2 (detail) and 242; IAEA Imagebank, CC-BY-SA 2.0: p. 311; Ijanderson977, PD: back endpapers; Johannes Jansson, CC-BY-2.5: p. 307; *Japanese Hero Portrait Encyclopedia*, PD: p. 196; Dennis Jarvis, CC-BY-SA 2.0: p. 130; Gustavo Jeronimo, CC-BY-2.0: p. 69; Joconde, PD: pp. 49, 253; Reginald Johnston, PD: p. 296; Jordanian Royal Hashemite Court, CC-BY-SA 4.0: p. 310; Maulwurfn Kalle, CC-BY-SA 4.0: p. 106; Gunawan Kartapranata, CC-BY-SA 3.0: p. 121; Dorfsh Kawayani, CC-BY-SA 3.0: p. 39; kladcat, CC-BY-2.0: p. 100; Ksss5pj, CC-BY-SA 4.0: p. 209; Kunsthistorisches Museum, PD: pp. 195, 211; Angel Lahoz, CC-BY-SA 2.0: p. 98; LeMill, PD: p. 105; Library of Congress, PD: pp. 287, 293; Los Angeles County Museum of Art, PD: p. 68; Louvre, PD: p. 188; Atelier Jacob Merkelbach, PD: p. 289; Petar Milošević, CC-BY-SA 4.0: p. 61; Kaho Mitsuki, CC-BY-SA 4.0: p. 80; Musée national du palais, PD: p. 174; Museo del Prado, PD: pp. 90, 112, 145, 153, 155, 168, 194, 225, 256; Myrabella, PD: p. 86; National Gallery, London, PD: p. 167; National Gallery of Art, Washington, DC, PD: p. 144; National Gallery of Denmark, PD: p. 241; National Library of Australia, PD: p. 255; National Library of New Zealand, PD: p. 294; National Library of Wales, PD: p. 260; National Maritime Museum, PD: p. 180; National Museum in Warsaw, PD: p. 208; National Museum Wales, PD: p. 95; National Palace Museum, Taipei, PD: pp. 6 (detail) and 103, 87, 91; National Portrait Gallery, London, PD: pp. 42, 161, front cover and 171, 197, 220, 230; *The National Portrait Gallery History of the Kings and Queens of England*, PD: p. 85; Nationalmuseum, PD: pp. 129, 140, 166, 181, 203, 252, 254; © Marie-Lan Nguyen, CC-BY-SA 2.5: pp. 29, 37 (PD), 59; autor nieznany, PD: p. 77; Bengt Nyman, CC-BY-2.0: p. 308; Orf3us, CC-BY-SA 3.0: p. 134; Osama Shukir Muhammed Amin FRCP(Glasg), CC-BY-SA 4.0: p. 38; *The Passing of Korea*, PD: p. 273; PHGCOM, PD: p. 175; Philip Pikart, CC-BY-SA 3.0: back cover, p. 23; Photo Dharma, CC-BY-2.0: p. 137; Portable Antiquities Scheme/The Trustees of the British Museum, CC-BY-SA 2.0: p. 46; Portraits of Kings, PD: p. 149; Presidential Palace, CC-BY-2.0: p. 309; Prime Minister's Office, Government of India, PD: p. 306; *The Prince Shotoku Exhibition*, PD: p. 63; Nguyen Thanh Quang, CC-BY-SA 3.0: p. 83; Emil Rabending, PD: p. 268; Carole Raddato, CC-BY-SA 2.0: pp. 45, 51; Rama, CC-BY-SA 2.0: pp. 18, 20; Pei Ranjun, PD: p. 142; *Rekishi Hakken*, Vol. 13, PD: p. 71; Rémih, CC-BY-SA 3.0: p. 35; Rijksmuseum, PD: pp. 70, 158, 206, 215, 279; © RMN-Grand Palais (Palace of Versailles)/Daniel Arnaudet, PD: p. 239; Rodhullandemu, CC-BY-SA 4.0: p. 75; Rosenborg Castle, PD: pp. 212, 232, 238; Joel Rouse (Ministry of Defence), Open Government Licence v3.0: p. 304; Royal Collection Trust, PD: pp. 210, 258–59; Saffronart, PD: pp. 182 (detail) and 219; Sailko, CC-BY-3.0: pp. 36, 148; Salisbury and South Wiltshire Museum, CC-BY-SA 4.0: p. 48; Satishk01, CC-BY-SA 4.0: p. 108; Scala Regia, PD: p. 240; Frederick Sears, PD: p. 291; Shakko, CC-BY-SA 4.0: p. 234; Richard Stone, PD: p. 299; J. Styfi, PD: p. 127; Surtsicna, CC-BY-SA 4.0: p. 133; tato grasso, CC-BY-SA 2.5: p. 65; Thesupermat, CC-BY-3.0: p. 82; Kim Traynor, CC-BY-SA 3.0: p. 89; Tretyakov Gallery, PD: p. 237; © The Trustees of the British Museum, CC-BY-SA 4.0: pp. 120, 125, 190; Kuichi Uchida, PD: p. 274; University of Southern California Libraries, anonymous, PD: p. 272; University of Toronto, PD: p. 157; Ron Van Oers, CC-BY-SA 3.0: p. 41; Victoria and Albert Museum, PD: p. 31; VladimirSlavik, PD: p. 52; Walters Art Museum, CC-BY-SA 3.0: p. 33; Web Gallery of Art, PD: p. 156; Weingartner Stifterbüchlein, PD: p. 73; Wellcome Collection, CC-BY-SA 4.0: p. 243; wmpearl, PD: p. 200; World Imaging, PD: p. 109; Yelkrokoyade, CC-BY-SA 4.0: p. 143; The Yorck Project (2002): pp. 131, 201; Franz Ziegler, CC-BY-SA 3.0: p. 282; YALE UNIVERSITY ART GALLERY, NEW HAVEN, CT: pp. 28, 32

SELECTED TINY FOLIOS™ FROM ABBEVILLE PRESS

American Impressionism · 978-0-7892-0612-1

Ansel Adams: The National Park Service Photographs · 978-0-7892-0775-3

The Art of Tarot · 978-0-7892-1306-8

Audubon's Birds of America: The Audubon Society Baby Elephant Folio · 978-0-7892-0814-9

Classic Cocktails · 978-0-7892-1381-5

Fashion: Treasures of the Museum of Fine Arts, Boston · 978-0-78921-380-8

Frank Lloyd Wright: America's Master Architect · 978-0-7892-0227-7

Illuminated Manuscripts: Treasures of the Pierpont Morgan Library, New York · 978-0-7892-0216-1

New York: Treasures of the Museum of the City of New York · 978-0-7892-1361-7

Norman Rockwell: 332 Magazine Covers · 978-0-7892-0409-7

Treasures of the Art Institute of Chicago: Paintings from the 19th Century to the Present · 978-0-7892-1288-7

Treasures of the Brooklyn Museum · 978-0-7892-1278-8

Treasures of Impressionism and Post-Impressionism: National Gallery of Art · 978-0-7892-0491-2

Treasures of the Museum of Fine Arts, Boston · 978-0-7892-1233-7

Treasures of the National Museum of the American Indian · 978-0-7892-0841-5

Treasures of the New-York Historical Society · 978-0-7892-1280-1

Treasures of the Prado · 978-0-78920-490-5

The Trees of North America: Michaux and Redouté's American Masterpiece · 978-0-7892-1402-7

Women Artists: The National Museum of Women in the Arts · 978-0-7892-1053-1